**OUR G**

# OUR GOD REIGNS

Tony Higton

**HODDER AND STOUGHTON**
LONDON SYDNEY AUCKLAND TORONTO

Biblical quotations are from the New International Version.
Copyright © 1973, 1978, 1984 by International Bible Society.


**British Library Cataloguing in Publication Data**

Higton, Tony, *1942–*
  Our God reigns.
  1. Christian Church
  I. Title
  260

  ISBN 0-340-42628-4

*Printed in Great Britain for Hodder & Stoughton Limited,
Mill Road, Dunton Green, Sevenoaks, Kent TN13 2YE by
Cox and Wyman Limited, Reading, Berks.
Hodder & Stoughton Editorial Office: 47 Bedford Square,
London WC1B 3DP.*

*Photoset by Rowland Phototypesetting Limited,
Bury St Edmunds, Suffolk*

Dedicated to those Christian leaders and church members who are praying and working for the restoration of the Church to biblical principles in the power of the Holy Spirit

# Contents

# Acknowledgments

I wish to thank my wife Patricia for her theological and prophetic insights and criticisms which have been vital in the writing of this book. My thanks are also due to Fiona Lindsay who has improved my grammar; Val Morris for her patient typing; and David Wavre of Hodder and Stoughton for his help and support throughout.

TONY HIGTON

# 1

## Introduction: Where is Your God?

It was a beautiful Lake District valley. From the caravan, that sunny August morning, I could see the distant hills sweeping down into the undulating green pastures. Nearby was a substantial grey stone farmhouse. A mile away a church tower rose above a tiny village. What a lovely setting for a really enjoyable family holiday! Then, as I looked at the farmhouse, it occurred to me that, from my knowledge of them, it seemed likely that the occupants were not involved in the church. In fact there must be many people in that beautiful area who have no time for God.

Most days we went fell-walking, climbing as high as possible to see the spectacular views and to be on our own. One day we climbed Great Gable. At about 2,000 feet we appeared to be alone in the mountains. Above us the rocky precipice of Gable Crag rose majestically for several hundred feet. Everywhere we looked there was beauty – mountains, valleys and lakes. Perhaps it was the view that prompted my son to ask a question which began a discussion on creation and evolution. Yet I found myself wondering how many people had climbed that mountain and failed to think of the Creator and to thank him for the beauty around them.

Another day, under a clear blue sky, we climbed Helvellyn by way of Striding Edge. One guide book describes it as 'a narrow ridge of naked rock, a succession of jagged fangs high above and between very steep and shattered cliffs'. It was breathtaking. We took it slowly along the narrow path.

A party of teenagers overtook us seemingly oblivious to the fact that a false step could have sent them plunging hundreds of feet down the mountainside. People have fallen to their death there. Such a prospect concentrates my mind on eternal issues. But how many others face that and other dangers when they are unprepared for, or even unconcerned about, eternity? I have frequently stood at the graveside of someone about whom I have no evidence of faith in Christ. One prayer in the new prayer book asks that we may be spared 'the bitter pains of eternal death'. And I wonder how ready the person was for death and about his eternal destiny. The vast majority of people seem totally unconcerned.

During this same holiday the newspapers reported the 'harmonic convergence' all over the world, when people gathered at sacred sites to celebrate the dawning of the Age of Aquarius. On Glastonbury Tor they meditated, hummed the Om mantra and 'tuned into earth energy'. These events were described as the 'gateway to the new consciousness' and were in aid of world peace. I had already written my piece on the New Age Movement (p. 124), and these widely reported activities focused my attention on the rapid promotion of occult religion in our society.

As I sat looking at our valley from the caravan, things began to clarify in my mind. There is a conspiracy afoot to keep active belief in God at best an optional hobby and at worst irrelevant, so that most people totally ignore their duty to him. This conspiracy is not human, it is demonic. God is rendered irrelevant by evolutionary philosophy. Belief in God is regarded as a subjective, personal opinion: the New Agers have their views, the Christians theirs. The idea of an exclusive way of salvation based upon an authoritative written revelation is alien to our tolerant and liberal age, and to the thinking of many Christian leaders. So the general population feels it does not matter what you believe so long as you are sincere – and tolerant. This often leads on to the rejection of the idea of God as a judge in favour of a

God who, in the end, accepts everyone (assuming there is life after death). Such a God is, of course, proclaimed in many pulpits. There is, therefore, no ultimate accountability, for there is no ultimate judgment or punishment. So, if modern man thinks of eternity at all, he does not think there is anything to worry about. God can safely be ignored and, if he does exist, he is all-accepting, whatever our creed or failings.

The church fosters the idea of the irrelevance of God because it falls far below the standards of the New Testament, in power, love, joy and holiness. The conspiracy is working efficiently. Over 90 per cent of the English population does not go to church. I am convinced that God's attitude to them is the same as that shown by Jesus: 'When he saw the crowds, he had compassion on them, because they were harassed and helpless, like sheep without a shepherd' (Matt. 9:36).

What of the church? All too often it undermines the idea of authoritative divine revelation and particularly the sufficiency of scripture. Doubts at this fundamental level mean the trumpet gives an uncertain sound and nobody takes any notice of it. As we shall see, Jesus was tough on his disciples when they lacked faith and he roundly condemned religious leaders as 'blind guides' (Matt. 15:14; 23:16). We teachers will have to give an account (Heb. 13:17) and will be judged more strictly (Jas. 3:1). Yet Jesus wept over the rebellion of Jerusalem and longed for her to return to him. He wept at the judgment she was to bring upon herself (Matt. 23:37; Luke 13:34).

This book is about these concerns. Each part examines the relevant biblical teaching, shows how it is undermined within the church, and gives an intensely practical chapter of advice on how to submit to God's sovereignty in the area covered. So about half of each part is concerned with examining and analysing the faults in today's church. By that I do not just mean liberal or traditional churches but evangelical and charismatic churches too. Some Christians tend simply to be negative – criticising the church but

offering no positive recommendations. I have been at pains
to avoid this. Others may feel that criticising the church is
uncharitable and unnecessarily controversial. But the New
Testament urges us to contend for the faith against those
who undermine the gospel or 'who change the grace of our
God into a licence for immorality' (Jude 3–4; cf. Phil. 1:27).
We are to 'have nothing to do with the fruitless deeds of
darkness, but rather expose them' (Eph. 5:11).

Modern Christians, even many who uphold the authority
of scripture, understand what is meant by a teaching,
pastoral and evangelistic ministry. But they have a blind
spot over a prophetic role, caused by years of neglect of this
ministry in the church. They might welcome suggestions of
practical ways forward for the church but react against any
stress on its faults. Yet so often a prophetic ministry must
bring bad news before good news. Lam. 2:14 states rel-
evantly: 'The visions of your prophets were false and
worthless; they did not expose your sin to ward off your
captivity. The oracles they gave you were false and misleading.'

So I have sought to expose the sin of the church. The
other half of the book concentrates on positive biblical
teaching and practical recommendations. I have a heart for
the welfare of the church. But my concern is primarily for
the honour of God whose sovereignty is being undermined;
and for the nation and world; and for all those who look at
the church and say, 'Where is their God?' (Joel 2:17; note
vv. 12–16).

# Part I

# GOD'S SOVEREIGNTY
# IN REVELATION

# The God Who Intervenes

Throughout the ages man has sought to create God in his own image and to reach him by human reason and tradition. In his pride man has thought that in such ways he can ascend to God. Cutting across this deception is the great self-revelation of God in Christ. As we shall see, it is the nature of a personal God to communicate. In this communication he reveals himself. Over the centuries the church has believed that God has not left us without a reliable permanent account of the truth we need to know about him and his requirements of us. Rather it has accepted the 'givenness' of scripture as inspired by God, and its permanently normative authority in matters of faith and ethics: for example, this is clearly taught in the canons of the Church of England. So Christianity proclaims the revelation by God to man, based upon divine initiative alone. By contrast we see within the church today a presumptuous rejection of divine revelation. Following are some examples of this.

## "The Nature of Christian Belief"[1]

This is the title of a Report published in 1986 by the General Synod House of Bishops. The Bishop of Salisbury, Chairman of the Doctrine Commission, said: 'One thing that could be said about this report is that . . . it sanctions a departure from the accepted sense of the universal faith as reflected in the creeds.' Admittedly the creeds do not have the same authority as scripture. But the early ecumenical councils of the church, in the midst of great controversy, established the interpretation of scripture over various basic beliefs – and this has been generally accepted by the universal church. (The exception is the dispute between the eastern and western churches over the 'filioque' clause, that is, the Spirit proceeding from the Son as well as the Father.) For the English House of Bishops (44 diocesans and 9 suffragans) to sanction a departure from the generally accepted sense of the creeds with respect to the virginal conception and the empty tomb is extremely grave.

The Bishops' Report states:

The divergences between Christian scholars on the relation of the Virginal Conception of our Lord to this great mystery [the incarnation], and on the question whether or not that conception is to be regarded as historical fact as well as imagery of divine truth, have been indicated, and they are reflected in the convictions of members of this House. But all of us accept: first, that the belief that Our Lord was conceived in the womb of Mary by the creative power of God the Holy Spirit without the intervention of a human father can be held with full intellectual integrity; secondly, that only this belief, enshrined in the Creeds, can claim to be the teaching of the universal church.[2]

Similarly, speaking of the resurrection, the Report states:

On the question whether, as a result of this divine act of resurrection, Christ's tomb that first Easter Day was empty, we recognise that scholarship can offer no conclusive demonstration; and the divergent views to be found among scholars of standing are reflected in the thinking of individual bishops. But all of us accept: first, that belief that the tomb was empty can be held with full intellectual integrity; secondly, that this is the understanding of the witness of Scripture which is generally received in the universal church.[3]

It may be that the House of Bishops was not aware of the presumption of this aspect of the Report. The main concern of some of the more conservative bishops was clearly to go as far as possible in a traditional biblical direction without 'unchurching' the liberals. This overwhelming desire to be inclusive and to produce a 'unanimous' report apparently blinded them to the gravity of its weaknesses.

David Jenkins, Bishop of Durham, who created the controversy which led to the Bishops' Report, had referred to the credal statements about the virginal conception and the empty tomb as 'various dated formulations' and 'mere formulae'.[4] Instead of correcting this, the Bishops' Report sanctioned it as legitimate for a bishop to hold his views.

Referring to the controversy over the virginal conception and the empty tomb the Archbishop of York, John Habgood, said 'the root difference lies between those with a questioning, exploratory faith and those who hold that essentially all the answers have already been given'.[5] The Archbishop is simplistic in his distinction. Many of those who believe that the answers have already been given have reached that position through much questioning and exploring. He is wrong to conclude – as he clearly does – that the answers on important matters, such as the virgin birth, have not been given. The whole thrust of biblical teaching clearly supports Article 6 of the Church of England: 'Holy Scripture containeth all things necessary to salvation.' And Articles 2 and 4 show that this includes the virgin birth and the empty tomb as historical facts.

In all these statements both the clear teaching of scripture and some two thousand years of agreed interpretation of scripture are set aside. Let us therefore look at what the Bible has to say about the way in which God has revealed – and continues to reveal – himself to man.

## Revelation through intervention: a biblical study

It is surely inherent to the nature of a rational, loving person to wish to communicate, especially with those he loves. It is only to be expected then that the Godhead is a fellowship of Persons. God is not, therefore, dependent upon human beings for the purposes of revelation, communication and love. But the three Persons of the Godhead have chosen not only to relate to each other: their love and desire to communicate overflows in creation of and revelation to human beings. Ultimately God so loved the world that he communicated; he sent his Word, the living Word – Jesus.

## Revelation through the incarnation

At the centre of this revelation is the incarnation of the Son of God. Belief in this doctrine is a supreme test of orthodoxy. 'Every spirit that acknowledges that Jesus Christ has come in the flesh is from God. But every spirit that does not acknowledge Jesus is not from God. This is the spirit of the antichrist' (1 John 4:2–3; cf. 2 John 7). Jesus is 'the Word' who 'became flesh and made his dwelling among us' (John 1:14). He is 'the Word of life . . . the eternal life which was with the Father and has appeared to us' (1 John 1:1–2). The incarnation is the ultimate self-revelation of God. As the Word, Jesus reveals the heart and mind, the very life and nature of God.

Christianity is therefore founded on revelation. This revelation is God's initiative, stemming from his grace and mercy. The whole direction of the initiative is from God to man. We respond to the revelation in faith and obedience and seek to explore its depths. But we do not add to it (Rev. 22:18; cf. Deut. 4:2; 12:32; Prov. 30:6). It is complete in itself for 'he is the image of the invisible God' (Col. 1:15); he is 'the radiance of God's glory and the exact representation of his being' (Heb. 1:3); 'God was pleased to have all his fulness dwell in him . . . for in Christ all the fulness of the Deity lives in bodily form' (Col. 1:19; 2:9). In Christ 'are hidden all the treasures of wisdom and knowledge' (Col. 2:3). So Jesus can say to Philip, 'Anyone who has seen me has seen the Father' (John 14:9; cf. 12:45).

## Revelation through the Spirit

God has also given his Spirit to us, who will guide us into all truth, revealing Christ to us and reminding us of his teaching (John 16:13; cf. 14:26; 15:26; 1 John 2:20–27; 5:6). 'The Spirit searches all things, even the deep things of God', he alone knows the thoughts of God and reveals them to men (1 Cor. 2:9–16). God has been pleased to reveal to us the mystery of his intention to unite all things under Christ (Eph. 1:9; cf. Gal. 1:11–12, 15–16). He further intends to reveal his wisdom through the church to the rulers and authorities in the heavenly realms (Eph. 3:4–11). Daniel praises God who 'reveals deep and hidden things' (2:22). He is 'a God in heaven who reveals mysteries' (2:28; cf. 2:47). Amos adds that he 'reveals his thoughts to man' (4:13).

## Revelation as essential to salvation

It is clear from the New Testament that God, in his infinite love, desires the eternal salvation of all men (1 Tim. 2:4). Jesus came into the world not to condemn (John 3:17) but to become the atoning sacrifice for the sins of the whole world (1 John 2:2). Repentance and faith are necessary conditions of the individual receiving the salvation achieved for him by Christ. But even then God patiently waits and delays judgment, 'not wanting anyone to perish, but everyone to come to repentance' (2 Pet. 3:9).

Nevertheless there is a mystery here. The salvation of the individual depends upon God in his sovereignty revealing the gospel to the individual. The Christian faith contradicts the wisdom of the world. In fact the wisdom of the world is foolishness in God's sight (1 Cor. 1:20,25). The world cannot accept the Spirit of truth for it does not recognise him (John 14:17). 'The man without the Spirit does not accept the things that come from the Spirit of God, for they are foolishness to him' (1 Cor. 2:14). The message of the cross is foolishness to such a man (1 Cor. 1:18). However,

what is hidden from the wise and learned has been revealed
to 'little children' by the Father (Matt. 11:25); 'no one
knows the Father except the Son and those to whom the
Son chooses to reveal him' (Matt. 11:27; cf. 13:11; Luke
10:22; Col. 1:26–27).

So revelation is central to the Christian faith and to the
nature of a personal, loving God. Furthermore the individual is dependent upon a personal revelation by God
before he can accept the truth of the gospel. In all this God
is sovereign and we are dependent. Human wisdom is
foolishness in God's sight. Our minds need to be transformed by the Spirit of God before we can understand the
wisdom of God and 'think God's thoughts after him'.

## Revelation is essentially historical

We have seen that the primary way in which God has
revealed himself is in Christ, the living Word. Of necessity
the incarnation is historical. In order to become one of us
the Son of God must enter the stage of human history. So
historical fact matters, as the New Testament writers
emphasise.

John writes: 'The Word became flesh and made his
dwelling among us. We have seen his glory' (John 1:14).
'That which was from the beginning, which we have heard,
which we have seen with our eyes, which we have looked at
and our hands have touched – this we proclaim concerning
the Word of life. The life appeared; we have seen it and
testify to it, and we proclaim to you the eternal life, which
was with the Father and has appeared to us. We proclaim to
you what we have seen and heard' (1 John 1:1–3; cf. 4:14).
John stresses that he writes as an eyewitness of the crucifixion and 'his testimony is true. He knows that he tells the
truth' (John 19:35). He makes a similar claim as a witness of
the resurrection (John 21:24). Similarly Luke refers to his
eyewitness sources and says that he has 'carefully investi-
gated everything from the beginning . . . so that you may
know the certainty of the things you have been taught'

(Luke 1:2–4). Peter writes as 'a witness of Christ's sufferings' (1 Pet. 5:1) that 'we did not follow cleverly invented stories when we told you about the power and coming of our Lord Jesus Christ, but we were eyewitnesses of his majesty' (2 Pet. 1:16). The writer to the Hebrews states that the 'salvation, which was first announced by the Lord, was confirmed to us by those who heard him' (Heb. 2:3).

Jesus himself 'after his suffering . . . showed himself to these men and gave many convincing proofs that he was alive' (Acts 1:3). He took pains to prove to Thomas the reality of his resurrection body (John 20:27). He sent his disciples out as witnesses who would proclaim these historical events (Luke 24:48; Acts 1:8). And so they did. The early sermons recorded in the Book of Acts emphasise the historical Jesus. He is Jesus of Nazareth (2:22; 3:6; 4:10; 10:38), a descendant of David (13:23). Peter accused the people of condemning him, handing him over to Pilate for him to be nailed to the cross (2:23; 3:13–15; 13:27–28) and buried (13:29). They had killed him but God raised him up (2:24; 3:15; 4:10; 5:30; 7:52; cf. 3:26; 17:18; 26:8,23). God 'caused him to be seen' (10:40) 'for many days' (13:31) and would not allow his body to decay (2:31; 13:34–37). The early preachers stressed that they were witnesses of the resurrection (2:32; cf. 4:20, 5:32) and of everything Jesus had done (10:39). They had seen him for many days after the resurrection as they 'travelled with him from Galilee to Jerusalem' (13:31) and they 'ate and drank with him after he rose from the dead' (10:41).

The gospel writers major on the physical suffering and crucifixion of Christ. Around one fifth of the accounts describe the final hours leading up to his death. And, of course, Jesus left us Holy Communion to focus our attention on his body and blood (1 Cor. 10:16; 11:23–25; Matt. 26:26–29, and so on). The New Testament writers similarly stress the importance of the physical suffering of his body and the shedding of his blood. He appeared in a body prepared for him (1 Tim. 3:16; Heb. 10:5). It was in his body that he bore our sins (1 Pet. 2:24). We were reconciled

'by Christ's physical body through death' (Col. 1:22); we
have access to God through his body (Heb. 10:20) and are
made holy through the sacrifice of his body (Heb. 10:10).

It is emphasised that 'without the shedding of blood there
is no forgiveness' (Heb. 9:22). We are bought or redeemed
with the blood of Christ (Acts 20:28; Rev. 5:9; Eph. 1:7;
Heb. 9:12,14; 1 Pet. 1:19; Rev. 1:5). It is through the blood
of Christ that we are reconciled (Eph. 2:13; Heb. 10:19),
justified (Rom. 3:25; 5:9; Col. 1:20) and purified (Heb.
12:24; 13:12; 1 Pet. 1:2; 1 John 1:7; Rev. 7:14).

It follows from this stress on the death of Christ's body
that the resurrection of his body is important too. 'He was
put to death in the body but made alive by the Spirit' (1 Pet.
3:18). 'He appeared in a body, was vindicated by the Spirit'
(1 Tim. 3:16). The resurrection was Christ's vindication for
he 'was declared with power to be the Son of God, by his
resurrection from the dead' (Rom. 1:4). 'God raised him
from the dead, freeing him from the agony of death,
because it was impossible for death to keep its hold on him'
(Acts 2:24). The resurrection would not have been a real
vindication had not his body been raised. It was in his body
that he had borne our sins. Therefore the historical and
demonstrable resurrection of his body, together with its
ascension to heaven, was a necessary vindication of the
sufficiency of his death to atone for our sins. Christ's bodily
resurrection showed that God accepted his sacrifice. That is
why the apostles stress that God did not allow Christ's body
to see corruption. Both Peter (Acts 2:27–31) and Paul
(Acts 13:34–37) proclaim that, unlike David's body, which
decayed after death, Christ's body did not. It is true that
Christ's resurrection body was not subject to the limitation
of his pre-crucifixion body. He could appear and disappear.
He could pass through locked doors. His transformed body
was not immediately recognised by the disciples on the road
to Emmaus. But his body could be touched (Luke 24:39);
he could break bread (Luke 24:30), make breakfast (John
21:9), give it to his disciples (John 21:13) and eat with them
(Luke 24:42–43). He had flesh and bones (Luke 24:39).

All of this makes it obvious that God's revelation in Christ is essentially historical. It is therefore a reasonable and logical assumption that God in his providence would give us a historically accurate and reliable account of the life, teaching, death, resurrection and ascension of Jesus.

## The undermining of revelation through intervention

We have seen something of the richness and majesty of biblical teaching on God's initiative and sovereignty in revelation. By contrast we now look at the impoverished rationalistic approach to the faith, which is still current in the church. There are various characteristics.

### The problem of presuppositions

Some church leaders display arrogance in their presuppositions about God. We all have fundamental assumptions, of course. Scientists assume that the universe is regular, orderly and reasonable; that logic and mathematics are reliable. Traditionally the church has assumed there is a personal God whose nature is to communicate; and that he has provided for us a reliable written account of absolute truth in matters of faith and morals. The Bible supports such an assumption. Liberal theologians on the other hand assume that their minds are sufficient to judge scripture and its teaching about God and so on, even to reject it.

So David Jenkins, Bishop of Durham, in his notorious speech to General Synod in July 1986 said:

> God, it is apparently alleged, works uniquely and directly in a divine intervention on physical matter, in order to bring about his basic saving miracles of incarnation and resurrection . . . The choice of physical miracles with what might be called laser-beam-like precision and power would, I suggest, not seem to be a choice which he cared, or would care, to use.[6]

We shall return to the rest of his argument but it is sufficient here to note how he summarily rejects the biblical description of God and substitutes a God of his imagination. In an interview in the *Sunday Times*[7] discussing the empty tomb he said: 'Although he *could* have done it, it doesn't seem to be the way he goes about things.' So he prefers his own subjective presuppositions about God to the revelation of God in scripture which is the generally received teaching of the universal church. Like many other Christians I would rather believe in the God of revelation than a God of the Bishop of Durham's imagination.

More extreme is Don Cupitt who states bluntly:

> It seems doubtful whether there is any immense cosmic or supracosmic Creator-mind. Even if there is, it is hard to see what it or he could have to do with religion[8] . . . So we cannot (and ought not to) believe in an objective deity who among other things antecedently prescribes our moral values and our spiritual itinerary from outside[9] . . . For on our account God is not really a person or a substance but (so far as we are concerned) an unconditionally demanding and inflexible principle which as we choose it and lay it upon ourselves generates certain effects within us; theistic faith, the drama of the spiritual life etc.[10]

Cupitt describes his views as 'Christian Buddhism'.[11] It seems that he is making up his religion as he goes along. But we include him in our consideration because (surprisingly) he is still a clergyman in the Church of England.

## An outmoded rejection of divine intervention

In the General Synod debate on *The Nature of Christian Belief* in July 1986 Professor Barnabas Lindars said:

> I think that everybody accepts that Jesus is an historical person because the historical enquiry, as far as anything

can be established, has established that a man named Jesus lived. Another fact that we know about Jesus is that he suffered under Pontius Pilate. There is the strongest reason for accepting as historical the fact of the crucifixion. Beyond that, we have as assured fact that, following the crucifixion, his followers preached the Resurrection as part of a messianic claim which, of course, has to be understood within the context of the Jewish expectations of the time. These can be regarded as assured facts. [He continues:] It is quite obvious that the virgin birth is one of those facts that cannot be established by historical science; it depends entirely upon the worth that is attached to what is said in the first two chapters of Matthew and Luke. There is bound to be a differing degree of understanding with regard to how far those opening chapters of the gospels are to be treated as straightforward reporting, historical accounts.[12]

David Jenkins, in his interview in the *Sunday Times*,[13] says:

I've been reading *Who Moved the Stone* by Frank Morison . . . That's exactly the wrong approach! It regards the New Testament books as providing undoubted historical evidence which leads logically to a supernatural conclusion! Our curse is that we live in a scientific age and we can't believe that anything is real, unless it has physical reality. St Paul wouldn't have any of our trouble, he'd have understood emotional truth and not been tied down to scientific facts. But suppose I were a judge sitting on an inquiry into the facts of the empty tomb. Suppose I'd heard all the witnesses, Mary Magdalene and her friends and the eleven disciples, everyone concerned. What would the correct verdict be? The verdict would be 'not proven'!

John Habgood, Archbishop of York, speaking on the TV programme *Credo*,[14] said that the birth of Jesus was a break in genealogical continuity which symbolised the newness of

God's action. But about the historicity of the virgin birth he said: 'There is no conceivable way in which we can disentangle this and get at the facts.'

We must ask why scholars distinguish between certain aspects of the story of Jesus being 'assured facts' and others not. The distinction sounds very scholarly – but is it? What is the difference between the evidence for Jesus' crucifixion and his bodily resurrection, which makes the former 'assured' and the latter not assured? There is the same documentary evidence for both. The argument from the effect of these supposed events on history is at least as high for the resurrection as it is for the crucifixion. So why the distinction? Is it based on objective facts? The answer is no. Rather it is based on presuppositions which doubt the supernatural intervention of God into the realm of physical matter. These presuppositions doubt that such things as bodily resurrection or virginal conception take place.

John Wenham[15] quotes F. G. Kenyon:

For all the words of classical antiquity we have to depend on manuscripts written long after their original composition. The author who is the best case in this respect is Virgil; yet the earliest manuscript of Virgil that we now possess was written some 350 years after his death . . . for Livy it is about 500 years, for Horace 900, for most of Plato 1,300, for Euripides 1,600. On the other hand the great vellum uncials of the New Testament were written perhaps some 250 years after the date when the Gospels were actually composed.

Wenham comments: 'The philosophers feel justified in laying great weight even upon minute turns of phrase in Plato in spite of the 1,300 year gap.'

The oldest manuscript of Caesar's Gallic wars was written some 900 years after the events it describes. For Tacitus' Histories the period is about 700 years; the History of Thucydides and of Herodotus over 1,300 years. But scholars accept their authenticity. Why is the Bible not afforded the same trust? It is because of the anti-supernatural presuppositions of some scholars. Such presuppositions were clearly displayed in the debate on *The Nature of Christian Belief* in the General Synod of July 1986. For example, David Edwards, Provost of Southwark, spoke of 'obvious difficulties' in the gospel stories which:

> present to our age of science stories about a baby who has no human father, of people who speak poetry closely echoing the Old Testament, of angels singing in the sky, of star-led men from the East with gold, incense and myrrh. The Easter narratives contain details which seem to make one gospel inconsistent with another. They tell of the rending of the great curtain in the temple, of the walking of many dead saints in the streets of Jerusalem, and of angels or a young man in white. They tell of a body which rises from its grave, but also disappears, which leaves behind its shroud but is also clothed normally, which holds conversations but is also unrecognised, which eats fish but also passes through doors. Such stories not only seem to belong to a world different from the world known in ordinary experience and described by science, they also seem to belong to a world different from the Nazareth where the carpenter's son is mis-understood by his own family, and different from the Calvary where he suffers under Pontius Pilate.

He went on to say that Jesus probably had a human father who probably emptied his tomb.[16] The Dean of St Paul's, Alan Webster, said: 'When we are asked to believe extraordinary facts, we need, as I think Hume said, an extraordinary amount of evidence.' He thinks the power of 'imaginative stories' provides extraordinary evidence.[17]

In the same debate, as already mentioned, David Jenkins spoke at length on the nature of miracle.

> The critical point is this: the claim that the miraculous and divinely produced transformation must be a directly

induced transformation of the precisely physical, in order for the Incarnation and the Resurrection to be believable, real and historical. God's power and presence and commitment must, so it is claimed, in these two particular cases have acted something like a divine laser beam, which fuses the physical particles into a reality which is both divinely produced and divine . . . We are faced with the claim that God is prepared to work knock-down physical miracles in order to let a select number of people into the secret of his Incarnation, Resurrection and salvation, but that he is not prepared to use such methods in order to deliver from Auschwitz, prevent Hiroshima, overcome famine or bring about the bloodless transformation of apartheid. Such a God, surely, is a cultic idol . . . If such a God is not a cultic idol produced by mistaken and confused worshippers, but actually exists, then he is the very devil, for he prefers a few selected worshippers to all the sufferers in our world. Such a God is certainly not worth believing in. [18]

If the bishop is calling the God of the Bible, who manifestly is selective in his miraculous intervention, a cultic idol or even the very devil, is that not blasphemous?

In the previously mentioned *Sunday Times* interview, speaking of the empty tomb David Jenkins says: 'Although he could have done it, it doesn't seem to be the way he goes about things. But the real point is that concentrating on the miraculous sidetracks people. It encourages them to believe in all sorts of other things like . . .' The interviewer comments that Dr Jenkins gave a small but visible shiver of disgust before saying: 'spiritual healing! And then miraculous claims put ordinary, sensible people off Christianity. They say, "Tell that to the Marines" and so they miss a great opportunity for good.'

Similarly Archbishop John Habgood[19] admitted he could not understand how prayer changes things. He found it difficult 'to believe in the kind of universe where there was some enormous heavenly computer logging a million requests a minute and then ordering the universe in some incredibly complicated way in order to see that the maximum number of requests was fulfilled without messing up everybody else's life.' Of course it is not necessary to believe in such a caricature to hold that God can change things through prayer.

Ironically Professor Pinchas Lapide, an orthodox German rabbi, has no problems with the bodily resurrection of Jesus. Dr Lapide does not recognise Jesus as Messiah but when interviewed by the *Sunday Telegraph*[20] he said:

> I cannot rid myself of the impression that some modern Christian theologians are ashamed of the material facticity of the resurrection. Their varying attempts at dehistoricising the Easter experience which give the lie to all four Evangelists are simply not understandable to me in any other way. For all these Christians who believe in the incarnation (something which I am able to do) but have difficulty with the historically understood Resurrection the words of Jesus of the blind guides, straining out a gnat and swallowing a camel probably applies.

The tendency of some Christian leaders to doubt or even reject certain parts of scripture because of anti-supernatural presuppositions, is really out of touch with what God has been doing in the church, particularly in the last twenty-five years. The Bishop of Singapore, Dr Moses Tay, writing to the Archbishop of Canterbury to express dismay and distress at the doubts expressed by English bishops, said:

> In view of our experience of the reality of God in our life situations, manifesting His love even in miracles of healing and deliverance, we cannot but affirm the basic beliefs of Christianity namely the Virgin Birth, the miracles of Christ and the Resurrection exactly as described in the Bible.

How sad that these liberal theologians have been so out of touch with the recent move of the Holy Spirit in the Charismatic Renewal which has been deeply affecting the historic churches since the 1960s! There have been countless examples of physical and emotional healings; striking deliverance from occult and other bondages; remarkable experience of supernatural gifts of knowledge and wisdom. Like thousands of other Christian leaders, I have seen these things with my own eyes. When I came to know more of the reality of God the Holy Spirit through an experience of Charismatic Renewal, it was like entering a whole new world – a world in which the supernatural and miraculous were, in a sense, normal. This underlined the biblical emphasis on miracles and the supernatural power of God. I have no problem with the major or minor miracles of scripture partly because God is working many miracles – some of them spectacular – today.

Of course there are many conservative Christians (Catholic, Evangelical or simply conservative) who are at a disadvantage here. They uphold the traditional doctrine of the creeds and defend the miracles of Christ and the apostles. They may believe in the miracle of the new birth and allow the possibility of other miracles happening. Many of them will seek to defend the Bible against an anti-supernatural rationalism. But they themselves are unaware that they have a fairly liberal approach to scripture themselves. They do not really face up to the clear teaching of the New Testament that the Christian life is to be lived on a supernatural level. The New Testament stresses the power of the Holy Spirit in the life of the believer (for example Acts 1:8) and that the believer will do the works Jesus did and even greater things (John 14:12; the context is miracles). The many gifts of the Holy Spirit should be the normal experience of the church – including healing and miraculous powers and the spoken gifts we have already referred to (see Rom. 12:6–8; 1 Cor. 12:8–11; 28–31; Eph. 4:11). Some conservative Christians even argue that the gifts of the Spirit died out with the apostles. There is nothing to support this view in the New Testament. In fact it is clear from 1 Corinthians 13:8–12 that the gifts will only cease 'when perfection comes'; when 'we shall see face to face' and we 'shall know fully'. This surely refers to the end of the age when we see Christ face to face. So this argument against the gifts of the Spirit is unbiblical and is in fact based on a lack of experience. How similar such an argument is to the arguments against the virgin birth and the empty tomb! The fact that some who experience the gifts mishandle them or neglect theology is no excuse for the rest of us to avoid the thoroughly supernatural challenge of the New Testament. And there is no excuse today. Many Christians are experiencing manifestly genuine gifts in the context of a biblical theology. One answer to the anti-supernatural rationalism of some Christian leaders is that other Christians are manifesting the power of the Holy Spirit as fully as the New Testament describes.

Sadly the anti-supernaturalism of some Christians really puts them out of touch with modern society. At the same time as the manifestation of God's power in the Charismatic Renewal there has been the explosion of its counterfeit in occult power. Where have David Jenkins and others been in recent years while interest in the supernatural, in religious cults with false prophets, messiahs and gurus, has mushroomed? How can they think that modern western man is embarrassed by the supernatural and the miraculous? A tiny minority is, of course, but the majority clearly is not. The main argument against the anti-supernaturalism of these Christians is not that of experience. This is far too subjective and, as we shall see later, can be seriously misleading. No, the argument is far more fundamental. We believe in a God who is all-powerful. He has revealed himself in history and chooses to intervene in his world. Natural law is simply a description of the way God normally works. If he wishes he can temporarily suspend that 'law' (or normal way of doing things). Some people make the mistake of elevating God's normal way of doing things into some sort of cosmic 'law of the Medes and the Persians' which cannot be broken, even by God. By this assumption, these people neatly rule out miracles but, unfortunately for them, it is false, as the testimony of scripture manifestly shows.

Liberal theology is based not so much on scholarship as on rationalistic presuppositions. These include the ideas that God has not cared to give us an historically reliable account of salvation history and that God does not intervene supernaturally in the realm of physical matter. These presuppositions are statements of faith or, to be more accurate, statements displaying a lack of faith. That is not to deny that many liberals are honest seekers after truth who have a definite faith in other areas. But the reality of these presuppositions – and the fact that they are assumptions, not proven scholarship – must be faced. It is my conviction that there is a blanket of unbelief over the western world, not least over Britain. It can affect all of us with scepticism and cynicism. It is ingrained in the church and its theological colleges, even in conservative ones, and needs to be recognised and dealt with – through prayer, letting the Bible speak to us and obedient openness to the Holy Spirit.

J. B. Phillips paraphrases Colossians 2:8 as: 'Be careful that nobody spoils your faith through intellectualism or high-sounding nonsense. Such stuff is at best founded on men's ideas of the nature of the world and disregards Christ!'[21]

## The God Who Speaks

### Revelation through the Word

We shall start this chapter with a brief study of what Jesus and the New Testament authors have to say about the scriptures.

Jesus saw himself as the one who would fulfil the law and the prophets, not abolish them: 'I tell you the truth, until heaven and earth disappear, not the smallest letter, not the least stroke of the pen, will by any means disappear from the Law until everything is accomplished' (Matt. 5:18; cf. Luke 16:17). In John 10:34–35 he refers to the Old Testament people as those 'to whom the word of God came' and added, 'the Scripture cannot be broken'. Interestingly Jesus says about his own words, 'Heaven and earth will pass away but my words will never pass away' (Matt 24:35; Mark 13:31; Luke 21:33).

He sees the Old Testament scriptures as testifying to him (John 5:39; cf. Luke 24:25–27) and specifies various prophecies being fulfilled in him. He declares that Isaiah's prophecy of the anointed servant of the Lord is fulfilled in him (Luke 4:18–21); his suffering is foretold (Matt. 26:56; Mark 9:12; Luke 24:44–46) as are his being hated without reason (John 15:25); his betrayal (Matt. 26:24; John 13:18); the desertion of his disciples (Matt 26:31) and his resurrection (Luke 24:46). Jesus clearly has a very high view of scripture as the unbreakable Word of God which must be fulfilled in detail. 'Everything must be fulfilled that is written about me in the Law of Moses, the Prophets and the Psalms' (Luke 24:44). He could call on angelic deliverance from his arrest 'but how then would the Scriptures be fulfilled that say it must happen in this way?' (Matt. 26:54; cf. vv. 24,56; Luke 21:22).

The New Testament writers have the same high view of scripture: 'All Scripture is God-breathed' (2 Tim. 3:16). In scriptural prophecy 'men spoke from God as they were carried along by the Holy Spirit' (2 Pet. 1:20–21). Paul teaches that the Jews 'have been entrusted with the very words of God' (Rom. 3:2; cf. Acts 7:38). The early church held that God spoke by the Holy Spirit through the mouth of David (Acts 4:25–26; cf. Rom. 4:23–24). It is not necessary to hold a crude dictation theory – that the Holy Spirit simply dictated words to the apostles. There are clear differences of style between the writers. Their minds and literary abilities were clearly functioning, and yet the Spirit so overshadowed them that what they wrote was the inspired Word of God.

It follows from all this that, like Jesus, the New Testament writers stressed Messianic prophecies. Matthew refers to Old Testament prophecies of the virgin birth (Matt. 1:22–23); the flight to Egypt, slaughter of the innocents and return to Nazareth (2:15,17–18,23); Jesus' ministry in Capernaum (4:14–16); his healing ministry (8:17; 12:17–21) and parables (13:34–35; cf. vv. 13–15); his entering Jerusalem on a foal (21:4–5) and being betrayed for thirty silver coins (27:9–10). John adds that the unbelief of the people in spite of Jesus' miracles was foretold (John 12:38) as were the casting of lots for Jesus' clothes, his thirst on the cross, his bones not being broken and his body being pierced (19:24,28,36–37). Peter sees Old Testament predictions of the replacement of Judas (Acts 1:16,20); Pentecost (2:16–21); the suffering of Christ (3:18); his bodily resurrection (2:25–28; cf. 10:43) and ascension (2:34–35). Paul refers to the prophecies about the suffering and resurrection of Jesus (Acts 13:27–40; 26:22–23; cf. 17:2–3; 18:28). The writer to the Hebrews refers to prophecies of the divine sonship of Jesus (Heb. 1:5–13; 5:5–6).

So far we have concentrated on the New Testament writers' high view of the Old Testament as the Word of God. However, their attitude towards their own words is striking: they see themselves as speaking the Word of God by the power of the Spirit (Acts 4:31; 12:24; Phil. 1:14). Paul commends the Thessalonians for receiving his teaching 'not as the word of men, but as it actually is, the word of God' (1 Thess. 2:13). Paul's letters are compared with 'other scriptures' (2 Pet. 3:15–16). This can only mean that they are put on a level with Old Testament scripture. Similarly Luke 10:7 is quoted as scripture (1 Tim. 5:18).

While avoiding any superstitious view of scripture the New Testament writers clearly believe that the power of the Holy Spirit is released through the proclamation and reception of the Word of God. The Word is a spiritual seed which bears spiritual fruit in the life of anyone who obeys it (Mark 4:14,20). It is through the Word that people are born again (1 Pet. 1:23). The Word convicts of sin (Heb. 4:12) and brings cleansing (John 15:3; 17:17; Eph. 5:26). It produces faith (Rom. 10:17; John 20:31; 1 John 5:13), hope (Rom. 15:4) and wisdom (2 Tim. 3:15–17).

## The formation of the canon of scripture

In order to answer the question as to whether the Bible still speaks to us today, we need to look briefly at the way in which the canon of scripture came into being. It is often said that the Jewish Synod of Jamnia fixed the Old Testament canon in about AD 100. But it seems clear that all that really took place then was a discussion as to whether the books already in the canon should remain there. It was simply a re-examination of the long accepted threefold form of the 'Law of Moses, the Prophets and the Psalms' (Luke 24:44). Books of the Apocrypha appear in some late fourth- or fifth-century (AD) manuscripts of the Septuagint. However, there is no consistent list, and it seems from early Jewish writings that the Jews knew the limits of the canon but read other books too. After apostolic times many Christians came to accept the Apocrypha. But a distinction was made between the Old Testament canon and the Apocrypha, for example by Augustine and Jerome, and this was confirmed at the Reformation. New Testament allusions to the Apocrypha (for example Jude 14, quoting the Book of Enoch) do not imply these books are canonical, any more than quotations from non-Christian writers imply they are canonical (Acts 17:28; 1 Cor. 15:33; Tit. 1:12). Orthodox Jews, Augustine, Jerome, the Reformers, and the Bible societies are united in accepting the Old Testament canon. The Council of Trent is therefore somewhat isolated in committing the Roman Catholic Church to accepting the Apocrypha as canonical.

The present New Testament canon was formally acknowledged in the Council of Hippo (AD 393) and the Council of Carthage (AD 397). Since then it has been accepted with virtual unanimity. Luther had some doubts about books which did not emphasise justification by faith (especially James). Zwingli had some doubts about Revelation. From the earliest times though, the Gospels, Acts, the Epistles of Paul (sometimes Hebrews was regarded as Pauline), 1 Peter, 1 John and (often) Revelation have been regarded as scripture. There has always been at least a high regard for James, 2 Peter, 2 and 3 John and Jude.

It is important to stress that the church did not give authority to the books of scripture. Rather it accepted the Old Testament on the basis of its acceptance by Christ and the apostles. It also recognised that the New Testament has an inherent spiritual authority together with apostolic authorship or approval: but the shorter and more personal epistles were only recognised later by the universal church. Although it is going too far to say that no Old or New Testament books were disputed, nevertheless it is clear that the majority were always universally accepted, and the disputed books became universally accepted in AD 397. So by the providence of God a collection of inspired books has been recognised by the church throughout the ages. In them is preserved the written revelation God intended us to know.

The text of the Old Testament is considered by many modern scholars to be very reliable. Jesus and the apostles accepted the copies that were current in their day as reliable. The Dead Sea Scrolls have since confirmed the amazing accuracy of copies, even those made a thousand years later. John W. Wenham writes:

> Much textual criticism is concerned about microscopic matters that have no bearing on the meaning of what is written. Amazing though it sounds, the Herculean labours of the textual critics are virtually concerned with discovering the true reading at about a hundred points where there are variants of some significance to the ordinary reader . . . in most cases the variants do not contradict one another.[1]

Wenham's book provides fairly detailed chapters on 'The Canon' and 'The Reliability of the Bible Text', to which I am indebted.

Before moving on, it is useful to record the approximate dates given to various books of the New Testament, since this affects views of their apostolic authorship and their closeness to the events they describe. F. F. Bruce (formerly Rylands Professor of Biblical Criticism and Exegesis in the University of Manchester) dates Mark around AD 64–65, Luke shortly before AD 70, Matthew shortly after AD 70 and John's gospel between AD 90 and 100. A majority of modern scholars would date Matthew between AD 85 and 90 and Luke between AD 80 and 85. Either way 'the first three Gospels were written at a time when many were alive who could remember the things that Jesus said and did, and some at least would still be alive when the fourth Gospel was written'.[2]

Acts is generally dated in the sixties and Professor Bruce accepts all thirteen Pauline Epistles as genuinely written by Paul. Some scholars would reject Ephesians as Pauline, fewer would reject 2 Thessalonians; more would deny the Pastoral Epistles (Timothy and Titus) are Pauline. Bruce dates the Pauline Epistles as follows: Galatians AD 48; 1 and 2 Thessalonians AD 50; 1 and 2 Corinthians AD 54–56; Romans AD 57; Philippians, Colossians, Philemon and Ephesians c. AD 60; the Pastoral Epistles c. AD 63–65. He concludes:

> At any rate the time elapsing between the evangelic events and the writing of most of the NT books was from the standpoint of historical research satisfactorily short. For in assessing the trustworthiness of ancient historical writings, one of the most important questions is: How soon after the events took place were they recorded?[3]

Professor Bruce argues convincingly that the fourth gospel was written by John[4]. He harmonises the apparent discrepancies between it and the synoptic gospels: that John describes most of Jesus' ministry as in Jerusalem, the synoptics in Galilee; the different chronology of Holy week;[5] and the differences in language Jesus uses compared with the synoptic accounts.[6] He concludes:

> There is, in fact, no material difference in Christology between John and the three synoptists[7] . . . Whatever difficulties some scholars have felt, most readers of the Gospels in all ages have been unaware of any fundamental discrepancy between the Christ who speaks and acts in the fourth Gospel and Him who speaks and acts in the synoptics.[8]

Bruce also refers to J. A. T. Robinson:

> The latest exhaustive enquiry into the dates of NT books . . . by J. A. T. Robinson argues that everything in the NT was written before AD 70, the latest book being Revelation, which he dates preferably under Galba (June 68–January 69). The pivot of his case is the Gospel

of John to the final form of which he gives a date no later
than AD 65. I should not go all the way with some of his
early dating, for I believe that one or two of the NT
documents do imply that the fall of Jerusalem (AD 70)
had already taken place. But Dr Robinson's case is so
well researched and closely reasoned that no-one from
now on should deal with this question of dating without
paying the most serious attention to his arguments.[9]

This reference to the later work of the author of *Honest to
God* (1963) demonstrates the change to a more conservative position which occurred towards the end of his life.

K. A. Kitchen, Reader in Egyptian and Coptic, School
of Archaeology and Oriental Studies, University of
Liverpool writes:

There is the Rylands fragment from a manuscript of
John's gospel . . . datable by its script to about AD 130 – a
little more than a generation after the NT period itself.
As this fragment came from Egypt, it is evident that
John's Gospel had been composed, recopied and begun
to circulate well beyond Palestine *before* AD 130. Hence,
on this evidence alone, it must have been composed (at
latest) by AD 90/100, and more probably earlier.[10]

For the sake of completeness, Dr Donald Guthrie dates the
other books as follows: Hebrews *c*. AD 64;[11] James AD 62 or
earlier;[12] 1 Peter the mid-sixties;[13] 2 Peter (he argues for
Petrine authorship) the late sixties;[14] 1, 2 and 3 John (he
argues for authorship by the apostle John) the late
nineties;[15] Jude AD 65–80;[16] Revelation (he argues for
authorship by the apostle John) AD 90–95.[17]

## The undermining of revelation through the Word

Unwarranted scepticism concerning scripture is currently
the principal way in which God's revelation to mankind

contained in the Word is being undermined. This is obviously a vast subject and we do no more than give one example of this prejudiced approach to the Bible.

It is common practice to criticise the accounts of the resurrection and the post-resurrection appearances of Jesus. Matthew records that Mary Magdalene with the other Mary went to the tomb. There was an earthquake and the angel rolled the stone away and sat on it. He tells the women about the resurrection and they hurry to tell the disciples meeting Jesus on the way.

Mark records that Mary Magdalene with the other Mary and Salome went to the tomb and found the stone already rolled away with a 'young man dressed in a white robe' sitting inside the tomb who tells them of the resurrection. They are fearful and flee, telling no one. Then Jesus appears to Mary Magdalene.

Luke's version is that 'the women' went to the tomb, found the stone removed and saw 'two men in clothes that gleamed like lightning'. Mary Magdalene, Joanna, Mary and others all reported back to the disciples who would not believe them. Peter went to the tomb.

Finally John describes how Mary Magdalene went to the tomb and found the stone had been removed. She ran to tell Peter and John, who ran to the tomb. They left but Mary Magdalene remained and saw 'two angels in white' who asked why she was weeping. Then Jesus appeared to her, after which she went to tell the disciples the news.

We have seen the importance of presuppositions, and in facing apparent contradictions like the post-resurrection narratives a lot depends on our attitude to scripture. If we are prepared to accept that it is God's nature to reveal himself and that, as part of this revelation, he would provide for us a reliable written account of absolute truth in matters of faith and morals, we shall look for a possible harmony of the supposed contradictions. The fact that we may not be able to achieve this will not cause us to believe such a harmony is impossible. Rather it will indicate that we do not have enough information. And if this be construed as irrational and naive, we must remember that scientists use the same principle with regard to the difficulties and contradictions concerning the theory of evolution, as we shall see later. However, if we decide that scripture is fallible, we shall not be too concerned to find an answer to the apparent contradictions.

It is a favourite attitude among liberals to stress the 'contradictions' of the resurrection narratives. After all, it bolsters up the presupposition that the tomb was not empty. I get the impression that these people are not really interested in the possibility of a harmony between the accounts. They assume that is impossible, for this suits their prejudices.

Now any such harmony is bound to be speculative. Therefore dogmatism is out of place. Equally if a satisfactory harmony is theoretically possible then New Testament critics cannot logically be dogmatic that the accounts are contradictory. There may be various possible harmonies: we mention just one which has been current for many years. It seems to harmonise the accounts, each of which, given the emotional turmoil of the resurrection morning, is understandably incomplete:

- Mary Magdalene, Mary the mother of James, and Salome start out for the tomb followed somewhat later by other women carrying spices (Mark 16:1; Luke 23:55–24:1).
- The three named women arrive first at the tomb (the earthquake, the rolling away of the stone and the angel's appearance [Matt. 28:2–4] had happened before they arrived). Mary Magdalene, seeing the stone rolled away, immediately leaves to tell the disciples (John 20:1–2).
- The other Mary and Salome see the angel then go to meet the other women who are following with spices.
- Meanwhile Peter and John, alerted by Mary Magdalene, run to the tomb, look in it and leave (John 20:3–10).
- Mary Magdalene, having returned to the tomb,

remains there weeping. She sees two angels. Then
she sees Jesus (John 20:11–17) and goes, as he tells
her, to tell the disciples (John 20:18).
- Meanwhile the other Mary has met the other women
  who were bringing spices and returns with them to see
  two angels (Luke 24:4–5; Mark 16:5). They also receive a message from the angels and, whilst going
  to report to the disciples, are met by Jesus (Matt.
  28:8–10).

It is important to note that all the accounts are incomplete.
So a reference to the two Marys does not exclude the
possibility of others being with them. A reference to one
angel speaking outside the tomb does not exclude the
possibility of another inside the tomb. Nor is it reasonable
to maintain that the angels did not change their posture
(sitting or standing) or position (inside or outside the
tomb). So the angel who sat on the stone may have moved
inside the tomb before the women arrived. The accounts
are also conflated. For example, Luke 24:10 says that the
two Marys, Joanna and others reported back to the disciples – but this did not necessarily happen all at the
same time. The fact that Mark 16:8 describes the women
as so fearful that they told no one, seems to conflict with
Matthew and Luke. Clearly, however, this would be only a
temporary silence. Maybe the women could not immediately bring themselves to tell the depressed, unbelieving disciples. Or it may be that Matthew and Mark refer to
different groups of women.

Another version of this harmony differs in suggesting all
the women arrived together at the tomb. Mary Magdalene
left before the rest of them saw two angels, the one who sat
on the stone having entered the tomb before they arrived.

Similar apparent contradictions arise in the resurrection
appearances of Jesus. Matthew describes the eleven going
to a mountain in Galilee where he commissions them to
evangelise the world. Some claim this conflicts with Mark
and Luke who only refer to post-resurrection events in the
Jerusalem area, although John describes certain events in

Galilee. It is not necessary to assume Matthew knew nothing of post-resurrection appearances in Jerusalem but, rather, implied that the ascension took place on the mountain in Galilee. It seems that on the day of the resurrection the Lord appeared to Mary Magdalene (John 20:11–17), then the other women (Matt. 28:8–10); to Peter (Luke 24:34); to the disciples on the Emmaus Road (Luke 24:13 –32) and to the apostles, in Thomas' absence (Luke 24:36–43; John 20:19–24). Eight days later he appeared the second time to the company of disciples including Thomas (John 20:24–29). Then he met them the third time (John 21:14) by the sea one morning. Perhaps the 500 witnesses (1 Cor. 15:6) were present on the Galilean mountains. After this Jesus appeared to James (1 Cor. 15:7), probably back in Jerusalem. Finally he met the disciples in Bethany (Luke 24:50–51; Acts 1:6–10).

It is not possible to be dogmatic about harmonies of the resurrection accounts and they may not completely answer every question. But the problems are at least reduced to a minimum and the harmonies are feasible. It is certainly not at all necessary to conclude that the accounts contain inaccuracies. It is fair and reasonable to say that the incompleteness and conflation of each story accounts for the apparent problems between them. There are those who begin with the assumption that scripture cannot be (or need not be) historically accurate in detail. Some of them may not trouble to consider the possible defences of its accuracy such as we have referred to above. It would be in their interest to undermine such defences, or dismiss them, in order to support their negative presuppositions.

Scepticism concerning scripture is not the only attitude which undermines the truth that God has provided us with an authoritative, complete and clear account of his revelation to man. Other attitudes are the desire for an agnosticism over doctrine; a desire for inclusiveness; and a capitulation to the emotions.

## Agnosticism over doctrine

Speaking to the York Convocation of Clergy in October 1984, Archbishop John Habgood said: 'Any theology which imagines that it can straightforwardly describe the realities to which it points is bound to be false, because it ignores the very dimension which makes it theology rather than science or literature or history . . . it is essentially tentative, exploratory, varied.' The logical implication of this statement is that the Bible is false because it straightforwardly describes the realities of the faith and is not tentative or exploratory.

David Jenkins in General Synod (July 1986) claimed: 'It is simply not true that there is anywhere a church which is guaranteed to get it right under God . . . there is no church with knock-down authority which can settle decisively and definitely declare for ever what God is like and what God wants.'[18] But this ignores the definitive authority of scripture which is available to the church. In fact the context was a consideration of the doctrines of the virginal conception and the empty tomb. Scripture describes a God whose nature and will is to perform such miracles but the bishop was doubting this. His words were therefore a denial of the authority of scripture to declare for ever what God is like and what God wants. This is clear because two paragraphs later he denies that Anglicanism is 'biblicist protestant'.[19]

He continues: 'We need to be clear that living together and serving the world is more important than being right and in the right.'[20] Such a statement is very popular in a tolerant age like ours, especially in a church which prides itself on its tolerance. But it is a contradiction of the New Testament. Paul strongly condemns those who proclaim a false gospel:

Even if we or an angel from heaven should preach a gospel other than the one we preached to you, let him be eternally condemned! As we have already said, so now I say again: If anyone is preaching to you a gospel other

than what you accepted, let him be eternally condemned!
(Gal. 1:8–9; cf. 2 Cor. 11:4–6,13–15)

The first epistle of John condemns as antichrists those who
deny that Jesus is Messiah (1 John 2:22–23). The same is
true of those who deny the incarnation (1 John 4:1–3;
2 John 7–11). Those denying the incarnation should not be
welcomed or given hospitality (2 John 10–11). It is clear
from these writers that correct theology does matter,
although they would never have favoured a dead, legalistic
orthodoxy.

These statements that all theology must be tentative,
exploratory and uncertain might seem humble. In fact they
are not. They are proud refusals to submit to the authority
and clarity of scripture as the reliable account of God's
complete revelation to man. It seems that some Christians
wish to make up their religion as they go along. If so, they
can hardly claim that their version of Christianity is the real
thing.

## The desire for inclusiveness

Then there is a passionate desire, especially in the Church
of England, to be inclusive: to retain in leadership those
denying fundamental beliefs. The Bishops' Report on *The
Nature of Christian Belief* is a classic example of this desire.
It affirms that the virginal conception and the empty tomb
are the teaching of the universal church and express the
faith of the Church of England. Yet it clearly allows bishops
who publicly doubt or deny these truths to remain in office.
Introducing the Report to General Synod in July 1986
Archbishop Runcie said:

That the vast majority of Christians throughout history
have accepted the empty tomb and the virginal conception as historical facts is not in dispute. Any other
interpretation is a departure from that held in the universal church. For this majority, such facts sustain and
illumine faith in the Resurrection and Incarnation. But

they are by no means the only facts on which those great central events rest. That is why it is possible to believe fully in the Resurrection and Incarnation while reserving judgment on these specific historical points.[21]

This is a masterly statement from the point of view of ecclesiastical politics but it is neither logical nor Anglican nor biblical. It is not logical to believe in the resurrection if Jesus' bodily remains are still lying in the tomb. It is not Anglican to deny the virginal conception and the empty tomb because the historical legal formularies of the Church of England require belief in these two doctrines. It is not biblical to deny their historicity. Yet the House of Bishops allowed this contradiction of logic, tradition and scripture in order to include bishops who doubt or deny these beliefs. Inclusiveness, therefore, takes precedence over submission to divine revelation. (It is heartening, therefore, that in the following Synod, the Houses of Clergy and Laity voted overwhelmingly to reaffirm these two doctrines as the faith of the Church of England.)

## Capitulating to emotions

One major factor which bedevils discussion of this whole area of controversy is the emotion which fogs the issues. David Jenkins' notorious speech to General Synod in July 1986, to which we have already referred, received a standing ovation. Yet, it seems, he described the God in whom we believe as 'a cultic idol or even the very devil'. I can only conclude that this ovation resulted from a mixture of politeness; English support for the under-dog; a few good things in the speech and the passion with which the bishop spoke (he almost broke down at one point). Clearly many who heard the speech allowed emotional considerations to cause them to applaud what was in fact a serious undermining of divine revelation.

Describing an earlier debate on the same issues in February 1985,[22] Donald Allister wrote:

Distortion was the order of the day in this debate: and it earned generous applause from Synod. On this occasion I will refrain from naming the so-called evangelical leaders who applauded enthusiastically as the Bishop of Winchester turned the whole Gospel upside down, the Archbishop of Canterbury emptied it of all content and the Archbishop of York blatantly preached another gospel. God help us all.

Two evangelicals present replied to this report, saying they had applauded because it was polite to do so. Somehow I cannot see St Paul doing this. When the gospel is at stake it is not enough (or even legitimate) to be polite. When the Senior Evangelical Anglican Clergy Conference (December 1984) discussed the Durham affair, some members wanted to emphasise peace, unity and friendly dialogue with theological opponents. Incredibly the whole House of Bishops including several convinced Evangelicals and Anglo-Catholics signed *The Nature of Christian Belief*, which effectively made belief in the virginal conception and the empty tomb optional. This polite easy-going compromise contrasts with the teaching and ethos of the New Testament. Again emotional considerations are allowed to undermine submission to divine revelation.

## Revelation through other means

It is apparent, even from a study of the biblical text, that God has chosen to reveal himself to man in a number of different ways. We shall now look at some of these.

### Through creation

God proclaimed that 'he has not left himself without testimony: He has shown kindness by giving . . . rain from heaven and crops in their seasons' (Acts 14:17). Paul goes on to state that 'since the creation of the world God's invisible qualities – his eternal power and divine nature –

have been clearly seen, being understood from what has been made, so that men are without excuse' (Rom. 1:20; cf. Ps. 19:1; 97:6).

## Through providence

One very effective means of revelation is through personal experience. With the eye of faith, believers recognise divine intervention in their lives (for example Isa. 25:1–5). This may take the form of a deep experience of love, joy, peace and awe which is consciously related to the presence of God. It may include what are seen as answers to prayer and, at times, unsolicited experiences of God's blessing and protection. Anyone who denies the legitimacy of faith or the reality of a God who intervenes will probably be able to satisfy himself that such experiences are either subjective or are produced by natural causes. But a person open to the possibility of faith can come to personal faith through an experience perceived to be one of divine providence. At times even decided sceptics have come to faith through this means: Paul was won to faith through his vision of Christ (Acts 9:1–19). The Philippian gaoler was won through the experience of the earthquake in the context of the witness of Paul and Silas (Acts 16:25–34). The writer to the Hebrews teaches that God testified to the message 'by signs, wonders and various miracles, and gifts of the Holy Spirit' (Heb. 2:4; cf. Mark 16:20). I have a friend who as an unbelieving soldier came to faith when his life was spared in a bomb attack on his army vehicle.

## Through the witness of the church

The New Testament teaches that every believer is part of the body of Christ and is meant to benefit from the various ministries God has put within the body. Clearly the corporate interpretation of the Bible by the church is more reliable than that of the individual member. He will therefore benefit from the teaching ministry of the church as it

seeks to interpret scripture with respect to local circumstances. The Council of Jerusalem in Acts 15 shows the
validity of the church doing this, though that gathering was
unique in that the apostles were present to govern the
proceedings. The implication is that subsequent councils of
the church are legitimate but any conclusions and traditions
they produce must be subject to apostolic scriptural
teaching. One of the great contributions of the church to
the understanding of biblical revelation are the creeds. The
Nicene Creed may have been produced by the Council of
Constantinople in AD 381. The Apostles' Creed reached its
final form by the Middle Ages. Both are in regular use
in modern liturgies and have aided the faith and understanding of many generations of Christians. The Athan-
asian Creed, generally not thought to have been produced
by Athanasius, probably dates from between AD 381 and
428.

## Through human reason and conscience

The human mind is important in the teaching of the New
Testament: we are to love God with our minds (Matt.
22:37); to be 'clear minded' (1 Pet. 4:7) and to prepare our
minds for action (1 Pet. 1:13). We are to be united in mind
(Acts 4:32; 1 Cor. 1:10; 2 Cor. 13:11) and to set our minds
'on things above' (Col. 3:2). But the devil 'has blinded the
minds of unbelievers' (2 Cor. 4:4). The sinful mind of a
person who lives according to the sinful nature is hostile to
God and cannot submit to his law (Rom. 8:5–7). God gives
persistent sinners over 'to a depraved mind' (Rom. 1:28).
So Paul can say: 'If anyone of you thinks he is wise by the
standards of this age, he should become a "fool" so that he
may become wise. For the wisdom of this world is foolishness in God's sight' (1 Cor. 3:18–19). Or as he puts it in
Romans 12:2: 'be transformed by the renewing of your
mind' (cf. Eph. 4:23).

Similarly conscience is important. Paul believes in living
according to conscience (Rom. 9:1; 13:5; 2 Cor. 1:12; cf.

1 Pet. 3:16,21). Faith must be held with a clear conscience
(1 Tim. 1:5,19; 3:9). Paul commends himself to the scrutiny
of other people's consciences (1 Cor. 4:2; 5:11; 10:27–29).
However, conscience is fallible (1 Cor. 4:4). It can be weak
and oversensitive (1 Cor. 8:7–12) or even seared (1 Tim.
4:2) and corrupted (Tit. 1:15). Consequently although God
can reveal himself through human reason and conscience,
these faculties need renewing and cleansing through
the power of the Holy Spirit. They are fallible guides
and therefore need to be educated by the Spirit of
truth, especially through submission to the teaching of
scripture.

## The spoken gifts of the Spirit

A consideration of divine revelation through the written
and spoken word would be seriously incomplete without
reference to the verbal spiritual gifts. The current renewed
experience of these spiritual gifts points again to the desire
of God to communicate with his people. They do not add to
scripture: rather they are to be weighed carefully (1 Cor.
14:29) to see if they are genuine and scriptural. It is a
characteristic of the sheep of the Good Shepherd that 'they
know his voice' (John 10:4). So it was that when the church
at Antioch 'were worshipping the Lord and fasting, the
Holy Spirit said, "Set apart for me Barnabas and Saul for
the work to which I have called them." So after they had
fasted and prayed, they placed their hands upon them and
sent them off' (Acts 13:2–3).

It would be unwise to be too dogmatic as to the exact
nature of these gifts. However some information can be
gained from the titles of the gifts in the New Testament,
especially when related to the various, apparently relevant,
supernatural experiences both of biblical characters and
modern Christians. The following definitions are suggested
as guidelines:

*The message of wisdom* (1 Cor. 12:8)
A supernatural revelation of the solution to a particular problem or crisis. The way Jesus answered the 'loaded' questions from Jewish leaders may be an example of this gift (Matt. 21:23–27; Luke 20:19–26; John 8:3–11) especially in view of the powerful effect on his audience (Luke 20:26). It is a fact of Christian experience that a sudden inspiration of wisdom can be given in very perplexing circumstances.

*The message of knowledge* (1 Cor. 12:8)
A supernatural revelation concerning a difficulty or need, of facts not known naturally. It seems likely that Jesus' knowledge of the background of the Samaritan woman in John 4:16–19 is an example of this gift. Many modern Christians have experienced similar revelations which have proved accurate, especially concerning people in need.

*Prophecy* (1 Cor. 12:10,28; cf. Eph. 4:11; Rom. 12:6)
A supernatural revelation of God's will for the present and plans for the future which challenges, encourages and comforts the people of God (1 Cor. 14:3–5) and convicts the unbeliever of sin (1 Cor. 14:24–25). As with other gifts, the speaker remains in control when he speaks (1 Cor. 14:30–33,39–40). The message may come through visions or dreams (Acts 2:17–18; 9:10; 10:3,11; 16:9; 18:9; 22:18; 23:11; 2 Cor. 12:1).

*Tongues and the interpretation of tongues* (1 Cor. 12:10)
Tongues is the supernatural ability to praise God in a language never learned; an earthly or a heavenly language (1 Cor. 13:1) not understood by the speaker (1 Cor. 14:14) or – normally – by the hearers (1 Cor. 14:2). Its primary use is private (1 Cor. 14:4,18–19) but it may be used with interpretation in public. The interpretation of tongues is the supernatural ability to interpret a public message in tongues (1 Cor. 14:13–17,27–28).

*Teaching* (1 Cor. 12:28; Eph. 4:11; Rom. 12:7)
Also a gift of the Spirit, perhaps lacking some of the high
level of direct inspiration of other gifts, being a ministry
of explaining biblical truth simply and accurately, and
ensuring that the hearers understand and obey.

Scripture is normative but God has not ceased to reveal
himself. He continues to do so through the Bible; through
spiritual experience; through the gifts of the Spirit; through
the mind and conscience (of individuals and the church)
transformed by the Spirit. But all human interpretation,
experience, gifts and thoughts must be tested by scripture
(cf. Acts 17:11).

# Submitting to God's Sovereignty in Revelation

Christians who have been brought up in a conservative theological tradition have to face the challenge of liberal theology. For some who have been unable to cope with it the challenge has undermined or even destroyed their faith. Others have not allowed it to get through to them and learn about it simply in order to reject it. Still others, through at least partial acceptance of liberal theology, have experienced a temporary sense of relief that they can still be Christians without having to accept everything the Bible teaches. They no longer have to accept all the miracles as historical; they no longer have to defend biblical teaching which does not harmonise with modern thinking; apparent mistakes or contradictions in the biblical text no longer matter. The relief leads on to a new sense of freedom; a new openness to ideas that once were threatening.

This apparently positive experience is, however, deceptive. Such people have stepped out on to a slippery slope. Some may move into an extreme liberal position. Others will lose something of their sensitivity to the Holy Spirit, though initially they are unlikely to be aware of it. Having rejected certain aspects of divine revelation they are open to spiritual deceit over other matters. They have capitulated to rationalistic presuppositions. To that extent their minds are not transformed by the Holy Spirit. Rather they have become prey to the spirit of unbelief – a subtle but demonic spirit – which particularly afflicts us in the western world today. What is thought to be intellectual or emotional acceptability too easily becomes the criterion for judging

truth and discerning error. Even those who retain a high
view of scripture will tend to judge its teaching using this
criterion. This, of course, is not the same as careful interpretation of scripture; it is changing its teaching to fit
humanistic presuppositions.

There are many people who have been brought up in the
liberal tradition. Even those who have read theology may
never have been presented with a good defence of a
conservative position. Given the tendency to caricature the
conservative position as naive and obscurantist, some liberals may have learnt about that position simply in order to
reject it. Such an approach contradicts the scholarly openness which is supposed to characterise the liberal position.

How can those affected by liberal theology become free
to accept scripture as the completely reliable, authoritative
and clearly written account of God's revelation to man, as
we have attempted to describe it? I include some important
steps in the following section.

## Check and renew your spiritual foundations

Some liberals (and some conservatives) have not come to
experience the reality and fulness of a saving faith. In
recent months I have met several Anglican incumbents who
have only come to a personal saving faith some years after
they were ordained. I know others who came to such faith
during theological training. Those who have not yet experienced this personal faith will often be sincere in seeking to
practise a Christian lifestyle: they may feel strongly about
Christian theology and be deeply committed to the church
and its work but they lack the personal intimate relationship with Christ in trust and love. They do not have the
assurance of a personal loving acceptance by God, for time
and eternity through repentance and faith, on the basis of
Christ's death. They have not experienced the supernatural
new birth by the action of the Holy Spirit. The Holy Spirit
will doubtless be influencing them, but since they have not
personally received him as the Spirit of truth, it is not

surprising if they have problems and doubts about biblical authority and reliability. (Conservatives in the same spiritual state will be experiencing an orthodoxy which lacks spiritual life.)

This living relationship with Christ is a gift of God's grace and not deserved by any of us. God wants everyone to enjoy it with its spiritual benefits. It takes real courage and humility to acknowledge that one's spiritual foundation is lacking. But even clergy have done this and been richly rewarded.

If this is relevant to you, pray for such faith; re-read the New Testament; ask God the Father to reveal himself to you personally through the Holy Spirit as you repent and commit your life in a new way to God the Son on the basis of his work of salvation. Lay down your presuppositions before God. Sincerely done, this is not an academic exercise. It can lead to real changes. Offer to God your intellect (for him to renew) and any rationalistic presuppositions for him to change as he wishes. Similarly offer him the presupposition that what he has given to us cannot be a completely reliable, authoritative and clear written account of his revelation in Christ. Offer your problems and doubts concerning scripture including divine intervention in the form of miracles. Tell God that you are willing for these things to be changed or, if they are wrong, removed. Repent of any attitudes you know to be wrong. For example, if you think you have fallen into a presumptuous rejection of part of God's revelation, repent of it. Repentance is a gift (Acts 5:31; 11:18; 2 Tim. 2:25) and can therefore be prayed for. It includes 'godly sorrow' (2 Cor. 7:10). So it is important to renounce unbelief, recognising that without faith it is impossible to please God (Heb. 11:6). Unbelief, even in Christians, is a sin.

Then ask God to release you from the spirit of unbelief. It may be helpful to ask an experienced discreet counsellor to pray with you. However, repentance also includes good deeds (Acts 26:20). So it is important to make a definite commitment to accept the authority of scripture.

The next step is to ask God to fill you with the Spirit of truth (John 14:16–17) which he is very willing to do (Luke 11:13). Deliberately open your heart, mind and spirit to Christ for this blessing. Again it may be good to seek some help.

The scriptures are the foundation upon which a renewed personal faith can be built. Make it a habit to read scripture regularly. Read it as a devotional exercise, asking God for a fresh understanding and appreciation of it. You may also find it helpful to read some books defending a high view of scripture (see Appendix 1).

# Part II

# GOD'S SOVEREIGNTY IN CREATION

# The God Who Created

We have looked at the way in which God's sovereignty in revelation is being undermined. But, as noted, one major way God reveals himself is through creation. However, the theory of evolution has had the effect of making many people feel God is remote from creation. Some have drawn the illogical conclusion that the theory does away with the need to believe in God. Yet, as we shall now see, God is Creator of the universe and all mankind should acknowledge this. First we examine the biblical teaching on creation.

## The majesty of creation

The majestic opening chapters of the Bible describe God creating the heavens and the earth by his powerful Word (Gen. 1:1,3,6,9,11,14,20,24,26). The Psalmist says 'he commanded and they were created' (Ps. 148:5); and 'by the word of the Lord were the heavens made, their starry host by the breath of his mouth' (Ps. 33:6). The writer to the Hebrews teaches that 'by faith we understand that the universe was formed at God's command, so that what is seen was not made out of what was visible' (Heb. 11:3). In fact the universe is sustained by the powerful word of Christ (Heb. 1:2–3); 'in him all things hold together' (Col. 1:17).

Here is no pantheism (God being everything and everything being God) or deism (a remote God leaving his creation to run by itself) or thought of matter always having

existed. Instead we have a transcendent, personal Creator
distinct from his creation yet personally sustaining it. He
created the universe out of what is invisible (Heb. 11:3).
The Son of God was the agent through whom God created
everything (John 1:3; Heb. 1:2–3). He was present with the
Father in the beginning (John 1:1–3) as was the Spirit of
God hovering over the formless, empty, dark water-
covered earth (Gen. 1:2). The wisdom by which God
created the universe (Prov. 3:19–20; Jer. 10:12) is personified in Proverbs 8:22–31. These rudiments of the doctrine of the Trinity, hinting at a fellowship of persons within
God, underlines the concept of a personal Creator.

The fact that God spoke the universe into being and
maintains it by his powerful word emphasises his sovereignty and power (see Jer. 10:13; 27:5; 32:17; 51:15).
Jeremiah's response to God as Creator is 'Nothing is too
hard for you' (Jer. 32:17). But God has a special purpose in
creation. Everything in heaven and earth, visible and invisible, every power and authority has been created for
Christ so that he might have the supremacy (Col. 1:16–18;
cf. Rom. 11:36; Heb. 2:10). The fact that God created the
universe for his own glory and especially that he created it
through and for Christ makes creation seem so personal. It
is created by persons, for personal reasons and particularly
for the motive of love.

The creation of man from the dust (Gen. 2:7) may stress
the frailty of men compared with the sovereignty of God,
but the great dignity given to man is shown in his special
creation in the image of God (Gen. 1:26–27); 'he is the
image and glory of God' (1 Cor. 11:7; cf. Gen. 9:6). Man is
the offspring of God (Acts 17:29), only a little lower than
the angels crowned with glory and honour (Ps. 8:5; Heb.
2:6–8). The Bible even frowns on cursing man who has
been made in God's likeness (Jas. 3:9). It is artificial to
divide up man in order to relate the image of God to one
aspect of his humanity. Man, the dignified high point of
creation, reflects the image of God in his thinking, feeling
and acting. The ability to reach the heights of love for God

and neighbour in communication and sacrifice is a key factor in the image of God – a factor spoilt by sin.

Man is given the authority to rule over creation (Gen. 1:26,28; Ps. 8:6–8); to take care of it (Gen. 2:15) and to enjoy it (Gen. 2:9; 1:29). He is a social being who needs companionship (Gen. 2:18). The most intimate human companionship is marriage. On the basis of a deep social commitment (leaving the parental home) a man and his wife may find fulfilment in sexual union (Gen. 2:24) and so perpetuate the human race through procreation (Gen. 1:28; 9:1,7). The essential equality of male and female is taught (Gen. 1:27; 5:1–2) as is the purity of sexual relations within marriage (Gen. 2:24–25).

The Psalmist praises God who knit him together in his mother's womb; God's eyes saw his unformed body (Ps. 139:13–16). The Servant was called by God before he was born (Isa. 49:1), as was Jeremiah (Jer. 1:5). John the Baptist was filled with the Holy Spirit 'from birth' (Luke 1:15): but perhaps before birth, because in Luke 1:44 his mother Elizabeth says to Mary, who is also pregnant: 'As soon as the sound of your greeting reached my ears, the baby in my womb leaped for joy.'

However, the most profound argument for the dignity and humanity of even the earliest embryo is from the incarnation. If the incarnation did not take place at the conception, when did it take place? Could there have been some intermediate state when the second person of the Trinity was united with something which was not fully human? Surely the incarnation took place at the virginal conception and this necessarily means the embryo was fully human, albeit not capable of independent existence. Interestingly the reaction of the unborn John the Baptist (Luke 1:44) must have taken place less than three months into Mary's pregnancy (Luke 1:26; cf. vv. 56–57). This implies the incarnation had already taken place at conception when the Holy Spirit came upon Mary and the power of the Most High overshadowed her (Luke 1:35).

The Bible requires a belief that the human race began

from a single couple. This is taught in Genesis 2–3 but it is confirmed in the New Testament. Paul, preaching in Athens, says, 'From one man (God) made every nation of men, that they should inhabit the whole earth' (Acts 17:26). He teaches that the whole human race is in Adam and therefore experiences death (1 Cor. 15:21–22; Rom. 5:12–19). Clearly he regards Adam as a real person (1 Cor. 15:45–49; cf. 1 Cor. 11:8–9; 2 Cor. 11:3; 1 Tim. 2:13–14).

## Moral implications

We have seen that God in his sovereignty made man as the high point of creation. The dignity this gives to man involves certain moral obligations.

### Man is responsible to obey God

In Genesis 2:17 God gives man a moral choice – whether or not to eat of the tree of the knowledge of good and evil. To eat means death. Faced with this moral responsibility man chooses to fall to temptation (3:1–6). The result is guilt, fear (3:7–11; cf. 2:25) and alienation from God (3:23–24).

### Man is responsible to preserve human life

Because man is created in the image of God his life is sacred. Hence the condemnation of Cain after he had murdered Abel (Gen. 4:10–12). In the covenant with Noah God makes it clear that anyone who takes the life of a man will face the death penalty (Gen. 9:5–6; cf. Exod. 21:12–14; Lev. 24:17,21; Deut. 27:24). These passages allow a man's life to be taken in exceptional circumstances, such as when he is convicted of murder. This responsibility to preserve human life of course applies also to the unborn human being.

## Man is responsible to maintain sexual faithfulness

We have seen that sexual union is for a heterosexual couple within marriage. Sexual immorality is condemned throughout scripture. The body is not meant for immorality (1 Cor. 6:13–20). Immorality is to be 'put to death' along with impurity and lust (Col. 3:5). Immoral church members must be avoided (1 Cor. 5:9–11). In fact God's judgment is coming on immoral people (Col. 3:6; 1 Thess. 4:3–6; Heb. 13:4). They will not inherit the kingdom of God (1 Cor. 6:9; Eph. 5:3–5; cf. Rev. 21:8; 22:15).

Fornication is specifically condemned in Deuteronomy 22:20–21. Adultery, which is destructive to marriage, is singled out for special condemnation (Exod. 20:14; Lev. 18:20; 20:10; Prov. 5; 6:29,32). Even adultery in the mind is taken very seriously by Jesus (Matt. 5:27–30). God will judge adultery (Heb. 13:4). Similarly homosexual practice is clearly condemned as 'detestable' (Lev. 18:22; 20:13); 'shameful . . . unnatural . . . indecent . . . perversion' (Rom. 1:26–27). Along with the sexually immoral and adulterers, 'homosexual offenders' will not inherit the kingdom of God (1 Cor. 6:9–10).[1]

## Man is responsible to promote human welfare

Isaiah 58:6–9 calls God's people to remove injustice; to set the oppressed free; to share food with the hungry, shelter with the homeless, clothes with the naked. The judgment of the nations is based on such criteria (Matt. 25:31–46). Oppression of the poor is condemned as showing contempt for God (Prov. 14:31; 17:5; cf. Deut. 24:14–15). He will take up the case of the oppressed poor (Prov. 22:22–23; 23:10–11; cf. Ps. 140:12; Exod. 22:22–24). So the sovereign Lord upholds the dignity of man, the high point of his creation.

## *Man is responsible to care for creation*

Man was commanded by God to rule over the animal kingdom (Gen. 1:28) and given seed-bearing plants and trees with seeded fruits for food (Gen. 1:29). The trees were pleasing to look at as well as good for food (Gen. 2:9): man was to tend and take care of his environment (Gen. 2:15). As a result of the Fall, this responsibility became arduous and painful (Gen. 3:17,19). Creation was spoilt, as was man's relationship with animals (Gen. 9:1–3). An original vegetarianism was changed by God (Gen. 9:3).

# 6

## Evolution Undermined

In the last hundred years the theory of evolution has often been used to undermine the sovereignty of God in creation. Christians are not called to be obscurantists or to oppose scientific enquiry. As scientists discover more about the created world, this can increase our appreciation of the greatness of God. God has given us minds, and therefore we must take scientific conclusions seriously and relate them to divine revelation in scripture. This process may lead us to recognise the inadequacy or inaccuracy of our previous interpretations of scripture. So science can help us understand more of God's revelation. For example, many Christians have become theistic evolutionists and have sought to harmonise the theory of evolution with belief in God and with biblical teaching.

However, science itself must be open to honest critical analysis. It is not scientific to call theory proven fact. Still less is it scientific to hold a theory with such emotional conviction that criticism of it is vehemently dismissed as irrelevant or stupid. Yet this sort of unscientific dogmatism does affect some scientists. For example, Dr Richard Dawkins (Lecturer in Animal Behaviour at Oxford) says: 'Darwinism is always under attack. Most people don't understand a truth like Einstein's relativity theory, but they don't seem to feel the same urge to lob ignorant criticisms at it.'[1] It is easy to label someone a 'fundamentalist' and so dismiss his views without argument or sufficient reason. But that too is unscientific. The same article refers to the views of the Archbishop of York: 'Fundamentalists have so far made little impact here with what Archbishop Dr John Habgood calls "transatlantic pseudo-science". A scientist by training, the Archbishop has hailed Dawkins for giving the *coup de grâce* to all sorts of "rubbish".' Dr Peter Adkins of the Department of Physical Chemistry, Oxford describes creationism as 'intellectual excrement of the first order and I don't think we need to worry about it any further'.[2] But is all doubt about evolution 'pseudo-science' and 'rubbish'? It would not worry me at all if evolution were to be proved tomorrow. But what are the facts about it today?

Michael Denton, a research molecular biologist at the Prince of Wales Hospital, New South Wales, has recently challenged not only Darwinian natural selection but the whole concept of evolution. In his book *Evolution: A Theory in Crisis* he accepts minor evolutionary change but states that the evidence is overwhelmingly against evolution between the major types of plants and animals. Scientists have almost completely failed to close the gaps in the fossil record.

In 1981 the Natural History Museum, London held an exhibition on Darwinism. The notices stated:

> One idea is that all the living things we see today have evolved from a distant ancestor by a process of gradual change . . . The exhibition in this hall looks at one possible explanation – the explanation first thought of by Charles Darwin . . . Another view is that God created all living things perfect and unchanging.

A leaflet included the phrase, 'If the theory of evolution is true . . .'. The scientific journal *Nature* strongly reacted against this particular wording. In its next issue was a letter signed by twenty-two biologists working at the museum:

> As working biologists at the British Museum (Natural History) we were astonished to read your editorial 'Darwin's death in South Kensington'. How is it that such a journal as yours that is devoted to science and its

practice can advocate that theory be presented as fact? This is the stuff of prejudice, not science, and as scientists our basic concern is to keep an open mind on the unknowable. Surely it should not be otherwise?

You suggest that most of us would rather lose our right hands than begin a sentence with the phrase 'If the theory of evolution is true . . .' Are we to take it that evolution is a fact, proven to the limits of scientific rigour? If that is the inference, then we must disagree most strongly. We have no absolute proof of the theory of evolution. What we do have is overwhelming circumstantial evidence in favour of it and as yet no better alternative.[3]

Some scientists, although remaining evolutionists, are very critical of evolutionary theory. Professor Stephen Jay Gould from Harvard says that most species arose within hundreds of thousands of years and then remained unchanged for millions of years.[4] He argues for 'punctuated equilibria', that is, evolution happening in short bursts separated by very long periods of time. Another group of biologists believe that animals should be classified according to observed biological facts and not according to the theory of evolution. This calls into question much evolutionary history. A French biologist, Professor Andrée Tétry criticises Darwinism and alternative evolutionary theories, as does Professor Pierre-Paul Grassé, Director of the Laboratory of the Evolution of Living Beings, University of Paris.[5]

The problem is that in the media and in education the theory of evolution is being put over as fact and many people uncritically conclude there is no need for God or creation. One good example is David Attenborough's TV series *Life on Earth*. Admittedly in the first programme he says it is legitimate to make 'informed speculations' and: 'It is a reasonable guess that these creatures evolved' and: 'Although we can't be sure of evolutionary pathways, relationships are clear.' But many later comments sound like a fairy tale, all too easily accepted uncritically as fact by many viewers. For example: 'Early in history spiders developed glands which produced silk'; 'In the course of time some plants developed that were able to grow upright and several feet tall'; 'Some insects turned their mouth parts into tubes so that they could reach deep into the flower'; 'The ray has flattened its body even more'; 'A group started constructing their skeletons not of cartilage but of bone'; '350 million years ago, one fish hauled itself out on to the land and from it developed frogs, lizards, mammals and, ultimately, ourselves'; 'one reptile insulated its body not with feathers but with fur'.

## The religious nature of evolutionary thinking

E. G. Conklin, a leading Darwinist, wrote: 'The concept of organic evolution is very highly prized by biologists, for many of whom it is an object of genuinely religious devotion, because they regard it as a supreme integrative principle'.[6] Professor L. H. Matthews states: 'Belief in evolution is exactly parallel to belief in special creation – both are concepts which believers know to be true, but neither, up to the present, has been capable of proof.'[7] Dr Colin Patterson of the Natural History Museum has said: 'Biology is being carried out by people whose faith is in, almost, the deity of Darwin.'[8] Professor G. A. Kerkut of Southampton University wrote: 'It seems at times as if many of our writers on evolution have had their views by some sort of revelation.'[9]

## The atheistic nature of evolutionary thinking

We have noted that there are many theistic evolutionists. But equally there is a large number of atheistic evolutionists. And the effect of the theory of evolution, especially as conveyed by many scientists and teachers, is to encourage many people to conclude that we no longer need to believe in God.

Professor Richard Dawkins is one atheistic evolutionist. He says 'God is a deeply untidy frill':[10]

Nowadays we have an alternative and in my opinion a more satisfying explanation for the existence of things like eyes, complicated things that have the appearance of being designed for a purpose. That answer is Darwin's Theory of Natural Selection. And my book *The Blind Watchmaker* is an attempt to explain Darwin's Theory . . . as it plays its role as, in a sense, replacing God in our world view . . . I think it does make God superfluous. I think it is possible to say that the Darwinian account of how life is, and how it came to be where it is, is entirely sufficient without the need for any additional postulate such as a God. But, of course, this doesn't rule out the possibility that there is a God. My own view is that where something is both superfluous and exceedingly complicated, and therefore improbable in its own right, we are better off being not merely agnostic about it, but positively sceptical about it.[11]

Dr Peter Adkins has said on television:

I see the role of the Creator as actually slowly slipping away and at the moment he's hanging on by his last finger nail . . . and is about to drop off into oblivion, which is where he belongs, of course. People will still go on believing that there is something out there, but the only justification they have, will be a yearning for it, not reality . . . I think the acid test of the battle that is going on between science and religion will be science's ability to show that the entire world could tumble out of nothing. It's already got back to within a photon's throw of the origin of the Universe, as we've gone back into the 'big bang', and almost to the point of talking about what happened before the 'big bang'. And I see no reason why we should not go beyond the 'big bang' and talk about its inception – how the Universe emerged from absolutely nothing – not just from empty space but from nothing, and how it did so without intervention. And if science can do that, then I think that the religions must concede defeat.[12]

On the same programme Alan Guth, Professor of Physics at Massachusetts Institute of Technology, said: 'It seems possible that the fundamental laws of nature can start with absolutely nothing and produce the universe that we see.' The programme concluded with the statement:

In the beginning the universe erupted spontaneously out of nothing. A featureless ferment of quantum energy inflated bubbles of space to cosmic proportions, filling the void with a fireball of heat. Out of this fireball came all matter and all physical features. As this fireball faded so the stars began to shine, generating planets and eventually life. Thus the universe became self-aware.

In a way Adkins and Guth are referring to the biblical concept of creation out of nothing (*ex nihilo*). It would be fascinating to know how they will *prove* it was without intervention. They ignore the spiritual world, of course, and seem unconcerned about the question of the meaning and purpose of the universe.

## The deification of evolution

One strangely illogical and even mystical aspect of evolutionary theory is that the process of evolution is seen as a distinct entity in itself. It is almost personified or 'deified' into some pantheistic presence in the whole of nature. I am convinced – especially as the inadequacies of evolutionary theory (particularly the atheistic version) become more widely acknowledged – that there will be a move towards pantheism. The influence of eastern religions, already strong in the West, will blend with evolutionary thinking. Some pantheistic force inherent in nature will be seen as the driving force of evolution. If anything this view will be more effective in leading people away from the Christian view of God, and therefore of eternal salvation.

Richard Dawkins entitled his book *The Blind Watchmaker*, referring to William Paley's famous eighteenth-century 'watchmaker' argument for the existence of God. Anyone finding a watch on the heath would realise its intricate mechanism had a purpose and a designer. How much more so must nature's complexity require a designer – God, the divine watchmaker. Dawkins says, 'The only watchmaker in nature is the blind forces of physics.'[13] He believes in cumulative natural selection:

> Natural selection is not random. In any generation random mutation in genes occurs randomly; natural selection means that successful organisms in that generation reproduce and pass on those mutations. The process continues cumulatively so that over a long stretch of time, the slight changes eventually lead to complex organisms.[14]

> Without the blind watchmaker there would be no chromosomes, no embryos, no eyes, no stick insects, fish, you or me and the dinosaurs would never have existed . . . Chance with natural selection, chance smeared out into innumerable tiny steps over aeons of time, is powerful enough to manufacture miracles like dinosaurs and ourselves.[15]

Dawkins generates figures he calls Biomorph on computer, by selecting from random variations produced by 18 quasi-genes. One gene dictates width, another length, another branchingness, and so on. You choose the most suitable figure from each 'generation' of figures produced by the computer. This operation would only seem relevant to reality if you 'personified' natural selection. But perhaps the most outstanding statement appearing to 'deify' natural selection is Dawkins' comment on life on other planets: 'If we do discover it, we already know the most important thing about it. It could only have got there by Darwinian means.'[16] Similarly David Attenborough in *Life on Earth* makes a statement of the sort common to many evolutionists: 'Evolution solved the problem of spherical aberration.' Professor Barry Cross, director of the Agriculture and Food Research Council's research into animal physiology and genetics, said, 'Evolution is no fool – it eliminates the weak bits.'[17] Surely evolution is simply a theoretical description: it cannot do anything. But this illogical 'personification' or 'deification' of evolution has a profound effect on many people. It seems to do away with the need of God. Actually it is a form of pantheism.

This tendency towards an impersonal, pantheistic God, is shown in statements made by two scientists on the Everyman programme *The Creation*. Paul Davies, Professor of Theoretical Physics of Newcastle University said:

> The traditional God has had to retreat further and further in the face of scientific advance. We now have a picture of the universe which runs itself perfectly satisfactorily without the need for any supernatural agency. We don't need a God to, as it were, oil the cogwheels of the cosmic machine. I think there is a particular difficulty about the idea of a God who answers prayer – a God who sits in judgment, a God who involves himself in the day to day affairs of the world. And the problem is that in the modern scientific version of the creation we see that space and time are themselves part of creation. So any God has to be outside of space and time and it's very hard to reconcile such a God with the notion of a personal God – one who answers prayer and so forth.

Peter Adkins believes that what explains the universe is not God but a set of simple mathematical rules:

> I find that very exciting and I find the thought that mathematics might be behind it all and for there to be a

resonance between mathematics and physical reality, emotionally and intellectually very rewarding, and that's enough, I think. Of course, you [could] go on beyond that if you really wanted to, and you could call that logical consistency 'God'. But that really would be the infinite emasculation of the previously omnipotent.

Christians will differ over belief in evolution. Some will, as we have noted, seek to harmonise belief in evolution with their interpretation of scripture. Others will see the two as incompatible. My concern here is that we remember evolution remains a theory and is not proven: in fact we have seen that some scientists do not accept the theory. We need to see through the unjustified dogmatism, even religious fervour, of some evolutionists. The 'personification' or 'deification' of evolution needs to be rejected as an unscientific superstition; and the idea that evolution does away with the need of God should be exposed as totally illogical. But there are other dangers. Evolutionary philosophy has led to an undermining of morality.

# Evolution in the Dock

The results of evolutionary thinking have been seriously damaging to religion and morality through the undermining of any awareness of God as Creator. For many the theory of evolution has undermined the sovereignty of God in creation. Some who do not believe in God see evolution as a preferable alternative. More believe in God but not as a transcendent, personal Creator; for them God is the impersonal force within nature and behind evolution. Others believe in a personal God but, since evolution appears to make him irrelevant to the development and maintenance of nature, he is a remote figure indeed and can safely be ignored. For very many people the theory of evolution has removed the sense of God's closeness in creation and in events. Everything can be 'explained' scientifically. It is not necessary for God to be intimately involved with nature, including man.

Paul stated confidently in Romans 1:19–20:

what may be known about God is plain to (men), because God has made it plain to them. For since the creation of the world God's invisible qualities – his eternal power and divine nature – have been clearly seen, being understood from what has been made, so that men are without any excuse.

On the demonic supernatural level, the purpose of the heavy emphasis on evolution since Darwin has been to undermine this human awareness of God in creation. And it has been very widely successful. We may argue that even if evolution is true it requires divine involvement throughout. But such theological argument is remote from much of the modern generation. Evolutionary theory has done immense spiritual harm.

Bernard Shaw graphically describes the spiritual effects of Darwinism. 'When its whole significance dawns on you, your heart sinks into a heap of sand within you. There is a hideous fatalism about it, a ghastly and damnable reduction of beauty and intelligence, of strength and purpose, of honour and aspiration.'[1] One could speculate on the possibility that such effects have contributed greatly to the insecurity, stress and neurosis of modern life.

## The devaluing of man

If man is merely a developed animal rather than a special creation in the image of God then much of the dignity of man is lost. The survival of the fittest is no basis for morality or loving relationships. It is certainly no basis for avoiding oppression. Not that most people think consciously in these ways. But the constant background brainwashing of evolutionary theory moves society in that direction.

We shall now look at some of the effects of this devaluing of man.

### Embryo research

The General Synod in July 1983 passed a motion stating 'that all human life, including life developing in the womb, is created by God in His own image and is, therefore, to be nurtured, supported and protected'. Lord Denning said in the House of Lords on October 31st 1984 that the legal rights of the unborn should begin from conception.

We have referred to relevant biblical material, especially the incarnation. In addition, from fertilisation the embryo is a distinct living being whose unique genetic make-up is

complete. Sex, colour of eyes and build are determined.
The fact that an early embryo is invisible and is not super-
ficially recognisable as a human being is irrelevant; and the
fact that it lacks certain abilities does not mean he or she is
subhuman. A person's abilities should never be the qualification for human status. It is true that a woman loses
embryos naturally and unconsciously. But the fact that
human beings die is no excuse for killing them.

The Warnock Committee recommends allowing experimentation on human embryos up to 14 days old. Such
experimentation would include testing lethal drugs, dissec-
tion and eventually disposal. This dehumanises the human
embryo. The test-tube baby pioneers, Patrick Steptoe and
Dr Robert Edwards, have said that valuable lessons could
be learnt from implanting human embryos into sheep or
rabbits. Warnock recommends that this should be illegal
but would allow the fertilisation of animal eggs from human
sperm. The Voluntary Licensing Authority for Embryo
Research says such experiments provide 'information on
the penetration ability and chromosomal complement
of sperm from subfertile men. They are considered ethi-
cally acceptable provided that development does not
proceed beyond the early cleavage stage.'[2]

Enoch Powell presented a Private Member's Bill to
Parliament on June 14th 1985. Its aim was to outlaw all
experimentation on human embryos except that which
would help a woman with problems of infertility. He had
discovered that one reason for embryo research was the
elimination of genetically defective embryos and research
on new methods of contraception. Sir John Dewhurst and
ten other obstetricians and gynaecologists wrote to the
*Daily Telegraph*:[3]

Enthusiasm for IVF (in vitro fertilisation) is now only
incidentally concerned with relief of infertility. What
is more important (to some) is that there should be
a plentiful supply of disposable human embryos in
the laboratories for testing drugs (and especially in

developing abortifacients) for experimentation in use of embryonic tissue for regenerating adult organs and for many frightening kinds of genetic manipulation. This is not scaremongering. This is what the pro-IVF lobby itself tells us; and we may suspect that much more is already happening inside some laboratories than we are told.

Steptoe and Edwards claimed that a technique enabling couples to choose the sex of their child 'to order' should be available in 1987.[4] Hugh Montefiore, then Chairman of the General Synod Board for Social Responsibility, said he was 'extremely worried' about this development. Mr Robert Winston, Consultant Gynaecologist at Hammersmith Hospital, said in an address to medical journalists on May 11th 1986: 'There is no question that male motherhood is possible, although the birth would carry grave risks to the life of the man.' It would be possible, he said, for homosexual couples to have a baby. In time it may be possible to inject genetic material from the male 'mother' into a donated egg so that the baby would genetically be the child of the man who gave birth to it. Interestingly Patrick Steptoe regards 'male motherhood' as thoroughly dangerous and unethical.

The letter from Sir John Dewhurst ended with the words:

> Mr Powell's Bill will put a stop to the worst forms of embryo abuse. It will uphold the precious principle that human beings should never be subjects of research and experimentation, which is not for their own benefit . . . We are being asked to go down a slippery slope which civilised society should find abhorrent.

However, the Archbishop of York, Dr John Habgood, opposed the Bill in favour of legislation along the lines of Warnock. In a letter to *The Times* he said:

> I know quite a lot about the subject, more than Mr Powell. I am a member of the ethical advisory committee on in vitro research and infertility, with the Medical

Research Council . . . There is no way of deciding on biological evidence alone whether a newly fertilised human ovum is or is not a human person. Nor are there valid grounds on which Christians can claim that theology solves the question.[5]

On September 4th 1985 in another letter to *The Times* the Archbishop said: 'It is . . . possible to hold, as I do, that innocent human life is sacred and must not be destroyed, while at the same time admitting a degree of uncertainty about the ethical significance of the earliest and most fragile stages of embryonic development.'

However it is a very serious matter that, having said he is not sure about the human status of the early human embryo, he is prepared to allow experiments on it for the first 14 days. Surely if there is any possibility at all that the newly fertilised human ovum is a human person, such experiments are abhorrent. The Powell Bill was lost through filibustering tactics.

## Abortion

The Office of Population Censuses and Surveys reported that there were over 141,000 legal abortions in England and Wales in 1985. That is 450 every weekday. Of these 87,000 were performed on unmarried women including 38,000 teenagers, 4,000 of them under sixteen.

An unborn baby can be surgically aborted (either cut to pieces, burnt with chemicals or simply removed and thrown away) at any time during its first 24 weeks (or even later) of development. Sometimes this is justified because the mother's life is at grave risk. But the majority of the two million or more unborn children slaughtered since David Steel's 1967 Abortion Bill became law have been disposed of for 'social reasons' (that is, convenience). Professor Malcolm Ferguson-Smith, Professor of Medical Genetics at Glasgow University stated in *The Times*: 'A number of mothers are actually giving wrong information so that they can get the tests' (pre-natal diagnostic tests which can determine the sex of the child). 'Some doctors then discover that women have had abortions in private clinics even if there were no foetal abnormalities because the child was not the sex they wanted.'[6]

Because an unborn baby is unseen, it is easy to think of it simply as a blob of jelly. But what are the facts? How does a baby develop after conception? Here is a brief summary:

Day 20     The foundation of the whole nervous system is established.

Day 21     The heart starts to beat.

Day 28     Arms, legs, eyes and ears start to form. The brain is distinctly human.

Week 6     The skeleton is complete and reflexes present. The liver, kidneys and lungs are formed. Electrical brain wave patterns are recorded. He really looks a lot like a minute baby.

Week 7     Milk teeth, fingers, thumbs, ankles and toes begin to form.

Week 8     *All* his organs are functioning; growth and maturity are all that occur from now on.

Week 9     Baby can make a fist and grasp an object stroking his palm; he will also leap up and down with co-ordinated movements.

Week 10    He can turn his head, frown, bend his elbow and wrist independently; he looks obviously like a human being.

Week 12    He can swallow; his fingernails are growing; his vocal chords are complete; his reproductive organs are advanced. Inherited physical features can be discerned. He can smile.

Week 16    He is half his birth length; his heart pumps 50 pints a day.

Week 20    Hair appears on his head; he weighs 1 lb and is 12 inches high.

Week 28    His eyes are open, eyelashes and eyebrows are growing. He can hear his mother's digestive

processes and heartbeat. His heartbeat can be
heard by stethoscope. He turns, kicks and can
suck his thumb.[7]

At any stage during those weeks he could be aborted.
David Amess MP stated in 1986 that babies weighing 5 lb
are being aborted at a London Clinic. He had the information from a gynaecologist who visited the clinic where the
babies are aborted by the dilatation and extraction procedure, which involves their being dismembered in the
womb. In 1986 doctors at Leiden University Hospital,
Holland who gave a woman fertility treatment later deliberately punctured the hearts of three ten-week-old embryo
quins she was carrying. Two days later cardiac activity was
detected in one of them and the puncture procedure was
repeated.[8]

In July 1983 the General Synod almost unanimously
expressed serious concern about the number of abortions
and called for the amendment of the Abortion Act. However, Bishop David Jenkins of Durham, speaking to
teenagers on BBC TV, said he did not believe that early
embryos are human, so abortion is permissible.[9]

Tolerating such carnage of unborn human beings alone is
sufficient for our nation to be under God's judgment. The
blood of over two million innocent unborn babies, most of
them killed unjustifiably, cries out for that.

## Infanticide and euthanasia

Once it is accepted that an unborn human being with
abnormalities may be aborted it is only a short step to
accepting infanticide. In 1981 Mrs Peggy Lejeune, mother
of a Down's Syndrome child and member of the Voluntary
Euthanasia Society, founded the Prospect Group. It has
drawn up a bill and sent it to MPs. The bill states that 'it
shall not be an offence if a registered medical practitioner
fails to administer or ceases to administer to a patient under
his care treatment necessary to preserve and/or prolong the
life of that patient'. It goes on that the patient should be an

infant under 28 days old; both parents or guardians must consent; two doctors must give certification and the child must be 'suffering from a severe physical and/or mental disability, which in their opinion . . . is irreversible . . . or of such gravity that the patient . . . would enjoy no worthwhile quality of life'.

R. B. Zachary, professor of paediatric surgery at Sheffield Children's Hospital, described the 'No Treatment' method in the *British Medical Journal* of December 3rd 1977:

> These babies are receiving 60 mg/kg body weight of chloral hydrate, . . . four times a day. This is eight times the sedative dose . . . recommended . . . and four times the hypnotic dose . . . No wonder these babies are sleepy and demand no feed, and with this regimen most of them will die within a few weeks . . . At another meeting I attended a paediatrician was asked by a medical student what was his method of management, and the reply was, 'We don't feed them.'

The bill further states: 'Nothing in this Act shall entitle the medical practitioners to withhold food or sustenance from the patient unless in the opinion of the practitioner formed in good faith, the provision of such food or sustenance shall directly increase the degree of pain and suffering occasioned to the patient.' One could easily argue that any food would increase pain and suffering because it would prolong life which the doctor has decided has no 'quality'.

A poll conducted by the BBC *Panorama* programme discovered that 86 per cent of people questioned did not believe a doctor should be found guilty of murder if, with the parents' agreement, he sees to it that a severely handicapped baby dies.

The Voluntary Euthanasia Society commissioned a National Opinion Poll in April 1985. It asked the same question as an earlier poll in 1971:

Some people say that the law should allow adults to receive medical help to an immediate peaceful death, if they suffer from an incurable physical illness that is intolerable to them, provided they have previously requested such help in writing. Please tell me whether you agree or disagree with this.

Overall agreement had risen from 69 to 72 per cent. (Those claiming to be Anglicans were 75 per cent in favour; Roman Catholics 54 per cent; atheists 89 per cent).

In October 1985 in the journal of the Christian Medical Fellowship Professor David Short wrote a warning that a voluntary euthanasia bill could possibly be presented to Parliament that year. This prediction proved correct. Although there was no report in the national press, the Suicide Act 1961 (Amendment) Bill was being put to the House of Lords for a Second Reading on December 11th 1985. The amendment concerned criminal liability for complicity in another's suicide. It read: 'It shall be a defence to any charge under this Act that the accused acted on behalf of a person who committed suicide and in so acting behaved reasonably and with compassion and in good faith.' Fortunately the bill was defeated.

However the battle is not over. In August 1985 a Dutch Government Commission recommended that euthanasia be allowed for any patient who is in great pain and who asks doctors for help to die. It is hardly helpful that we learnt in November 1986 that King George V's physician administered a fatal dose of cocaine and morphine into the king's jugular vein three quarters of an hour before his death. This was on the authority of the Prince of Wales (Edward VIII) and was partly timed to assist the morning papers to do justice to the king's memory. The *Daily Telegraph* editorial of November 28th 1986 found it difficult readily to condemn this action.

## Violence

A MORI poll in January 1986 rated violence as the second highest concern (the first was family moral standards). The poll specified mugging, physical abuse of children and violent videos. Interestingly the concern was somewhat lower in London; among readers of the *Telegraph* and *The Times*; and among Conservative voters.

Sir Kenneth Newman, Metropolitan Police Commissioner, pointed out in January 1986 that crimes involving guns doubled from just over 1,000 a year in 1975 to just over 2,000 a year from 1981 to 1984. The use of knives increased by 38 per cent between 1982 and 1984.[10]

The younger generation is increasingly violent. For example, in November 1985 an elderly woman died after being attacked by a schoolboy mugger.[11] A boy of eleven was accused of battering to death a 58-year-old polio victim.[12] The following month a teenager robbed and killed two elderly men.[13] A girl of eight squirted bleach in the eyes of an 85-year-old woman, stabbed her and hit her on the head with a piece of wood.[14] In June 1984 Dr Jean Lawrence and Mr David Steed, lecturers at Goldsmith College, London published a report on primary school violence. They had interviewed 85 primary head teachers in 38 inner city areas and discovered 312 disruptive incidents by reception class infants in a single day: for example fighting producing injuries; a five-year-old pushing another child's face into clothes pegs. They also heard of an eight-year-old who kicked and punched a teacher.

On the other hand physical abuse of children by their parents is rising. The NSPCC reported on December 9th 1986 that the number of children seriously or fatally injured by parents rose by two-thirds within a year (although part of the increase may be because more cases are being reported). Between three and four children are dying each week as a result of parental abuse or neglect. When BBC TV launched its 'Childline' switchboard in October 1986 over 1,000 children phoned within the first five minutes, and 50,000 called within the first three days. A nationwide survey mentioned on the programme said 1.5 million children could be suffering abuse.

In December 1986 the Bishop of Whitby reported that clergy in depressed areas in the north of England are facing increasing violence and many are close to breaking point. He was grateful for priests willing to go into urban black spots but said, 'I cannot keep them there indefinitely, and I reckon that four to five years is the maximum time for a priest to stay in such a parish.'[15]

Television has often been blamed for contributing to the increase of violence. Lord Chief Justice Lane, speaking to the Lord Mayor's dinner for judges in July 1985, said people were imitative in character, and the weaker the character, the more imitative they were likely to be: 'So thanks to TV and quite often thanks to TV News reports, violence is self-perpetuating.' It is 'now accepted as common form that once you have your victim on the ground, you kick him, preferably in the stomach or on the head where the blows are likely to do maximum injury'. Attacks on old people are a comparatively new and particularly horrifying manifestation 'of the increasing nastiness of crime'. The Prime Minister responded: 'The amount of violence to be seen on TV is bound to have an effect on those least able to adjudge it.'

In autumn 1985 the National Viewers and Listeners Association monitored all four TV channels between 6.30 p.m. and close-down for one week. They covered 165 hours of television and watched 220 out of 225 programmes. The results showed:

1 that nearly 30 per cent of those programmes contained violence, in some cases in gruesome detail;
2 that two-fifths of the programmes showing violence were shown before 9.00 p.m.;
3 that violence is equally divided between news/documentaries, drama and films;
4 that violence is shown being committed by people in

positions of authority as well as by those breaking the law.[16]

The International Coalition Against Violent Entertainment says that 'the average child will have witnessed 200,000 acts of violence and 50,000 attempted murders by the age of 16. 33,000 of the murder attempts will have been with guns'.[17]

We might also have looked at other aspects of the devaluing of man such as unjust political structures which remove human freedom, for example totalitarianism; or which oppress the poor, for example the North-South divide in Britain; or racism which is growing in society. But perhaps the above examples are sufficient to show that human beings are being increasingly devalued. It would be claiming too much to say that this is completely caused by evolutionary thinking. But it is a more important factor than many realise, stressing as it does man as an evolved animal, the survival of the fittest, and the irrelevance of belief in God. All of this undermines the dignity of human beings.

## The decline of sexual morality – heterosexual

Between 1974 and 1984 the number of illegitimate births to girls between eleven and twenty rose almost 60 per cent from 20,900 to 33,100. Venereal and other sexually transmitted diseases are running at more than 500,000 a year – half of them in persons in their late teens or early twenties. The number of abortions in girls between eleven and seventeen rose from 10,380 in 1973 to 14,038 in 1982. In 1964 16 per cent of persons aged fifteen to nineteen engaged in sexual intercourse at least once. By 1974 this had risen to 51 per cent.

On April 27th 1981 Sir George Young, Parliamentary Under-Secretary to the Department of Health and Social Security, said in a speech:

New cases of primary and secondary syphilis among the 16–19 age group increased by 38% between 1970 and 1979 and new cases of gonorrhoea for the same age group increased by 12%. This should be contrasted with increases of only 35% and 3% respectively for all age groups. The increase in syphilis and gonorrhoea is quite modest however when compared with the overall rise in all categories of sexually transmitted disease – up by 69% over the decade and there is no reason to suppose that young people have been exempt from this trend.

## The problem of sex education

The government-sponsored Newsom Report 1963 recommended that 'boys and girls should be offered firm guidance on sexual morality based on chastity before marriage and fidelity within it' (para. 164). But this has not been done. In 1972 the Royal College of Obstetricians and Gynaecologists said:

> Practically nothing is known about the effect of sex education programmes, either in regard to the future health and happiness of the individual children or in relation to unplanned pregnancy. It was suggested that wrongly-orientated sex education could be having a result which was the exact opposite of what it was desired to achieve, in that it was arousing curiosity and the desire to experiment. The rapidly rising incidence of unplanned pregnancies in the young age group gives some support to the idea.

In 1978 Professor Eysenck and Dr Nias repeated: 'Sex education is potentially dangerous . . . little is in fact known about the advantages and dangers of sex education.' In 1981 Professor Thomas Szasz, a child psychiatrist said:

> Sex education, as presently practised, is a mass of misinformation, misrepresentation, and outright fraud . . .

many thoughtful and well-meaning people now endorse sex education (especially in schools) as a good thing. They should, instead, oppose it as one of the most deplorable consequences of the combination of 'liberal' policies with medicalised morals.[18]

Another child psychiatrist, Professor Louise Eikhoff, 'found a correlation between the provision of sex education and increased sexual activity, which was itself associated with suicide attempts and delinquency'.[19]

With this sort of sex education and the influence of the media, which regularly and vividly portray a variety of sexual immorality, it is little wonder that there is a huge growth in promiscuity and living together. Adultery is widespread.

## Sexual abuse of children

Incidents of sexual abuse of children reported to the NSPCC increased by 90 per cent (from 1,500 to 2,850) during 1985. Of these 14 per cent were children under five. How much this is an increase in abuse and how much in reporting is difficult to tell. Young girls are five times more likely to be sexually abused by their stepfather than by a natural father, according to Dr Raine Roberts who works with Greater Manchester Police.[20] The existence of an organisation known as the Paedophile Information Exchange shows how far human sexuality has departed from the standards of the Bible.

## Rape

Anyone who reads a newspaper will be well aware of the growing incidence of rape. This is one of the ultimate ways of degrading another human being. The influence of violence in society, which we have already noted, must contribute here – as must pornography:

Rape . . . which had begun to decline (both in the
country as a whole and in London) in the early sixties,
increased by over 100% (from 422 cases to 998) in the ten
years following the 'liberation' of pornography – and this
in spite of a growing tendency for victims not to report
rape cases to the police.[21]

## Marriage breakdown

The divorce rate rose by 11 per cent in 1985 to 160
thousand. In fact the number of petitions rose by 50 per
cent soon after the law was changed to allow petitions to be
filed after one year of marriage instead of after three years,
as previously. At current rates one in five children will see
their parents divorced before they are fifteen. England and
Wales has one of the highest divorce rates in Europe. The
number of divorces in 1983 was two and a half times the
number in 1980.[22] The number of one parent families rose
to 940 thousand in 1984 compared with 570 thousand in
1971. Twenty years ago most single parents consisted of a
widowed partner, today most are as the result of divorce.
One in eight families are one-parent and one and a half
million children are involved.[23] Second marriages are
statistically more at risk than first ones and re-divorce is on
the increase.[24]

## The church's response

The attitude of a good number of church leaders is summed
up in a letter in the *Church Times* entitled 'Fornication
always wrong?':

It is not enough to say 'The Bible says this is wrong, and
so that can never change.' The whole question of socio-
economic and historical context needs to be taken into
consideration. The Biblical writers lived in a context
where there was no effective contraception except for
cruel forms of abortion or infanticide, and where there

was no welfare state. Thus family life had to be kept rigidly intact, to ensure that your children took responsibility for you in old age. Illegitimate children would have no clear responsibility for anyone. Hence the Biblical writers would have seen any form of sex outside marriage as unthinkable.

We must see sex as a societal affair, as involving a complex nexus of human, social and economic relationships, and not as some form of personal taboo. The nexus of relationships in our culture is very different from that of the Biblical writers, and so our sexual ethics need to be re-explored. Modern Christians do need a sexual ethic, but one that does justice to modern knowledge and avoids any form of repression or guilt-association. Our ethic must also do justice to the eternal principle of love contained in the Gospels.

Perhaps a workable ethic for today is to see marriage as the most stable and ideal base for sexual relations, whilst recognizing that a tender, caring relationship can exist out of wedlock.[25]

This view is widespread in the church and is found, for example, in the British Council of Churches Report *God's Yes to Sexuality*. But what do these carefully reasoned arguments really do? They undermine the authority of scripture in its teaching on sexual matters, and inevitably they encourage people to fall into fornication.

The Bishop of Manchester in his diocesan newsletter of December 1986 wrote:

In these days many couples who have been living together come to our altars. Provided they can sincerely make the commitment to lifelong marriage, excluding all other sexual partners, then I believe it is right for the church to pronounce the blessing of God on the vows they make to each other. But such a marriage does not mean that the Church is saying that living together is all right.

This statement is amazing for its naïvety. The nation will conclude exactly the opposite – that the church is soft on living together. For such a couple to have a white wedding in church with all the celebrations is saying 'living together is fine', whether the church intends to say that or not. It adds to the lowering of sexual standards in the country. Unless such a couple repent (which includes ceasing to live together), they should not be married in church.

In September 1986 one couple who had been living together got married in church and had the baptism of their six-month-old son at the end of the ceremony. The priest who took the service said:

> It may not, in fact, be quite as unusual as it may appear. When a couple go to a vicar to put up the banns, they don't always tell the full story of their circumstances. It may well be that an incumbent married a couple who have been living together. Such are the facts of life in 1986.

Such an event makes a mockery of biblical standards and discipline. An incumbent should take reasonable care to ensure a couple are not living together. If even then he is deceived by them, that is one thing. Not to bother to find out or to marry a couple he knows to be living together is quite another. Church law allows him to refuse to officiate.

On BBC television the Bishop of Durham answering questions from an audience of teenagers said it was possible that Joseph had sex before marriage with Mary and then said: 'But I am not saying he did, though.'[26] In spite of this agnostic comment the bishop's answer, in addition to being deeply offensive to Christians, could only have the effect of further undermining biblical morality. I have heard this idea concerning Joseph and Mary being used as an excuse by those living together.

A few years ago Graham Turner interviewed about twenty Anglican bishops for a series of articles in the *Daily Telegraph*. He quoted one bishop (anonymously for reasons which will become clear) as saying:

The definition of chastity which I like best is 'emotional integrity' . . . It means that you and I retain our integrity so far as our feelings are concerned, that I respect you as a person, not just somebody I'd like to go to bed with. That's a much better definition than just 'no sex'.

Turner asked if the definition meant you could in fact go to bed with the other person. The bishop replied: 'I think I'd prefer this to remain off the record, but, yes, it does.'

However it is not just bishops who are helping to undermine biblical standards of morality. Bearing in mind the problems resulting from sex education (already noted), it is interesting to read the January 1987 *News Review* of the Christian World Centre in Manchester. Speaking of recent books it says:

Suddenly evangelicals were experts in the field of sex. Christians had no need to visit general bookshops or station bookstalls in order to satisfy their appetite for romance and the rest . . . Those who sought the titillation of the senses in such areas had ample opportunity to find it under the cloak of Christianity. [One divorced evangelical writer] seemed to be so pleased with both his wives – past and present, that at times, it was difficult to know whom he was applauding . . . Buzz magazine believed that they should run an extended series of articles on Twentieth Century Sex. Every explicit aspect was explored . . . Christian bookshops began subjecting their better judgment as to the suitability of the books to the fact that certain titles were bestsellers.

Some people will react to this by accusing the writer of the article of being prudish. However some years ago I produced a Family Life Course for our church which included explicit details of sexual intercourse. The aim was to help husbands to ensure their wives experienced sexual fulfilment. I have since begun to see that this sort of sexual explicitness, certainly when generally published, is unhelpful in that it encourages an obsession with sexuality.

Another problem is the personal example of church leaders. In 1983 an association called 'Broken Rites' was formed and very soon 110 divorced or separated clergy wives had joined it. The association estimated that in 1984 there were 500 broken marriages among the ten thousand Church of England clergy. The secretary, herself a separated clergy wife, claimed that increasing numbers of clergymen were getting involved in extra-marital affairs, confident that if discovered and divorced they could go on working in the church. She said: 'Many clergy intend and expect to go on working in the Church after a divorce; they think they can get away with it and they do. They think of all sorts of things to justify themselves and their behaviour.' Even before I did any research or sought information I had heard about a dozen cases of clergymen who had fallen into serious immorality. Some of these men have indeed remained working in the church, in circumstances where this should not be the case.

## The decline of sexual morality – homosexuality

Since homosexual acts between consenting adults over twenty-one were legalised in 1967, we have been subjected to an increasing campaign of propaganda to accept homosexuality as normal. TV programmes, films and newspaper articles constantly bombard us with the subject. Hardly a meeting of General Synod goes by without each member being circulated by the Lesbian and Gay Christian Movement or similar bodies.

### Homosexual education

All twelve of London's Labour boroughs plus Leicester, Manchester and Nottingham in 1987 had 'pro-gay commitments'. Haringey election material in June 1986 included the statement: 'The Council is to establish a fund for curriculum projects from nursery through to further education to promote positive images of lesbians and gays.' They argue that since between 4 and 10 per cent of people are 'naturally' homosexual, 300 thousand to 700 thousand children in British schools at any one time will be 'naturally' homosexual when they grow up and have a right to be instructed in their sexuality.

One of the books used in some schools and aimed at the very young is *The Playbook for Kids About Sex*. It states: 'When grown-ups choose someone to be one of their sexual partners, they sometimes choose a person of the same sex and they sometimes choose a person of the other sex.' Another book, *Jenny Lives with Eric and Martin*, shows a girl of five sitting up in bed with her father and his homosexual lover. The Education Secretary told the Inner London Education Authority that the book should be banned. The Authority issues a 'resources guide' to schools of 150 books, plays and films to help schools handle homosexual matters. It includes sexually explicit books promoting homosexuality.

Five thousand Haringey parents signed a petition against the council's policy in summer 1986. They have been subjected to death threats on the telephone and face to face and have been spat upon. There has been violence and egg-throwing when they have attempted to put their case to the council. Bernie Grant MP, then the council leader, said: 'I don't think there is any difference between homosexual and heterosexual parents as far as the child is concerned.'

## Homosexual politics

Until thoughts of a General Election became dominant the leader of the Labour Party, Neil Kinnock, refused to get involved. However more recently the more extreme actions of some Labour councils have been toned down – for the time being. But the 1986 Labour Conference by a 590 thousand majority instructed the executive to draw up a 'Lesbian and Gay Rights Policy', which would include the repeal of all criminal laws which discriminate against homosexuals. This would involve lowering the age of consent for homosexuals from twenty-one to sixteen. The mover of the motion said heterosexism was like sexism and racism 'in perpetuating oppressive and discriminatory ideas that one sexuality – heterosexuality – is the only normal sexuality'. Neil Kinnock wrote to the Lesbian and Gay Pride Carnival 1985: 'We must all work to rid society of the fear and guilt that has victimised gays and lesbians and to create conditions in which people can conduct their personal relationships without persecution.'[27]

The GLC Gay Rights Charter (which is perpetuated by the London boroughs) recommends:

1   Intolerance of lesbians and gay men by leaders of members of organised religions should not be regarded as excusable on grounds of 'tradition', 'ethnic freedom', or 'moral leadership'.
2   Financial or civic protection to religious organisations which demonstrably discriminate in their hiring or caring policies against homosexuals should be withdrawn. The example set by New York City recently in seeking to require declarations of non-discrimination on grounds of sexual orientation as a pre-condition of state financial assistance should be emulated.
3   The law should be amended to permit the removal of charitable status from religious organisations or enterprises which provably practise and/or teach discrimination against lesbians and gay men. (p. 19)

Such recommendations, if carried out, would mean financial problems for churches opposing homosexual practice. They would have to pay full rates on church buildings and would not be eligible for covenanted giving. More chilling however is the idea of the removal of 'civic protection'. Does this mean the police would not step in over violence against those opposing homosexual practice?

Clause 28 of the 1988 Local Government Act rules out the promotion of homosexuality as normal by local authorities.[28]

## The church's response

In 1974 the General Synod Board for Social Responsibility set up a working party to consider homosexuality. It reported in 1978 but it was not until 1979 that the Report *Homosexual Relationships* was published, with what amounted to a disclaimer by the Board. The working party was chaired by the Bishop of Gloucester and contained no evangelicals. The Report deals with the biblical evidence and seeks to weaken the impact of the passages concerned. But it draws this conclusion:

> Nevertheless, what evidence there is seems clearly to show condemnation of homosexual behaviour. For many this will settle the matter. They will hold that the Bible so plainly indicates the divine disapproval of such behaviour, that it must be wrong in all circumstances, and especially so for Christians, who recognize the Bible as an inspired collection of writings which gives authoritative guidance for the conduct of human life. But this at once raises the very large and disputed problem as to the kind of authority we are to give to Bible statements, particularly in the moral and ethical spheres[29] . . . what is being claimed is that the question cannot be settled by reference simply to biblical texts that deal directly with homosexuality. These have to be considered in the light of the underlying message of the Bible, especially the New Testament, and in assessing and interpreting this, we need to take account of knowledge not available to biblical writers and moral intuitions formed in the Christian tradition. Thus the bearing of the biblical material . . . has also to be evaluated in the light of those other theological, philosophical, medical and social insights which are discussed in other chapters of this Report.[30]

The Report admits that Paul and the other New Testament writers reinforce the Old Testament condemnation of homosexual practice, but says: 'Paul, too, was a child of his age and was as limited by its outlook as were men of the Old Testament.'[31] Thoughtful and reasonable as this appears, it is in fact a sophisticated attempt to undermine the authority of scripture as the expression of God's sovereign Word. Arguments like this mean that whenever we come across something in the Bible we do not like we can explain them away as 'culturally conditioned'. To do this and to claim any submission to the authority of scripture as God's Word is to be at best self-deceived and at worst hypocritical. Little wonder the Report concludes:

> In the light of some of the evidence we have received we do not think it possible to deny that there are circumstances in which individuals may justifiably choose to enter into a homosexual relationship with the hope of enjoying a companionship and physical expression of sexual love similar to that which is found in marriage. For the reasons which we have given such a relationship could not be regarded as the moral or social equivalent of marriage; it would be found to have a private and experimental character which marriage cannot and should not have. Nevertheless, fidelity and permanence, although not institutionally required, would undoubtedly do much to sustain and enhance its genuinely personal commitment and aspirations.[32]

In 1982 in a Methodist Report on *A Christian Understanding of Human Sexuality* a majority of the twelve working party members believed that homosexual Christians could choose a partnership which involved physical expression.

The present Archbishop of York, when Bishop of Durham, was quoted in the *Daily Telegraph* as saying that Christian opinion was divided on the issue of homosexuality and there was 'quite a legitimate fuss about moving towards a society where it was no more odd than marriage'. On the other hand a good deal had been lost by persecuting homosexuals and 'not allowing them to make morally risky moves in order to create a viable life for themselves'. As for homosexual priests, 'I try to make it clear that if they were aggressive or indiscreet, they will bring wrath on their heads and make it impossible to minister.' Asked if his concern was to avoid public scandal, he replied:

Well, you can go quite a long way so long as you don't flaunt things in people's faces. There may be situations where, say, a priest has a lodger. Now I don't know what goes on in the privacy of their own home. As soon as one raises questions in that way, one is inevitably putting oneself in the position of making judgments, and we don't make judgments about the quality of each other's marriages. [He continued:] We are learning to be more relaxed about things, without departing from the standards we have always held to.

We now knew a good deal more about homosexuality as a condition than they did in biblical times, and realised that a hard core were inherently so. That had not come up in the Bible, so to that extent, it was 'a new one'. Caught between upholding the standards of Christianity and facing the facts about society as it is, he remarked, one was always forced into a compromise – but then he did not regard compromise as a bad word.[33]

This is typical of the weak and ineffectual response of many bishops and other Christian leaders to homosexual practice within the church. Meanwhile some clergy are known to be practising homosexuals; some priests bless the relationship between homosexuals (although this normally, but not always, receives an episcopal rap on the knuckles). The Lesbian and Gay Christian Movement campaigns actively in the synod and church, advertising in the official *Church of England Year Book* and selling books which allow promiscuity, orgies and sado-masochism.

The attitude of some bishops has seemed to be to 'fiddle while Rome burns' especially as there is a danger of waking up one day to find it is illegal to speak against homosexual practice. So I took the initiative in 1987 of tabling a Private Member's Motion on Sexuality for General Synod. It stated:

> This Synod reaffirms the Biblical Standard, given for the well-being of society:
>
> 1   that sexual intercourse should take place only between a man and a woman who are married to each other;
> 2   that fornication, adultery and homosexual acts are sinful in all circumstances;
> 3   that Christian leaders are called to be exemplary in all spheres of morality, including sexual morality, as a condition of being appointed to or remaining in office;
>
> and calls upon the Church to show Christ-like compassion to those who have fallen into sexual sin, encouraging them to repent and receive absolution, and offering the ministry of healing to all who suffer physically or emotionally as a result of such sin.

The Synod accepted an amendment which substituted 'gentler' language and passed it by a 98 per cent majority. It states:

> This Synod affirms that the Biblical and traditional teaching on chastity and fidelity in personal relationships is a response to, and expression of, God's love for each one of us, and in particular affirms:
>
> 1   that sexual intercourse is an act of total commitment which belongs properly within a permanent married relationship;
> 2   that fornication and adultery are sins against this ideal, and are to be met by a call to repentance and the exercise of compassion;
> 3   that homosexual genital acts also fall short of this

ideal, *and are likewise to be met by a call to repentance and the exercise of compassion*;

4 that all are called to be exemplary in all spheres of morality, including sexual morality, and that holiness of life is particularly required of Christian leaders.

The good news is therefore that Synod voted by a 98 per cent majority that fornication, adultery and homosexual genital acts are wrong and are 'to be met by a call to repentance'. So the Church of England, after years of sitting on the fence, after the 1979 Bishop of Gloucester's Report, which (though never approved by the church) said certain homosexual relationships were acceptable, has decided for biblical and traditional sexual morality. Synod also rejected a 'pro-homosexual' amendment by a devastating 85 per cent majority. At that vote the secretary of the Lesbian and Gay Christian Movement was heard to gasp in horror and say 'Oh, no!'

It is true that an attempt to specify the need for 'appropriate discipline among the clergy . . . in cases of sexual immorality' was defeated. Had the Synod voted as one body this would only have been lost by 13 votes. As it was, Synod voted 'by houses' – bishops 5 for, 14 against (the rest abstained); clergy 82 for, 138 against; laity 136 for, 84 against. It must be understood though, that the reason for this is that most members probably favoured discipline but wanted to leave it to the bishops – not tell them what to do. The massive majorities mentioned above provide a great challenge and encouragement to the bishops in the difficult task of discipline.

The bad news is that the wording passed confused many in the church and nation. This is a very serious failing. The original amendment moved by the Bishop of Chester, Michael Baughen, was very weak concerning homosexual acts. It did not even include the words in italics (clause 3 of the motion passed), calling for repentance which were added during the debate. There is no biblical justification for such weak language. For all its claim to greater compas-

sion the amendment omits reference to the assurance of
forgiveness and the availability of emotional and physical
healing. It is in fact less compassionate than the original
motion. Amazingly Michael Baughen (and other bishops)
claimed it was unreasonable to call for Christian leaders to
be exemplary.

The question now is whether the church will really put its
house in order, ensuring that those accepted for ordination
or remaining in office uphold biblical sexual morality.
Some encouraging signs were seen immediately after the
debate, with those responsible for recommending candidates for ordination and those responsible for theological
colleges reconsidering procedures and so on.

However, Archbishop John Habgood, in an article written before the debate but published after, said concerning
my original motion:

> The drawing of such rigid lines, and the hounding from
> office of those who offend, are deeply alien to the
> character of our church . . . for the church to commit
> itself inflexibly to such rules would be to take a big step
> along the road to becoming a persecuting sect. [He
> continues:] . . . in the field of sexual behaviour the facts
> have changed . . . many Christian people, for reasons
> which seem good to them, do not find traditional Chris-
> tian teaching about sex fully answers their questions, and
> are not impressed when the only word which comes
> across to them with any conviction is the word 'don't'.
> This is especially true of homosexuals. Many are not
> prepared to accept the fact that St Paul settled the
> matter once and for all by condemning homosexuality as
> understood in his own day . . . It is now known that many
> homosexuals have no choice at all about their sexual
> orientation. The question facing them is . . . whether,
> given their sexuality as it is, any form of sexual ex-
> pression is permissible. So far most churches have not
> found it possible to give a clear answer to that question.
> (Refer to *Sexuality and the Church* edited by the author,

distributed by Kingsway, for medical evidence that homosexuality is 'learned behaviour' and that the concept of the 'inverted' or 'natural' homosexual was known before N.T. times.)

He goes on to say that my motion 'would have closed the door on many puzzled heterosexual adolescents . . . who cannot see that it is necessarily wise or helpful to postpone all sexual activity until marriage'.[34]

Meanwhile the country is increasingly moving towards an acceptance of homosexual practice. As someone put it, 'If God doesn't judge us for this sin, he'll have to apologise to Sodom and Gomorrah.' It is a detestable perversion according to scripture and the church must give a clearly understood message to this effect within the nation. At the same time we need to make it clear that we are against persecution or intimidation of practising homosexuals and that we love them as people. There must be no condemnation of homosexual tendencies as opposed to practice. If we do not give this clear message (and practise what we preach) then, alongside its other sins, many of which we have outlined above, the nation will suffer God's judgment, but it will begin with the 'household of God', the church.[35]

Soon after the General Synod debate a number of diocesan bishops followed the lead of the Bishop of Ripon in banning active homosexual clergymen and ordinands from their dioceses. The Archbishop of Canterbury also backed the Bishop of Ripon. Then the Revd Jeremy Younger, vicar of St Mary, Bow and a practising homosexual, resigned amidst national publicity. He claimed that he had told three bishops he had worked under that he was living with a male partner. He gave the debate and its aftermath as the reason for his resignation.

# 8

# Submitting to God's Sovereignty in Creation

Paul in Romans 1:18 speaks of 'the godlessness and wicked-ness of men who suppress the truth by their wickedness'. He is clearly referring to the tendency of men to ignore the revelation of God in creation – a revelation which has been plain since creation. Many people are using the theory of evolution for this purpose, either to try to do away with the need for God or to make him remote and irrelevant. Paul teaches that God's wrath is being revealed from heaven against these attitudes. Doubtless there is a further fulfil-ment of this revelation of wrath. But an immediate result of it is 'futile' thinking. 'Although they claimed to be wise, they became fools' and fell into idolatry (vv. 21–23). In-terestingly the 'deification' (as I call it) of evolution is a form of idolatry. It sounds so reasonable but when analysed it is foolish.

Another effect of the wrath of God is in sexual perver-sion, which follows on the 'futile' thinking. That is not of course to say that all atheistic or agnostic evolutionists have low moral standards, but that sexual perversion, including homosexual practice, is encouraged by the denial of God's revelation in creation and subsequent idolatry (vv. 24–27).

God giving men over to a depraved mind is another aspect of his wrath. The result of this is to degrade human beings and human relationships. It is characterised by 'wickedness, evil, greed and depravity . . . envy, murder (the various pro-life issues fit here), strife, deceit and malice. They are gossips, slanderers, God-haters, insolent, arrogant and boastful . . . they are senseless, faithless, heartless, ruthless' (violence fits here) (vv. 28–31).

The context of this passage however is Paul expounding the gospel 'because it is the power of God for the salvation of everyone who believes'. So there is salvation from this list of ugly things which increasingly characterise modern life. What can the individual do to be effective in counteracting the evil and spreading the message of salvation? We shall be examining that in Part III.

*Meditate on God as Creator*. Instead of succumbing to the spirit of the age which tends to push God partly or wholly out of creation, meditate on the great biblical passages about creation, and let creation itself point you to God and inspire worship. Paul says:

> The God who made the world and everything in it is the Lord of heaven and earth and does not live in temples built by hands. And he is not served by human hands, as if he needed anything, because he himself gives all men life and breath and everything else. (Acts 17:24–25)

'The earth is the Lord's, and everything in it, the world and all who live in it' (Ps. 24:1). 'How awesome is the Lord Most High, the great King over all the earth' (Ps. 47:2). 'The Lord reigns, he is robed in majesty . . . and is armed with strength' (Ps. 93:1).

Evolutionary theory can make creation seem rather impersonal, so meditate on Christ who is 'sustaining all things by his powerful word' (Heb. 1:3). Remember 'all things were created by him and for him.' (Col. 1:16).

*Recognise the inadequacy of evolutionary theory*. Reject the indoctrination that it is fact. Remember it is only theory and there is no proof of evolution across the species. Recall that some scientists are rejecting not just Darwinism, but evolution itself. Ensure that your children and others you know are aware of these facts.

*Take a stand on the pro-life issues (embryo research, abortion, infanticide, euthanasia)*. Join one of the pro-life organisations and encourage others to do the same (see Appendix 1). Make sure people are aware of the facts and that the government is urged to maintain or introduce pro-life legislation, and to revise the abortion law. Be involved with schemes to care for single mothers and their children, or with hospice care for the dying.

*Repent if you have had an unjustified abortion.* An abortion can be justified if a mother's life is at grave risk. If you have had an abortion for lesser reasons than this, repent of it before God. Then be assured that God forgives you. No sin is too great for God's forgiveness, even the unjustified taking of another person's life. For example Moses (Exod. 2:11–12) and David (2 Sam. 11:14–17; 12:9) were guilty of murder but God not only forgave them but used them greatly. It may help to discuss the matter with a discreet counsellor, particularly if you cannot be sure of God's forgiveness. (The same would apply if you have been involved with euthanasia or infanticide.)

*Limit your exposure to media violence.* Bear in mind this can include documentary programmes/articles as well as fiction. You can also make representations to the media and government about such violence.

*Have a wholesome attitude towards sex.* All that God created and ordained including sexual relations within marriage is not only good but very good (Gen. 1:31; cf. 27–28; 2:24). God intended there should be no shame in sex (Gen. 2:25) but the fall brought in guilt (Gen. 3:7–11, 21). The fact that the Bible contains the Song of Songs which, in spite of often being spiritualised, is really a beautiful description of physical love, shows what a positive, joyful attitude we should have to sexual matters.

*Repent of sexual immorality.* This may include sex before marriage, adultery, sexual abuse of another person, indulgence in pornography, and so on. The Lord forgave the woman caught in the act of adultery (John 8:1–11). Again, if you cannot be sure of God's forgiveness, consult a discreet counsellor.

*Seek healing of sexual trauma.* Christ does heal such trauma through prayer for inner healing, as I know from ministering to such people. The trauma is often caused through sexual abuse as a child, but may happen in later life.

*Check on the sex education given in local schools.* The 1986 Education Bill stipulates that sex education should give proper regard to 'moral considerations and the value of family life'. You can discuss the matter with children, with the teachers or head. You could join the Parent Teachers Association or become a parent governor. It may be necessary to take matters up with the education authority, your Member of Parliament or the Secretary of State for Education.

*Maintain a high view of marriage.* Christians who have a high view of scripture differ about the grounds for divorce allowed by the New Testament. In my understanding the clear exception to the general disapproval of divorce is when one partner has committed sexual immorality (Matt. 5:32; 19:9). Even then, given repentance, it may be possible for the marriage to be saved. Prayer and Christian counselling should figure prominently in marriages facing difficulty. The church should teach on marriage; the responsibilities of husbands, wives and parents; the nature of love; repentance and forgiveness, and so on. Clergy and ministers should maintain a high standard with respect to wedding couples, for example not taking the wedding of a couple who persist in living together before they are married.

*Repent if you have experienced a marriage breakdown or divorce.* Even if you feel you were the innocent partner, repent of any way in which you may have contributed to the breakdown. Ensure you have the right attitude to your former partner and that you have fulfilled all your responsibilities to him or her and the family. Deal with any resentment and seek healing for the hurts involved.

*Take a stand against homosexual practice.* First ensure you have the right attitude and let it be known that you reject persecution or intimidation of practising homosexuals and that you love them as people, just as you do other sinners. Regard homosexual acts in all circumstances as sinful, and encourage people to repent as part of your help to them. If you have homosexual temptations yourself remember that temptation is not sin (Jesus was tempted to sin). But it is possible so to indulge in the feelings of temptation that the indulgence amounts to sin (cf. Matt. 5:27–30). If you have fallen to temptation, repent and receive God's forgiveness, which is readily available. Biblical, compassionate counselling and support, if not available locally, is available from various national sources (see Appendix 1). Do not limit the power of prayer, especially in the context of biblical, compassionate counselling. There are those who testify to a remarkable deliverance from homosexuality through prayer. Take note of the pro-homosexual political lobby. Keep informed about the attitudes and actions of local government and national political parties. Consider standing as a borough or district councillor to be a good influence in this and other matters.

*Church leaders should take disciplinary action for those who persist in immorality.* If after all the love, help, advice and warnings a church member or leader persists in immorality (whether heterosexual or homosexual) then the disciplinary measures outlined in the New Testament should be taken. Jesus taught that an offending brother should be approached privately. If that failed to correct him, a few other witnesses should be involved. If that failed, the church should be informed. (This should probably only be committed members, not the general Sunday congregation. The essential, proven non-confidential facts need to be conveyed and members encouraged to pray for and to urge the offender to repent.) If the offender failed to heed the church, then he should be regarded as out of fellowship (Matt. 18:15–17). Similarly Paul urges the Corinthians to expel an immoral brother from the fellowship (1 Cor. 5:11). It is important though, that other (non-sexual) blatant sins should be dealt with similarly. This may include offences in the pro-life area or in a totally different area, for example, divisiveness in the church. Whenever a person repents they should be readily forgiven and restored.

# Part III

# GOD'S SOVEREIGNTY IN SALVATION

# 9

# The God Who Saves

In this chapter we shall look at the biblical basis for the teaching that salvation is only possible because of what Jesus Christ accomplished on the cross. The exclusiveness of the Christian gospel is not an easy concept today, but is however central to the gospel which is no myth but historical fact.

## Jesus is a historical figure

We have already seen that divine revelation is essentially historical. Emphasis is laid in the New Testament on eye-witness accounts and on the importance of the physical reality of Jesus. F. F. Bruce writes:

> Some writers may toy with the fancy of a 'Christ-myth', but they do not do so on the ground of historical evidence. The historicity of Christ is as axiomatic for an unbiased historian as the historicity of Julius Caesar. It is not historians who propagate the 'Christ-myth' theories.[1]

In addition to the New Testament material various non-Christian historians who lived very near to the time of Christ testify to his historicity. Tacitus, a Roman born about AD 52, wrote of 'Christians, who were hated for their enormities. Christus, the founder of the name, was put to death by Pontius Pilate, procurator of Judea, in the reign of Tiberias.'[2] The Jewish historian Josephus, born AD 37, referred to Jesus as 'a wise man' and 'doer of wonderful works'.[3] The details of the reference are disputed but not his reference to the historicity of Jesus. Writing in AD 112 Pliny, Roman Governor of Bithynia, referred to the Christians and their courageous beliefs.[4] And there are other similar references among ancient writers and historians.

## Jesus is God's only Son

Jesus is referred to as God's 'one and only Son' in five places in the New Testament. God 'sent his one and only Son into the world that we might live through him'. He was the 'atoning sacrifice for our sins' (1 John 4:9–10). He was the divine, eternal Word who 'became flesh and made his dwelling among us . . . the One and Only (Son), who came from the Father, full of grace and truth' (John 1:14). 'No-one has ever seen God, but God the One and Only (Son), who is at the Father's side, has made him known' (John 1:18). Those who believe in God's one and only Son may have eternal life. But those who do not believe stand condemned already (John 3:16,18). It is God's unique ('One and Only') Son who reveals God to us and becomes the atoning sacrifice for us. It is only by faith in God's unique Son that a person is saved from condemnation and receives eternal life.

The full divinity of Jesus is also taught. The eternal Word was God (John 1:1). When he said 'I and the Father are one' the Jews regarded this as a blasphemous claim to be God (John 10:30–33). He commended Thomas for addressing him as 'My Lord and my God' (John 20:28–29). Jesus is similarly worshipped in Philippians 2:10–11; 2 Peter 3:18; Revelation 1:5–6; 5:11–14. Paul teaches that 'in Christ all the fulness of the Deity lives in bodily form' (Col. 2:9; cf. 1:29). In the light of all this and other textual considerations, the New International Version of the Bible feels justified in translating Titus 2:13; Hebrews 1:8 and 2 Peter 1:1 as describing Jesus as God. The translators are so sure of their ground as to mention no alternative readings.

## Jesus' sacrifice is complete

Jesus 'does not need to offer sacrifices day after day, first for his own sins, and then for the sins of the people. He sacrificed for their sins once for all when he offered himself' (Heb. 7:27). 'He entered the Most Holy Place once for all by his own blood, having obtained eternal redemption' (Heb. 9:12; cf. v. 28). He tasted death for everyone and 'became the source of eternal salvation for all who obey him' (Heb. 5:9). 'We have been made holy through the sacrifice of the body of Jesus Christ once for all . . . because by one sacrifice he has made perfect for ever those who are being made holy' (Heb. 10:10,14).

After Jesus had 'provided purification for sins, he sat down at the right hand of the Majesty in heaven' (Heb. 1:3). This 'heavenly session' of Christ vividly illustrates the completeness of his sacrifice and its acceptance by God. (See also Matt. 26:64; Mark 16:19; Col. 3:1; Heb. 8:1; 1 Pet. 3:18.)

Another theme which emphasises the completeness of Christ's sacrifice is that of his death being a ransom. Jesus said he had come to give his life 'as a ransom for many' (Matt. 20:28; Mark 10:45). The word 'for' in Greek is 'anti' which means 'in exchange for'. In 1 Timothy 2:6 Christ's death 'as a ransom for all men' is described as an 'antilutron', that is, substitute-ransom for all men, sufficient to ransom us from sin, death and hell. 'Therefore he is able to save completely those who come to God through him' (Heb. 7:25). Because his sacrifice is complete, when he appears a second time it will be 'not to bear sin, but to bring salvation to those who are waiting for him' (Heb. 9:28).

## Jesus is the only way to God

'There is one God and one mediator between God and men, the man Christ Jesus' (1 Tim. 2:5). This is a categorical statement of Jesus being exclusively our mediator, priest and saviour. Jesus himself affirmed: 'I am the way and the truth and the life. No-one comes to the Father except through me' (John 14:6). He is the mediator of the new and superior covenant (Heb. 8:6; 9:15). Through him we have access to the Father (Eph. 2:18; 3:12; cf. John 10:9). We enter the Most Holy Place by the blood of Jesus (Heb. 10:19–20). Consequently Peter proclaimed: 'Salvation is found in no-one else, for there is no other name under heaven given to men by which we must be saved' (Acts 4:12). We shall return in Chapter 10 to recent attempts to make John 14:6 and Acts 4:12 not mean what they say.

## The reality of Jesus' incarnation

We have already touched on the importance of the physical body and blood of Jesus. Here we expand on this subject which is vital to that of salvation. The New Testament clearly describes the reality of Jesus' humanity. Although his conception was miraculous his birth was normal, as was his development as a child (Luke 2:40). He experienced hunger (Luke 4:2), tiredness (John 4:6; Luke 8:23), sadness (John 11:35) and anguish (Luke 22:44). He was 'tempted in every way, just as we are – yet was without sin' (Heb. 4:15).

It is true then, that the Word became flesh (John 1:14); 'he appeared in a body' (1 Tim. 3:16); his disciples touched him (1 John 1:1–2). He was 'born under law, to redeem those under law' (Gal. 4:4–5) by becoming 'obedient to death – even death on a cross' (Phil. 2:8). He shared humanity 'so that by his death he might destroy him who holds the power of death – that is, the devil – and free those who all their lives were held in slavery by their fear of death' (Heb. 2:14–15). 'Therefore, when Christ came into the world, he said. "Sacrifice and offering you did not desire, but a body you prepared for me"' (Heb. 10:5). So Jesus bore our sins in his body (1 Pet. 2:24) and 'we have been made holy through the sacrifice of the body of Jesus Christ' (Heb. 10:10). This great fact is fundamental to the sharing of bread in communion (Matt. 26:26; Mark 14:22; Luke 22:19; 1 Cor. 11:24).

Similarly the New Testament emphasises the importance of the shed blood of Christ. The OT sacrificial system taught the truth fulfilled in the cross, that 'without the shedding of blood there is no forgiveness' (Heb. 9:22). Unlike the priests of old Jesus entered the Most Holy Place once for all by his own blood (Heb. 9:12). Following OT imagery his blood is seen as sprinkled before God (Heb. 12:24) and as sanctifying the people (Heb. 13:12). Paul affirms that we are 'justified by his blood' (Rom. 5:9), reconciled to God through his blood shed on the cross (Col. 1:20; Eph. 2:13) and redeemed through his blood (Eph. 1:7; Col. 1:14; Acts 20:28); also Peter in 1 Peter 1:19 (cf. Rev. 5:9). John affirms that 'the blood of Jesus . . . purifies us from all sin' (1 John 1:7; cf. Rev. 1:5; 7:14). Compared with animal sacrifices 'how much more . . . will the blood of Christ, who through the eternal Spirit offered himself unblemished to God, cleanse our consciences from acts that lead to death' (Heb. 9:14). Paul affirms that 'God presented him as a sacrifice of atonement, through faith in his blood' (Rom. 3:25). It was through the blood of the eternal covenant that God raised Jesus (Heb. 13:20) so we can 'have confidence to enter the Most Holy Place by the blood of Jesus' (Heb. 10:19). We can therefore partake of the sacrament of the blood of Christ (Matt. 26:28; Mark 14:24; Luke 22:20; 1 Cor. 11:25,27). We can overcome the condemnation of the accuser (the devil) 'by the blood of the Lamb', that is, by knowing the blood of Christ cleanses us from all sin (Rev. 12:10–11).

So Christ was our sin bearer. 'God made him who had no sin to be sin (or a sin offering) for us' (2 Cor. 5:21; cf. 1 Pet. 2:24). Christ redeemed us from the curse of the law by becoming a curse for us, for it is written: 'Cursed is everyone who is hanged on a tree' (Gal. 3:13). We are saved from God's wrath through Christ (Rom. 5:9; 1 Thess. 1:10). It is against this background that we can understand Jesus' cry of dereliction on the cross: 'My God, my God, why have you forsaken me?' (Matt. 27:46). We shall examine God's wrath in greater detail in Chapter 17. Jesus bore God's judicial wrath on our sin. He was our penal substitute. His death was equivalent to the death of all of us (2 Cor. 5:14) and death is the wages of sin (Rom. 6:23).

## Faith in Christ Jesus is essential

The New Testament teaches that in order to receive and experience eternal life it is necessary to have faith in Christ. After all Jesus is the eternal life which was with the Father and appeared to the first disciples (1 John 1:1–2). He himself claimed to be life (John 11:25; 14:6). So 'He who has the Son has life, he who does not have the Son does not have life' (1 John 5:12) but is condemned already (John 3:18,36). Eternal life is to know God and Jesus Christ (John 17:3). Whoever believes in Christ has eternal life (John 3:15–16; 5:24; 6:47). This includes believing he is the Son of God (1 John 4:15) and the context, as we have seen, is that he is the 'one and only Son' of God (1 John 4:9–10); the Messiah (1 John 5:1). To deny the truth about Jesus is to be antichrist (1 John 2:22). No one who denies him 'has the Father' (1 John 2:23; cf. John 8:19; 14:7). Anyone who denies the reality of the physical incarnation of Christ is antichrist and 'does not have God' (2 John 7,9; cf. 1 John 4:2–3).

## Jesus lives in us through the presence of the Spirit

At the Last Supper Jesus promised his disciples he would soon dwell in them and they in him (John 14:19–20). The Father also will indwell them as they dwell in him by virtue of being in Christ who dwells in him (John 14:23). Paul teaches that Christ indwells the believer (Rom. 8:10; 2 Cor. 13:5; Gal. 2:20; Col. 1:27). Ephesians 3:17 makes it clear that Christ dwells in our hearts through faith. The context (verse 16) shows that this is achieved by the indwelling Holy Spirit. (See also the context of Rom. 8:10, especially vv.

9,11). 'We know that we live in him and he in us, because he has given us of his Spirit' (1 John 4:13; cf. 3:24). Jesus promised that the Holy Spirit would bring glory to him (John 16:14) by testifying about him and reminding the disciples of his teaching (John 14:26; 15:26; 16:15).

## Jesus will return!

Jesus foretold that many false messiahs would arise (Matt. 24:4–5,11). They may perform great signs and miracles but they are not to be believed (Matt. 24:23–24; cf. Mark 13:5–6,21–23; Luke 17:23; 21:8). Jesus warns his disciples to watch out for false prophets, checking them out by their fruits, that is, their obedience to God's Word (Matt. 7:15–27). In fact there will be a major false Christ (the antichrist or 'lawless one'). He will come in the context of 'all kinds of counterfeit miracles, signs and wonders' and will deceive many people. Christ will destroy him at his second coming (2 Thess. 2:3–11); parallels may be drawn with the beast out of the earth who works miraculous signs (Rev. 13:13; cf. 16:14; 19:20).

However the return of Christ will be as obvious (and sudden) as lightning flashing across the sky. All the inhabitants of the world will see him in his power and glory. Many will mourn (Matt. 24:27–30; cf. 16:27; 25:31; 26:64; Mark 13:26; Luke 17:24; Rev. 1:7). The Lord will descend and call to himself all believers whether dead or alive (1 Thess. 4:16–17). He will bring the fulfilment of their salvation as they remain with him for ever (Heb. 9:28). But he will also come 'in blazing fire with his powerful angels. He will punish those who do not know God and do not obey the gospel of our Lord Jesus' (2 Thess. 1:7–8).

## Christ's kingdom is not of this world

Jesus explained to Pilate: 'My kingdom is not of this world. If it were, my servants would fight to prevent my arrest by the Jews. But now my kingdom is from another place'

(John 18:36). Earlier when he had realised the people wanted to make him king by force, he had withdrawn to the hills (John 6:15). He rebuked Peter in the Garden of Gethsemane for attacking the high priest's servant, 'for all who draw the sword will die by the sword'. Turning to the crowd he asked: 'Am I leading a rebellion, that you have come out with swords and clubs to capture me?' (Matt. 26:52–55).

Jesus and the early church preached that the kingdom was near (Matt. 3:2; 4:17; 10:7). He said: 'The kingdom of God does not come with your careful observation, nor will people say, "Here it is," or "There it is," because the kingdom of God is within (or among) you' (Luke 17:20–21). Only those who are born again of water and the Spirit can enter the kingdom of heaven (John 3:3,5; cf. 1 Cor. 15:50). Those who are obedient; the poor in Spirit; those with child-like trust (Matt. 7:21; 5:3,10; 19:14; cf. Gal. 5:21; Jas. 2:5). The kingdom is shown in powerful signs and wonders (Luke 11:20; 1 Cor. 4:20). However the consummation of the kingdom will take place when Jesus returns. The signs of the End Times are signs that the kingdom of God is near (Luke 21:31). The Son of Man will come in his kingdom (Matt. 16:28). He will reward the righteous on the day of judgment by allowing them to take their inheritance in the kingdom prepared for them since the creation of the world (Matt. 25:34).

So whether we think of the present manifestation of the kingdom or the future consummation, it is clear that flesh and blood (and human methods) cannot inherit the kingdom. Only supernatural intervention can bring the individual into the kingdom (the new birth) or bring the consummation of the kingdom (the second coming). Human methods of violence and rebellion are not part of the kingdom of Christ.

## The Bible condemns other gods and gospels

The Ten Commandments rule against the worship of other gods (Exod. 20:3–5) and this condemnation of idolatry is repeated many times. It includes the worship of the sun, moon and stars (Deut. 4:15–19). Isaiah mocks idols (Isa. 40:19–20; 41:7; 44:9–20; 46:6–7). God is angered by idolatry because it involves sacrifice to demons (Deut. 32:16–17). So if someone enticed Israel to idolatry he was to be executed (Deut. 13:10). Rather the people of God were to break down the altars, sacred stones and items of worship of other religions (Exod. 34:13). Israel experienced God's judgment for making the idolatrous golden calf (Exod. 32:4,8) and ultimately they were exiled because of their idolatry (2 Kgs. 17:1–23). In the New Testament idolatry is also condemned (1 Cor. 5:10–11; 6:9; Gal. 5:20; 1 Pet. 4:3). It is a degrading of religion (Rom. 1:21–25). An idol is nothing (1 Cor. 8:4) and in fact pagans sacrifice to demons (1 Cor. 10:20–21; cf. Deut. 32:17; Ps. 106:37).

We have already noted the condemnation of those who deny the truth about Jesus, especially the truth of his incarnation. Paul, facing the challenge of false teachers who wanted to turn the believers back to justification by works, speaks very strongly against them in Galatians 1:6–9. He describes the 'different gospel' as 'really no gospel at all' and continues: 'even if we or an angel from heaven should preach a gospel other than the one we preached to you, let him be eternally condemned!' (v. 8) and repeats this condemnation in the following verse.

# 10

## Salvation Undermined

There is a growing movement throughout the world seeking to further the cause of peace through co-operation between the various religions. The Dalai Lama is a patron of the World Congress of Faiths (WCF), whose object is:

> To promote a spirit of fellowship among mankind and to do so through religion – through religion, however, interpreted in its universal and widest sense, a sense far transcending its particular expression in any one of the world's faiths, and penetrating to that divine essence we believe to be common to all.

Similarly Archbishop George Appleton preaching at the annual service of the WCF in 1974 said:

> World religions have a vital task today of creating a world community . . . We are living at a creative moment of divine action, when a world community is in the making. The time for comparative religion is past: now the world religions must together seek the meaning of true religion.

A similar interfaith group is the World Conference on Religion and Peace, which organises the annual Week of Prayer for World Peace, drawing together at least ten of the world's religions. And there are other such groups. One is Prayer for Peace, which encourages people round the world to pray for one minute at noon:

Lead me from Death to Life, from Falsehood to Truth.
Lead me from Despair to Hope, from Fear to Trust.
Lead me from Hate to Love, from War to Peace.
Let Peace fill our Heart, our World, our Universe.
Peace. Peace. Peace.

The idea is to 'create a dynamo of positive thought and directed hope'. Announced in 1981 by Mother Teresa of Calcutta in St James's, Piccadilly, it was used in 1982 by the 900 delegates to the Assembly of World Religions in Moscow: 'Maybe the first time the world's leading religions had prayed together the one prayer.' This all seems a beautiful idea. But the leaflet about it causes concern: 'The words of the Prayer, adapted from a passage in the Upanishads' (holy books) 'are witness to the selfless and yet self-centred quality of peace . . . the Prayer for Peace is uniquely addressed to the universal *inner* dimension.' This very widely used prayer is deeply associated with Hinduism as is shown by its being printed in the form of a prayer mandala in the leaflet. That too is a Hindu concept. This may not seem a cause of great concern but it is part of the subtle spread of Hinduism throughout the western world which is furthering syncretism (the amalgamation of religious beliefs).

On October 27th 1986 leaders of the world religions, including Robert Runcie, Archbishop of Canterbury, at the invitation of Pope John Paul II gathered at Assisi for a day of Prayer for Peace. In the first part of the day the members of each faith prayed in separate places. After that followed an act of worship in a multi-faith context. Prayer was offered separately by representatives of each world-faith successively in the presence of all. There was however no common prayer of all religions.[1]

On May 28th 1986 the Archbishop of Canterbury delivered a lecture at Lambeth Palace on 'Christianity and World Religions'. He expressed pleasure at doing so during the fiftieth anniversary year of the WCF. 'Religious diversity has often been disruptive of community, and it remains the root cause of tensions and deep divisions between different human groups,' he said and compared this with the keynote of the first WCF Congress in 1936 – 'World Fellowship through Religion'.

Now of course Christians are deeply concerned for world peace and for harmony between races and understanding between those of different religions. These are laudable aims for people to work towards. If they can be achieved through co-operation between people from different faiths, well and good. But there are dangers. Peace, although a high priority, is not the highest one for Christianity. It is not as high as the priority of truth. So using religion for the cause of world peace and racial harmony must not be allowed to compromise truth. Jesus said, 'Do you think I came to bring peace on earth? No, I tell you, but division' (Luke 12:51). Division is an evil but is sometimes a necessary evil when people refuse to accept the truth which Christ taught. The great danger in interfaith relations is of compromising the truth. In his lecture Archbishop Runcie said we should:

> recognize that other faiths than our own are genuine mansions of the Spirit with many rooms to be discovered, rather than solitary fortresses to be attacked . . . All the centuries that the Spirit of God had been working in Christians, he must also have been working in Hindus, Buddhists, Muslims and others . . . We must learn to recognize the work of the Spirit at the centre of each of our faiths . . . and . . . to explore together the moments of revelation and the spiritual treasures which our respective faiths have handed down to us . . . We need both courage and humility to recognize this work of the Spirit among us in other faiths.

Dr Runcie was speaking shortly after a visit to India, which had clearly had a profound spiritual effect on him: 'India can be a stunning experience . . . which leaves one dazed and uncertain of one's bearings. Before, there were the certainties of an encapsulated western Christianity: after, there are new ways of thinking about God, Christ and the world.' It is clear that his certainties about some basic Christian beliefs had been undermined as his speech continued: 'Christians recognize that other faiths reveal other aspects of God which may enrich and enlarge our Christian understanding . . . Encounter with other faiths can deepen and enrich us. [We can] emancipate ourselves from the isolationism which limits religion to the insights and errors of one stream of tradition.' The Archbishop then referred to the story of a lady missionary who passed a Hindu shrine and remarked: 'I'm always very sad to see the piety with which those Hindus worship at that shrine.' Asked why, she replied: 'There's no one there to hear them.' The Archbishop commented, 'That "simple finality" has no place today.'

Seemingly unaware that he had just undermined one of the main motives for most of the sacrificial missionary work in recent centuries, he continued:

there is a certain incompleteness in each of our traditions . . . ultimately all religions possess a provisional, interim character as ways and signs to help us in our pilgrimage to Ultimate Truth and Perfection.

Did Dr Runcie realise his words were undermining the uniqueness of Christ as the full and final revelation of God and the only Saviour? He denied this charge but continued:

Christian theology must face . . . the question of the universality of Christ and his mission: the question as to the meaning and significance of the incarnation within the context of religious pluralism. There exists no easy answer to these questions . . . We will have to abandon any narrowly conceived Christian apologetic, based on a sense of superiority and an exclusive claim to truth . . .

This will mean that some claims about the exclusiveness
of the Church have to be renounced.

The Archbishop ended his speech by quoting (whether with
approval is unclear) the prediction of Arnold Toynbee
that the twentieth century would be remembered 'as the
time when the first sign became visible of that great
interpenetration of eastern religions and Christianity,
which gave rise to the great universal religion of the third
millennium AD'.

The Archbishop claimed not to be questioning 'the
uniqueness of God's revelation in Christ, nor the universal
significance of his incarnation and redemption', but most of
his speech contradicts this claim. And if the Archbishop of
Canterbury can be led into such serious error by interfaith
dialogue it is a warning to the rest of us to be very careful.

## Exclusivism, inclusivism or pluralism?

In June 1984 the Board for Mission and Unity (BMU)
of the General Synod published its Report, *Towards a
Theology for Interfaith Dialogue*. It describes three current
attitudes towards other faiths: exclusivism – that other
religions are 'either wholly in error, or simply inadequate
for salvation . . . For Exclusivism, then, the absolute supremacy of Christ is a given part of the data of Christian
identity'[2]; inclusivism – other religions are forerunners of
Christianity and Jesus is active in other religions, hidden
but bringing salvation; pluralism – that the different religions are 'different human interpretations of the revelation of the One God according to cultural limitations'.[3]
Jesus is normative for some pluralists but 'some Christians
can assent to this theory because they believe that the full,
true and reliable revelation of God in Christ may not
necessarily entail a belief in his ultimate supremacy'.[4]

The Report rightly warns against taking biblical texts out
of context, or out of the context of the whole witness of

scripture. But, as we shall see, the writers themselves
ignore the context of some of their 'proof-texts' and refuse
to see the relevance of some verses which, even after
consideration of the context, are clearly exclusivist. It is
interesting that the World Council of Churches (WCC)
*Guidelines on Dialogue*[5] says 'we are aware of problems
concerning the authority of the Bible remaining unsolved
among us'. Commenting on Acts 4:12 the British Council of
Churches (BCC) Guidelines *Can We Pray Together?* says:
'Yes, "sufficient" are the Scriptures provided we understand their adequacy rightly. They are not a manual of
proof-texts, nor a final verdict on realms and themes outside their time and geographical setting.'[6] Unfortunately
the booklet uses this consideration to try to change the clear
meaning of Acts 4:12. Similarly Kenneth Cracknell, Executive Secretary of the BCC Committee for Relations with
People of Other Faiths, writes:

Recent trends in our subject seem to show that Christians
in various ways are finding the Biblical images of the end
[he would include here the idea of eternal separation
from God for those who reject Christ] as well as the more
lurid developments of these images in the history of
doctrine, no longer adequate to deal with the perceived
facts. What we are beginning to discern is a theological
framework emerging in which the great traditional faith-
communities will not have disappeared.[7]

This means that at the end Jews, Muslims, Buddhists,
Hindus, and so on will still belong to their religion but 'will
sit down in the Kingdom of God, yet without first becoming
"Christians" like us'.[8] With this high handed attitude to
scripture, it is not surprising that all these publications
contain other errors as they explore relationships with
other faiths. Like the Archbishop, they regard Christianity
as one religion among many, rather than as the full, unique
and supreme divine revelation in Christ the living Word,

and scripture the written Word. To regard Christianity as
supreme would be the height of arrogance were it not that
the Christian faith is divine revelation given to undeserving
human beings, and that this is asserted, as we have seen, at
the very core of its message, by Jesus himself.

The BMU Report[9] points out that the Old Testament
was influenced by Egyptian, Canaanite, Assyrian, Baby-
lonian, Persian and Greek cultures and religions, and
instances sacral kingship influencing the Messianic concept; Hosea opposing the fertility cults but referring to
Israel as the bride of the Lord; the personification of
wisdom. Kenneth Cracknell in *Why Dialogue?*[10] refers to
the OT approval of the religious experiences of various
people outside the people of Israel. There is Melchizedek
(Gen. 14:18) who as 'priest of God Most High' blesses
Abram; Abimelech king of Gerar (Gen. 20:4) has a vision
of God and God guides him; Jethro, priest of Midian
(Exod. 18) offers acceptable sacrifice to God and speaks
the word of the Lord to Moses; Balaam (Num. 22:31)
communicates with the Lord; the widow of Zarephath
(1 Kgs. 17:7–24) and Naaman (2 Kgs. 5) both receive miracles from the Lord; and there are Ruth the Moabitess
and Job the Edomite sheikh. However these are weak
arguments for God revealing himself to people of other
faiths. Melchizedek, Jethro, Balaam, Ruth and Job clearly
believed in the Lord. The widow of Zarephath and Naaman
received miraculous provision from God and, it seems,
both came to faith in the Lord through those experiences.
Abimelech was in a special situation where, because of
Abraham's deceit, he was in danger of death. God simply
had mercy on him as an innocent man.

More than one of these publications quote Malachi 1:11
(RSV) 'from the rising of the sun, to the setting, my name
is great among the nations, and in every place incense is
offered to my name, and a pure offering, for my name
is great among the nations'. It is claimed that this shows
people in other religions are worshipping God acceptably.
But this is by no means clear from the passage, and in any

case the BMU Report says we should not rely too much on single proof texts! It has been interpreted as referring to the Jews in the Diaspora or to Gentile converts to Judaism. However the NIV translates it all in the future tense as a prophetic vision. Cracknell quotes Max Warren[11] as saying the Old Testament is very reserved on condemning idolatry outside the covenant people. But surely this is to be expected. The Old Testament was primarily written to the covenant people. However it makes it clear in the Ten Commandments and elsewhere that idolatry is wrong, including as it does the worship of demons (Deut. 32:16–17), and that the symbols of Canaanite idolatry are to be smashed. Idols are 'gods that are not gods' (Jer. 5:7). These gods will perish (Jer. 10:11). Warren also says the idols of the nations were conceived as symbols of the nations, so that judgment on a nation was described as judgment on its god. This no doubt means that the judgment on the nation was also a judgment on the demonic power that nation worshipped. To say, with Cracknell, that the Old Testament is not as unequivocal or unambiguous as it might appear at first sight, is an argument without foundation.

The BMU Report continues[12] that because the divine covenants with Adam, Noah and Abraham were for the benefit of the whole of humanity 'all humanity is the people of God'. But the Bible never teaches this. The Report quotes as evidence that God brought the Philistines from Caphtor and the Syrians from Kir (Amos 9:7). Also it claims the Assyrians and Egyptians are related directly to God (Isa. 19:25). The former reference is in the context of God condemning Israel and means no more than that God controls world events. The latter reference is a prophecy concerning the future of Assyria and Egypt when they turn to Yahweh. Both are irrelevant to the matter in hand and quoted without due reference to context.

Then the BMU Report lays great stress on the teaching in John 1:9 that the Word (Logos) 'gives light to every man', and argues that we must take seriously 'other manifestations of the Logos in other places and at other times' than in Jesus. This, the Report argues, means in other religions. But John does not teach that there are other manifestations. Rather, like Paul in Romans 1:20, he teaches that God has ensured there is a basic knowledge of his eternal power and divine nature inherent in creation. This is quite different from the idea of manifestations of the Logos in other religions which are similar (if inferior) to the manifestation in Jesus. The Bible does not teach such other manifestations. And if there were such surely this would undermine the uniqueness of Christ. A more extreme version of this argument is found in John Hick's essay 'Jesus and the world religions'.[13] Hick rejects the historicity of the fourth gospel and sees Jesus as simply a man who was 'intensely and overwhelmingly conscious of the reality of God'.[14] He says:

The different religions have their different names for God acting savingly towards mankind . . . *All* salvation, within all religions is the work of the Logos and . . . under their various images and symbols men in different cultures and faiths may encounter the Logos and find salvation. But what we cannot say is that all who are saved are saved by Jesus of Nazareth. The life of Jesus was one point at which the Logos – that is, God-in-relation-to-man – has acted; and it is the only point that savingly concerns the Christian; but we are not called upon nor are we entitled to make the negative assertion that the Logos has not acted and is not acting anywhere else in human life . . . The specifically Christian gift to the world is that men should come to know Jesus and take him into their religious life – not to displace but to deepen and enlarge their relationship with God to which they have already come within their own tradition.[15]

In Acts 4:12 Peter states: 'Salvation is found in no-one else, for there is no other name under heaven given to men by which we must be saved.' One would have thought that this was a clearly exclusivist statement. But the BMU Report argues[16] that for 'salvation' we should read healing and for 'saved' healed, since the context is healing and the word for 'saved' is translated in verse 9 as 'healed'. But Peter is arguing in verses 10–11 that the healing is proof that Jesus was raised from the dead, the stone the builders rejected has become the capstone. The context therefore requires that the verse be translated as it is (NIV) because it is an evangelistic context. It was this evangelism which had got Peter and John in trouble with the authorities to begin with (see Acts 3:11–26). The BCC Report *Can We Pray Together?*[17] asks about Peter: 'Are we to understand him as rejecting totally the cultures of India and the Far East of which he was completely ignorant?' It prefers to paraphrase the verse, making it a statement to the Jews that Jesus is the Messiah. But the question ignores any idea that Peter was inspired by the Holy Spirit. The paraphrase is a rather presumptuous treatment of scripture since it has no justification in the text. Acts 4:12 remains unscathed as an exclusivist statement that 'Salvation is found in no-one else, for there is no other name under heaven given to men by which we must be saved'.

The BMU Report then turns to John 14:6: 'I am the way and the truth and the life. No-one comes to the Father except through me.' It points out that the context is Thomas' question about how the disciples can know where Jesus is going. The answer is he is going to the Father and to have seen Jesus is to have seen the Father, that is, Jesus is assuring them in verse 6 that to have seen him is to have seen God. But, says the Report, 'there is no suggestion in the context that Jesus is claiming to be "the whole of God", that outside him there is no truth or life to be found'.[18] However we have seen that the life is exclusively in Jesus (see 'Faith in Christ Jesus is essential', p. 108). Significantly the BMU Report ignores the second half of the verse 'No-one comes to the Father except through me'. On the same page the Report makes this incredible statement concerning the Syro-Phoenician woman:

When the woman protests that even children and dogs share the same diet, she shows that Jesus is making a false distinction between Jew and Gentile. Jesus marvellously accepts the argument and confirms her view. He learns from her, his own boundaries are being enlarged, his attitudes shifted by a woman, a voteless pagan, who for his disciples was just a nuisance.

This interpretation is degrading to Jesus, implying he had to be argued into an inclusivist attitude.

After this the Report claims that the story of Cornelius shows the inclusiveness of God's saving activity. Cornelius fears God and does right. Peter sees that 'God does not show favouritism but accepts men from every nation who fear him and do what is right' (Acts 10:34–35). It is true that God deals with people who do not yet know Christ. But they are not thereby saved any more than Cornelius was. Peter preached the gospel to him, Cornelius and his household received the Holy Spirit and were baptised (Acts 10:36–48). The angel had told Cornelius to send for Peter saying: 'He will bring you a message through which you and all your household will be saved' (Acts 11:14).

Christians have often claimed that sincere seekers after God, who through no fault of their own have never heard the gospel, will be saved, though I can see no specific biblical justification for this view. However reasonable it may seem to say that God would not penalise such a 'seeker' for involuntary ignorance, all we can do is to trust such people to the justice of God. One thing is clear: such a person could not be saved through their own works or religious beliefs. Rather their religious beliefs are likely to be a hindrance.

The BMU Report calls us to be open to other faiths: 'We may be called to acknowledge the light shining there that reveals to us a deeper and truer understanding of the Christ to whom we would bear authentic witness.'[19] Again this undermines the inspiration and authority of scripture. The Report has been criticised (with justification) for being

weak on the atonement and resurrection. This is a serious
weakness for we have seen the stress on these doctrines in
the New Testament. Ironically other world religions, for all
their respect for Jesus, omit any reference to the atonement. But to underemphasise the cross is no way forward in
interfaith dialogue: it undermines the gospel. How dare
any Christian underemphasise the importance of the
Second Person of the Trinity going to the cross for us. Why
would God have done this if there were any other way of
salvation? It is an affront to God to imply there might be.

Don Cupitt writes: 'as soon as we begin to see our
religious values in relation to some particular doctrinal
system, we lose something of universality . . . and begin to
introduce local cultural distortions'.[20] He therefore calls
for a totally subjective, experiential religion in which
doctrine is relatively unimportant. Such religion would
emphasise spirituality and values, not theology. He says:

> There is much more overlap between the religions in this
> area of spirituality and values than there is in the realm of
> doctrine. Historically, doctrine has tended to become
> ideology and has been used to exclude the heretic and to
> separate the believer from the infidel. In so far as this use
> of doctrine has been emphasized, the religions have
> inevitably come to seem closed, mutually exclusive and
> irreconcilable ideological blocs. Not surprisingly, people
> then began to see religion in general as an ugly, obscur-
> antist and divisive force in human affairs.

However on Cupitt's view of faith:

> a much more congenial picture emerges. The major
> religious traditions need not be considered as excluding
> each other. None is 'pure' for history tells that they have
> all been unashamed borrowers at one time or another in
> their pasts. They are complex, many-dimensioned tra-
> ditions of faith, spirituality and values to live by, and they

overlap each other. Separation is irrational in our world. Why not move freely among them?[21]

Cupitt reaches this position by rejecting the literal truth of biblical teaching about God and the incarnate Christ. He calls himself a Christian Buddhist, even though he remains a practising Church of England clergyman. However his views lead us naturally to another important area where the sovereignty of God in salvation through Christ is being undermined.

## The New Age Movement

A large and increasing number of people in the world believe we are at the end of the Christian era and have entered the Age of Aquarius. In 1962 all eight planets were in the constellation of Aquarius, which had not occurred for nearly two thousand years. This was seen by occultists and astrologers as signifying the beginning of the New Age, when a messiah would bring peace. Many of them believed this messiah was born in 1962.[22] The New Age Movement is a loose network of groups working for global unity and peace on the basis of religious views and experiences founded on Hinduism and related eastern religions or occultism. People involved sometimes call it the Aquarian Conspiracy. St James's Church, Piccadilly has often been described as a New Age church. The Rector, the Revd Donald Reeves, has refused to give permission for his published sermons and leaflets to be quoted. In a sermon on October 20th 1985 he defined the New Age as a reaction to the rationalistic scientific materialism of the Enlightenment. He went on to state that men have failed to solve such problems as the arms race, terrorism, the North–South divide, the rape of the environment and so on. According to New Agers a new era is dawning; it is characterised by an awareness of the interdependence of nations; men and women; men and nature. The word 'planet' is a key word used by New Agers to stress this interdependence. The religious content of the New Age focuses on a search for the interrelatedness of creation and for wholeness.

On the face of it one can applaud these sentiments. What Christian would not be concerned about such matters and ideals? However the way in which the New Age Movement pursues these aims is often by occult and related means. It is easy to see how many individuals and groups concerned for peace, ecology, health and wholeness can innocently be drawn into a movement which is a Satanic deceit. In fact it is also known as the Human Potential Movement, Holistic Movement, Humanistic Psychology, and so on.

The New Age Movement is a development of the ideas of the Theosophical Society founded in 1875 by Helena Blavatsky. The society extended the idea of evolution to point to the existence of spiritual 'masters' who communicated telepathically with people like Blavatsky. The Theosophists were hostile to Christianity and other religions which believe in only one God. Madam Blavatsky wrote in 1875: 'The Christians and scientists must be made to respect their Indian betters. The Wisdom of India, her philosophy and achievement *must* be made known in Europe and America and the English be made to respect the natives of India and Tibet more than they do.'[23] One of Blavatsky's successors was Alice Bailey. In 1922 the Lucifer Publishing Co. was established to circulate her works, but the name was soon changed to the Lucis Publishing Co. She continued to receive messages from the spiritual 'masters' and encouraged her followers to infiltrate groups and to 'network' them together into the New Age Movement. The teachings about the New Age Christ and the 'spiritual hierarchy' were to be kept secret until 1975 – the centenary of the society.

In 1962 (the year the New Age Christ was said to have been born) the Findhorn Community was set up in Scotland by Peter and Eileen Caddy. It is a New Age community built on the intersection of ley lines (lines of energy said to cross the earth, which produce extra power where they intersect). The community, as we shall see, is into pantheism and animism, with remarkable results. It is a model community proving the reality of New Age thinking.

In 1982 a series of meetings called 'Turning Points' was begun at St James's, Piccadilly, and still continues. Its aim is to form networks of people committed to the transformation of the individual and of the planet. Participants may be humanists, radical Christians or New Agers who work together in groups to achieve the transformation of consciousness through exploring and expressing themselves. Donald Reeves often speaks on the relationship between Christianity and the New Age – not only in St James's; he spoke at the Festival of Mind-Body-Spirit at Olympia, which included many kinds of mystical and occult groupings.

Networking is most important in the New Age Movement: the Turning Point session of October 1st 1984 was about forming a major Network out of individual networks. These networks were not to be like ordinary organisations with structure and aims; rather their aim is to stress relationships and processes which help people to realise their personal potential. Networkers are people who seek to link those who share these beliefs the world over.

One leading New Ager, Marilyn Ferguson, begins her book *The Aquarian Conspiracy*: 'A leaderless but powerful network is working to bring about radical change in the United States.' She claims it ranges across every level of income, education and background. All of them are linked by an experience of inner personal transformation. They do not see themselves as part of a conspiracy but they do sense they are part of something bigger. She claims there are tens of thousands of entry points to the conspiracy. This may well sound exaggerated if we regard it as a human conspiracy. I have read of powerful and sometimes secretive international political groups like the Bilderbergers and the Trilateralists who (it is claimed) aim to take control of the world, and are linked in with the New Age Movement.

However I do not find the idea of a human conspiracy to take over the world convincing: rather I see it as a Satanic plan. The real conspiracy is occult; it is Satanic power that is drawing together this network of New Agers. Many of those involved are unaware of this. Some are idealists who care about justice, conservation, holistic health and the like. Such is the deceit of the devil. What we are examining is a major factor of the deceit in the End Times foretold by Jesus in Mark 13:5–6, 21–23.

We can now briefly examine some of the main beliefs of the New Age Movement.

## The unity of humanity, nature and God

New Agers refer to Plato who taught that there was a world of Ideas existing independently of the things we see and touch. Following from that they assert their need to tune in to the ideas of our time so that they can achieve personal and corporate transformation.

New Agers believe everything is interconnected. This is holistic thinking, or the Doctrine of Wholeness. 'All is One' is the motto. It follows that 'All is God'. There is no distinction between God and nature or between man and nature. We therefore need to become aware of our 'godhood' and oneness with nature through meditation, which will achieve altered states of consciousness. Individual people or things are all part of the One as are good and evil.

The Findhorn Community sees itself in co-operation with the Devas (Hindu gods) and the nature spirits who inhabit their flower and vegetable gardens. This may sound slightly ridiculous but in the early days it led to their growing cabbages weighing 40lb. Many have pointed out how plants thrived amazingly in spite of poor soil and severe weather conditions, exposed as the Findhorn Community is to harsh and frequent winds from the North Sea. In 1966 the community realised it was also co-operating with the god Pan (who indwells everything – hence panthe-

ism). I have watched these people on television holding
hands in a ring in the garden and meditating to tune in to the
nature spirits. In 1970 a prominent New Ager, David
Spangler, joined the Findhorn Community. He received
communications from spirit beings. He later wrote a book
*Reflections on the Christ* in which he speaks of the true light
of Lucifer, who works within all of us to bring us to
wholeness and the New Age. He states that all of us need
'Luciferic initiation' to experience wholeness and the fulness of light. Spangler is a leader in a New Age organisation
called Planetary Citizens which grew out of the 1970 Conference on Human Survival held at the United Nations in
New York. U Thant was one of the original organisers as
was Donald Keys who was associated with the Findhorn
Community. He has been described by one researcher[24] as a
disciple of Alice Bailey. Keys spoke at St. James's Piccadilly
on April 15th 1986.

New Agers seek to discover the God within. Donald
Reeves in his sermon 'Findhorn and Christianity' describes
the practice of attunement, which the community follows.
He quotes a revelation given to Eileen Caddy, co-founder
of Findhorn, which states that the answer to every problem
is to be found not by reading books or consulting others but
by seeking the answer deep within oneself – where God is.

It is little wonder therefore that the New Agers in general
are into various forms of alternative medicine which stress
energies within the body. On October 15th 1984 one
psychic speaker at St James's spoke about various such
energies including chakras and auras. The church also
offers acupuncture. Interestingly Dr Fritjof Capra, author
of *The Tao of Physics*, believes there are striking parallels
between twentieth-century physics and ancient mystical
traditions. He relates it to Taoism, 'an ancient Chinese
philosophical and religious system concerned with reaching
a state of self-awareness through mysticism and occult
practices'. This can only help forward the New Age Movement.

The New Age way of salvation – seeking the God within

through meditation and enlightenment – completely undermines God's sovereign provision of new birth by faith in Jesus Christ, crucified and risen.

## Jesus was an ordinary man who became a master of wisdom

In *The Aquarian Gospel* Marilyn Ferguson says: 'Jesus was not always Christ. Jesus won his Christship by a strenuous life . . . We have a record of the events of his Christing, or receiving the degree Christ . . . We recognise the facts that Jesus was man and that Christ was God . . .' The theory is that Jesus attained enlightenment through mystical experiences. He was trained by the Essenes (the community who produced the Dead Sea Scrolls) and other esoteric (secret) groups, and he may have gone to India and Tibet between the ages of twelve and thirty, to learn wisdom. Then he taught about 'Christ consciousness' which he possessed and we can attain.

Benjamin Creme of the Tara Centre in London mounted a massive publicity campaign in 1982 saying the return of the Christ was imminent and that in fact he was already in the world. The Christ is not Jesus but 'he manifested through his disciple Jesus (who is now the Master Jesus) by a process of overshadowing'. Jesus incidentally is below Buddha in the spiritual hierarchy. In order to maintain this belief New Agers claim that the apostles, especially Paul, perverted Christ's teachings. His true teachings were preserved by the gnostics (an ancient esoteric cult) who were in contact with the 'ascended masters'. But the early church suppressed the gnostics and created the New Testament which is biased against the teachings of Jesus. The New Age (or occult) teaching on Christ consciousness is not focusing on Jesus – for he himself had to gain Christ consciousness. Rather it is to replace Jesus Christ with a subjective experience of another supernatural 'christ'.

It is here that we can note some remarkable parallels

between New Age teachings and the views of certain radical theologians like Don Cupitt. In *Taking Leave of God*[25] Cupitt, a Christian Buddhist, says: 'Our Christian Buddhist speaks also of Jesus, but he does not think of Jesus as the divine Christ of the Church who lives and reigns in a higher world . . . Instead he studies the tradition of the words of that neglected spiritual master, the historical Jesus.' In *The Myth of God Incarnate*[26] Cupitt writes: 'If in Jesus the fullness of God himself is permanently incarnate, Jesus can be directly worshipped as God without risk of error or blasphemy. A cult of Christ as distinct from a cult of God, thus becomes defensible and did, in fact, develop.' He disagrees with this idea of Jesus and continues: 'it is my contention that the doctrine of Christ as God's divine son has here humanized deity to an intolerable degree'.[27]

Needless to say, all this undermines God's sovereign provision of salvation through Jesus Christ his One and Only Son.


## The goal of humanity is to become gods

For the New Ager salvation is not from sin so the cross of Christ has no relevance. God's sovereign provision for salvation is therefore ignored. Instead salvation is enlightenment. Man needs to realise and experience his divinity, his godhood. The idea is that we are to become 'gods', in spite of the fact that this was the sinful aim of Adam and Eve (Gen. 3:5). Salvation is to attune to the god within and so to become gods. Malcolm Stern, programme director of Turning Points at St James's Piccadilly, has stated that he didn't want Jesus to be portrayed as the only Son of God as though divinity was not attainable by everyone else. Rather he was the model of perfected man.[28]

Again Cupitt is remarkably close to the New Age view. He is very much against the idea of an objective, personal, metaphysical God. 'We cannot (and ought not to) believe in an objective deity who among other things antecedently prescribes our moral values and our spiritual itinerary from outside.'[29] In fact if such a God did present himself we must reject him.[30] Cupitt's main concern is human autonomy, which no one, not even an objective God, must infringe. So he sees obedience as sin.[31] 'Traditional Christianity is now our Old Testament,' he claims. 'The third dispensation, the Age of the Spirit long promised by certain visionary figures, has in a sense already begun.'[32]

So Don Cupitt calls us to internalise our religion and our God. It is God-within, not a God out there.[33] Our destiny is:

> to become spirit, that is, precisely to attain the highest degree of autonomous self-knowledge and self-transcendence[34] . . . God's will for us is precisely that we should become fully-realized spiritual individuals through the overcoming of any distinction between him and us[35] . . . There is no god, but the religious requirement: the imperative *Become Spirit!* is the presence of God within us, and for us it is God, it is the goal as well as the requirement[36] . . . [the fall of man is] in the long run a step upwards[37] . . . Religion is about holiness, exaltation, power, Lordship, spirituality, autonomy, freedom, knowledge, blessedness, universality and transcendence over nature . . . we say to ourselves, it is obviously absurdly presumptuous to suppose that the divine attributes could be for *me*. Even to think such a thing would be to flirt with the sin of Lucifer and to court damnation.[38]

But he continues:[39]

> Suppose then that those great qualities and powers, the divine attributes, are spiritual goals for us to pursue, then we must straight away register the fact that the tradition warns us that there is a right and a wrong way to go about it. The wrong way, symbolized by Lucifer, snatches at

equality with God. The right way is the way of humility,
disinterestedness and self-surrender . . . The real sin of
Lucifer lies in pursuing divine freedom, knowledge,
power and so on, not with a pure heart, but with the
intention of using them to bolster a still-unregenerate
self.

This is straightforward New Age teaching on salvation
through enlightenment and man realising his divinity. So
we see a range of teaching from Luciferianism to Cupitt's
stress on purer motives but, nevertheless still promoting
deification of self. This contrasts with biblical teaching on
the transcendence of God who indwells human beings by
his Holy Spirit given to believers. They must be careful to
use this power for the glory of God and not for self-
fulfilment. Various methods are used in New Age circles
to further the process of self deification. Some people
innocently become involved in the techniques without
realising their origin or purpose. Hence they unwittingly
become caught up in the New Age Movement with its
demonic associations. One widespread technique is transcendental meditation, which is:

that meditation in which a person transcends thought,
reason and the consciousness of his individuality to
become aware of the Creative Intelligence of God (also
called the Self or Pure Consciousness). One is not aware
of any thought or thing, but only aware of the Pure
Consciousness which is God.[40]

The Maharishi Mahesh Yogi, who started the transcendental meditation group, claimed it was not religious; but
on October 19th 1977 the United States courts judged that
it was a religion. The Maharishi accepts traditional monistic
(all is One) Hinduism. Each teacher has to sign an in-
vocation of various Hindu gods. The mantras (meditation
words) given to participants in TM are invocations of these

gods. Unwittingly many thousands of people are being initiated into Hinduism.

Then there is yoga, innocently practised even by Christians. But the Hatha Yoga, which is what most people are involved in, is really a branch of Hinduism. It is an ancient system of controlling body, breath and mind in order to achieve union with the universal soul. Each posture has a symbolic mystical and secret meaning in Hinduism. Some are silent invocations to Hindu deities.

Another technique based on Hindu ideas is 'rebirthing', where people experience a pre-natal state. This is achieved by hyperventilating, meditation and breathing control. It is not to be confused with an experience some people have had when receiving Christian prayer for inner healing, when God heals very early experiences in an individual's life. If such an experience happens spontaneously in the context of Christian prayer, well and good. But it should not be induced. This would be to come dangerously near to the New Age rebirthing.

There are various other New Age techniques which are claimed to lead individuals on to self-knowledge, to awareness of their divinity and to unity with God. In one Turning Points address at St James's Piccadilly, people were encouraged in self-acceptance through discovering the inner sound in each of them through relaxation, breathing techniques and movement.[41] Another used music to move people to enter sacred inner spaces for the first time.[42]

Guided imagery involves a person following an imaginary guide with whom he can converse and who will lead him into fantasy. The distance between this practice and acquiring a spirit-guide is very short. On March 3rd 1986 St James's held a visualisation session using a technique which sought to explore the imagery beneath the conscious mind. The aim was to integrate the conscious and the subconscious in order to achieve life goals.[43]

On September 14th 1987 Turning Points offered participation in dances from the Sufi tradition (Islamic mysticism) and included a whirling dervish experience. The following two sessions featured an astrologer and a practitioner of ancient Inca healing arts. The latter included learning how to use the Inca wheel of medicine for spiritual healing.[44]

And so on. Again guided imagery is not to be confused with Christian inner healing when past experiences may be brought to mind and healed by the power and presence of Christ. However, there should be no deliberate psychological manipulation or fantasising.

One sinister development of the New Age concerns the emergence of a new species of humanity. In the *Sunday Times* of August 25th 1986 Mick Brown interviewed Sir George Trevelyan, founder of the Wrekin Trust and a lecturer on 'The holistic view of the universe', who regards the earth as a living creature and humans as its brain and nervous system. He believes we are witnessing the emergence of MULIER HOMO SAPIENS NOETICUS, a human directed by consciousness, a new species embodying male and female sensibilities, and dedicated to building a society based on 'seizing the possibility of a new form of knowledge'. This idea of humans with special powers is constantly being conveyed by science fiction. It includes the power of mind over matter – which is one idea in the New Age Movement. However in some New Agers it is linked with the ancient Aryan race myth, which was behind Nazism.

## The expectation of a Messiah

Benjamin Creme produced his Information Sheet 'The Reappearance of the Christ and the Masters of Wisdom' in 1982. It would be foolish to dismiss him as a crank for he represents many New Agers and what he says seems to fit uncannily into New Testament predictions of the antichrist and the 'man of lawlessness'. Creme writes:

A new spiritual age is dawning: under the guidance of the Spiritual Hierarchy, those members of the human family who have made the evolutionary journey ahead of us, who have perfected themselves, and whose energies and ideas have been stimulating factors behind our evolution. For the first time for many thousands of years, the Masters of Wisdom are beginning to emerge from their retreats to guide us into the Aquarian Age . . . with their Head and Leader, the World Teacher, the One we call the Christ. The Christ, from the esoteric point of view, is not the One and Only Son of God, but the Head of the Hierarchy of Masters . . . awaited by Buddhists as the Lord Maitreya, by Muslims as the Imam Mahdi, as the Bodhisattva by Hindus and as the Messiah by the Jews . . . He manifested through His Disciple Jesus (who is now the Master Jesus) by a process of overshadowing. This time He comes Himself, as World Teacher for the Aquarian Age.

Creme sees the revealing of the Christ as imminent: 'Recognition is up to each of us individually, through the Christ Consciousness in us and through our own spiritual intuition.' The Christ will 'indicate the solutions to man's dilemma – political and economic, religious and social.'

One is reminded of a statement of a leading politician in the UN and NATO: 'Send us a man who can hold the allegiance of all the people, and whether he be God or devil, we will receive him.' Both the New Age Movement and the world situation make the appearance of such an antichrist figure seem very credible.

In *Considering Dialogue*[45] Kenneth Cracknell quotes Professor Donald Dawe of Union Theological Seminary concerning the religious renewal and fulfilment of human existence which he calls 'new being':

Other traditions live out of the power of this new being in accordance with the names by which they encounter and participate in ultimate reality. This does not make them crypto-Christians or members of a 'hidden' or 'latent

church'. They are and remain what they are – Hindus,
Buddhists, Muslims or devotees of a multitude of other
religions. This is possible because the 'name of Jesus' is
translatable.

At the end of the BMU Report[46] Bishop David Brown is
quoted: 'Christ will provide the link by which the different
religions will be brought into a deep and mutually enriching
relationship with each other.' The question is, which
Christ? It is my conviction that it will not be Jesus Christ,
God's One and Only Son, but the antichrist.

So we have seen how many have been deceived because
of a lack of submission to God's sovereign provision of
salvation through the atonement achieved by his unique
incarnate Son, Jesus Christ. Instead of submitting to God's
Word and salvation, some have deliberately turned to
subjectivism: to finding the god within and becoming gods:
these include New Agers and theologians like Don Cupitt.
Or out of false humility they seek to make Christianity one
religion among many, rather than God's final revelation to
unworthy men. Behind it all we have recognised a Satanic
conspiracy, deliberately aided by many New Agers spreading occult influence and preparing for a false occultic
Christ. Still more are being drawn into this conspiracy
unwittingly through involvement in various oriental cults
and practices and certain branches of alternative medicine.

Many of these people are, at best, preaching 'a different
gospel – which is really no gospel at all' (Gal. 1:6–7). Paul
says 'the gospel I preached is not something that man made
up. I did not receive it from any man, nor was I taught it;
rather, I received it by revelation from Jesus Christ' (Gal.
1:11–12). We need to take seriously, and fearlessly proclaim, what Paul said in Gal. 1:8–9 which is so relevant
today: 'Even if we or an angel from heaven should preach a
gospel other than the one we preached to you, let him be
eternally condemned! As we have already said, so now I say
again: if anybody is preaching to you a gospel other than
what you accepted, let him be eternally condemned.'

Hopefully some of these people will realise the error of their ways, repent and receive God's forgiveness. Until then, these awesome words of Paul apply to them, especially to those who profess Christianity.

# 11

## Submitting to God's Sovereignty in Salvation

As we have seen, salvation was achieved by God's only divine Son becoming incarnate as the historical Jesus of Nazareth; dying in our place as a complete, redemptive sacrifice; and rising triumphant over sin, death and hell. Salvation is received by response to the action of the Holy Spirit bringing the individual to new birth, repentance and the commitment of faith in Christ and his work.

### Submit to the authority of scripture

The grave danger in what we have considered so far is subjectivism. The remedy is to accept that the Bible is objectively the Word of God, as we saw in Part I. It is not simply that the Bible *becomes* the Word of God as the Holy Spirit applies it to our mind and heart, but that the Bible *is* the Word of God.

### *Regard biblical teaching as foundational*

Many of those we have quoted in this section do not place much emphasis or importance on doctrine. This allows them to follow their chosen path into subjectivism. You need to know the teaching of scripture and to test all teaching and experience (however convincing, attractive and 'Christian' it appears) by the teaching of scripture, with due regard for the way the church interprets it. In dealing with other faiths it is essential to know biblical teaching in order to assess their teaching.

*Unashamedly proclaim the need by sinful man of substitutionary atonement by the unique incarnate Son of God.* This is at the centre of the gospel, and it is ignored or denied by other faiths and the cults. It is undermined by some of the theologians we have quoted. Without this teaching, there is no gospel. The need of sensitivity and humility in proclaiming it does not alter its truth.

*Know the biblical teaching on the return of Christ.* The views of the New Age Movement (and cults such as Jehovah's Witnesses) are specifically contradicted in the New Testament. The way to recognise Christ when he returns is not by some subjective Christ consciousness but by acknowledging the clear (and spectacular) criteria of the New Testament being fulfilled.

## Do not be carried into error by idealism

Any Christian favours world peace, justice and harmony, and will oppose racism and other forms of oppression. But the means as well as the aims must be biblical. It is very easy to be swept along by a tide of fervent idealism, without realising one is being led into error. Peace and harmony are not the highest good. The highest good is loving and obedient submission to God through his revealed truth. And that will sometimes undermine peace and harmony. Much as we desire and work for peace and unity, it is doubtful if God could trust sinful mankind with global unity and government. The story leading up to the Tower of Babel would surely repeat itself. It is arguable that God could not trust us with global church unity either. Not only are all Christians imperfect, but it is obvious that much of the Christian church does not submit to the sovereignty of God through his revealed truth. In such circumstances total church unity would be at best a mixed blessing. These comments are not to deny the biblical teaching on the need for unity. Rather it is to say that without a common and wholehearted submission to the whole of God's Word, such unity would be dangerous. God desires not simply unity, but unity in the truth.

## Do not compromise through misguided humility

We are greatly influenced by democracy and by a desire to see the good in another person's views. It therefore seems arrogant to say we know the truth and those who disagree with us do not. And it *is* arrogant unless we believe that the Bible is God's Word revealed to unworthy sinners. We are not claiming superiority for ourselves; rather, as the gospel teaches, we are sinners deserving God's condemnation. What we are saying is that God in his grace and mercy has sovereignly revealed his salvation in Jesus the living Word, and scripture the written Word, to unworthy people like us. We have accepted this revelation by faith as true not only for us, but all humanity. It is therefore misguided humility to say that Christianity is only one religion among many, and that other religions are alternative ways to God. It is clear that God has given what is often called 'general revelation' (see Rom. 1:20), but it is evident from scripture and experience that this is not sufficient to bring an individual to salvation. Such misguided humility can in fact lead us arrogantly to dismiss the most amazing event in history – God entering the world to die for the sins of mankind.

## Beware of subjective and experience-based religion

This applies to Christian groups who underemphasise or even scoff at doctrine or who do not subject their experiences (including charismatic gifts, signs and wonders) to the scrutiny of scripture. But it applies even more to involvement in non-Christian groups – human potential organisations; holistic health groups; alternative medical practices, some of which can subtly lead people into occult experiences. Even conservation groups have been known to lapse into pantheism and earth worship. More serious are activities like yoga, transcendental meditation, rebirthing, imaging and similar non-Christian techniques, especially those which encourage a person to let his mind go blank. These are short cuts to occult involvement.

*Repent of errors in this area.* If you have been involved in any of these activities or have compromised the authority of scripture by soft-pedalling the truth of the gospel (especially the atonement), in interfaith relations, or by idealism or misguided humility:

(a)    repent of these sins before God;
(b)    renounce the wrong views and attitudes in the name of Christ;
(c)    seek counsel and prayer especially if you have had occult involvement (even 'innocently');
(d)    ask God to fill you with the Holy Spirit, the Spirit of truth (again seek counsel and prayer if necessary).

Part IV

# GOD'S SOVEREIGNTY IN THE CHURCH

## Characteristics of the Local Church

# 12

## Obedience and Holiness

Jesus said he would build his church and the gates of Hades would not overcome it (Matt. 16:18). He is therefore the architect of the church and has the blueprint for it. As stated earlier, it is to be expected that the God of revelation would give a clear and reliable record of the important principles on which he wanted his church built. Paul calls the church God's building and temple (1 Cor. 3:9,16,17). It is built on the foundation of Christ (1 Cor. 3:11) who is also called the cornerstone or capstone of the building (1 Pet. 2:4–7). A slightly different picture is given in Ephesians 2:20–22: it is 'built on the foundation of the apostles and prophets, with Christ Jesus himself as the chief cornerstone. In him the whole building is joined together and rises to become a holy temple to the Lord.' It follows that the church in every age should be built upon the principles the apostles taught. While the New Testament does not give us every detail of church structure and life it does give many principles which have all too often been forgotten by the church throughout its history.

Paul laid the foundation of the Corinthian church as 'an expert builder, and someone else is building on it' (1 Cor. 3:10). He warns that 'each one should be careful how he builds' because on the day of the Lord the fire of the Lord's judgment 'will test the quality of each man's work' (1 Cor. 3:10,14).

The Church of England officially accepts the supremacy of biblical authority. Canons A2–4 are at pains to stress that the Thirty-Nine Articles and the doctrine of the Book of Common Prayer are 'agreeable to the Word of God' and that the worship and ordination services are 'not repugnant to the Word of God'. Canon A5 states that 'the doctrine of the Church of England is grounded in the holy Scriptures, and in such teachings of the Ancient Fathers and Councils of the Church as are agreeable to the said Scriptures'. Article 20 of the Thirty-Nine Articles states:

> The Church hath power to decree Rites or Ceremonies and authority in Controversies of Faith: And yet it is not lawful for the Church to ordain any thing that is contrary to God's Word written, neither may it so expound one place of Scripture, that it be repugnant to another.

Apart from the issue of Christ's authority as architect of the church whose plans are communicated through the apostolic scriptures, there is another practical reason for restoring the church to biblical principles. The early church was growing (Acts 2:47; 5:14; 6:1,7; 9:31,42; 11:21,24; 14:1, 21; 16:5; 17:12): it is therefore sensible to look at the principles by which it was growing, and seek to apply them in our own situation. It may be argued that the early church was not meant to be normative for later ages, especially as it existed in a very different culture and at a time of a special outpouring of the Holy Spirit. But this argument is unconvincing. The early church was built on apostolic and scriptural principles. These are relevant and authoritative for all ages and cultures. And, as we shall see, one of these principles was that the church should be a supernatural body, filled with the power of the Holy Spirit and seeing that power manifested in 'signs and wonders'. In any case we are today witnessing what must be the greatest movement of the Holy Spirit – a truly worldwide movement – since Pentecost.

Furthermore God in his providence did not just give us a list of principles and theory, such as in the epistles. He gave us the Book of Acts to show us how the church worked these principles out. So although we may use new methods of working out biblical principles we would do well to examine the methods of the early church to see if some of them are better than our own. For example, in 1981 the Bible Society published statistics of church growth and decline, relative to the theological position of their minister. The survey was conducted in Baptist churches. It showed that in recent years churches with a 'radical' minister experienced decline by 22 per cent; 'middle of the road' by 15 per cent; interestingly, 'charismatic' by 2 per cent. On the other hand 'conservative evangelical' grew by 5 per cent and 'conservative evangelical and charismatic' by 25 per cent.[1] So those who sought to be open to the renewing power of the Spirit and to be true to biblical principles experienced the greatest growth. This is surely the theological position closest to that of the Book of Acts.

Similarly Roy Pointer[2] quotes statistics on 'Growth and Decline of British Denominations' from the UK *Christian Handbook* 1983. The two groups showing the highest growth in recent years are the Pentecostal 8 per cent; and Afro-West Indian 7 per cent. Roman Catholic, Anglican and other Protestant denominations all showed decline. These statistics seem to point in the same direction as the previous ones. To return to the principles of the New Testament in the power of the Holy Spirit is a recipe for church growth. We must now examine some of these principles. But first it is worth saying that they can be worked out in any church today – whether Anglican or other denominations or independent churches. My own church has been working them out extensively in recent years, and other churches do the same. The good effects have been dramatic. In this part I am concentrating on the local church; so, for example, in discussing the unity of the church I am referring to local church unity, not ecumenical unity.

Some years ago I introduced an outline of biblical teaching on the Nature and Mission of the Local Church (see Appendix 2). These principles are being worked out fully, although imperfectly, in Hawkwell:

1  Be wholeheartedly committed to Christ as Lord.
2  Act on the Word of God.
3  Experience the power of the Holy Spirit.
4  Live adventurously by faith.
5  Seek holiness before God.
6  Offer wholehearted praise and worship to God.
7  Be involved in intercession and 'hearing' God.
8  Discern and encourage every member's gifts.
9  Be a deeply committed fellowship:
   (a)   submitting to one another
   (b)   being loyal to and trusting one another
   (c)   encouraging and correcting one another
   (d)   sharing needs and possessions.
10 Be involved in urgent evangelism and spiritual warfare.

We shall examine these principles in the same order, except for linking no. 5 with no. 2.

## The local church should be wholeheartedly committed to Christ as Lord

When large crowds were following Jesus he did not compromise his call to discipleship, that is, to love God with all our heart, soul, mind and strength. He puts the challenge starkly that no one can be a disciple of his who does not 'hate his father and mother, his wife and children, his brothers and sisters – yes, even his own life' (Luke 14:25–26). Clearly the statement does not mean literally to hate our relatives, but rather to challenge us to put Christ definitely and sacrificially before anyone else. Elsewhere Jesus says, 'Do you think I came to bring peace on earth? No, I tell you, but division. From now on there will be five in one family divided against each other, three against two and two against three' (Luke 12:51–53; cf. Matt. 8:21–22; 10:34–36; Luke 9:59–62). He clarifies the challenge in Matthew 10:37: 'Anyone who loves his father or mother more than me is not worthy of me; anyone who loves his son or daughter more than me is not worthy of me.'

A disciple must practise self-denial and take up his cross (Matt. 16:24–26; Mark 8:34–38; Luke 9:23–26). He is to 'give up everything he has' (Luke 14:33) which, at the very least, means to renounce the ownership of our possessions; to regard them as simply entrusted to us to 'manage' for God, so that he can use them or dispose of them as he will. A disciple will not seek popularity and praise from men (John 5:44). Rather he will beware when all men speak well of him (Luke 6:12) and not shrink from following Jesus who lost most of his followers because of his hard teaching (John 6:60–66). He will rejoice when he is persecuted, excluded and insulted because he follows the tradition of the prophets who also were persecuted. He will rejoice because he anticipates a heavenly reward (Matt. 5:10–12; cf. Luke 6:22–23). Far from resenting his persecutors, he will pray for them and bless them (Matt. 5:44; Luke 6:27).

## The local church should act on the Word of God

'Why do you call me, "Lord, Lord," and do not do what I say?' asks Jesus. He goes on to tell the story of the man who hears the Word but does not obey it; such a person is like a man building his house on sand (Luke 6:46–49; cf. Matt. 7:24–29). At the Last Supper Jesus states five times that anyone who loves him will obey him (John 14:15,21,23,24; 15:14). We do not love him, nor are we his friends if we do not obey him. We are to 'live by the truth' (John 3:21). In fact a willingness to obey God is a prerequisite for knowing that Jesus' teaching is true (John 7:17). So he sends his disciples out to 'make disciples of all nations . . . teaching them *to obey* everything (he has) commanded' (Matt. 28:19–20). We are not to be content with simply teaching everything Jesus has commanded us. We must teach people to obey it.

## The local church should seek holiness before God

Christ died not only that we should be forgiven but also that
we should be holy: 'He himself bore our sins in his body on
the tree, so that we might die to sin and live for righteousness' (1 Pet. 2:24; cf. Rom. 6). In the context of referring to
immorality, Paul says to the Corinthians: 'Do you not know
that your body is a temple of the Holy Spirit, who is in you,
whom you have received from God? You are not your own;
you were bought with a price. Therefore honour God with
your body' (1 Cor. 6:19–20).

An emphasis on repentance is to be a characteristic of the
church, as it was in the preaching of Jesus (Matt. 4:17), and
of the Twelve before and after Pentecost (Mark 6:12; Acts
2:38; 3:19). In fact Jesus commanded that repentance was
to be preached in his name to all nations (Luke 24:47)
because God commands all men everywhere to repent
(Acts 17:30). God shows kindness, tolerance and patience,
not because he does not care about sin, but in order to lead
people to repentance (Rom. 2:4–5). 'He is patient . . . not
wanting anyone to perish, but everyone to come to repentance' (2 Pet. 3:9). On the other hand God sometimes allows
us to go through difficulties which act as a discipline to bring
us to greater holiness; this of course includes necessary
repentance.

Repentance involves wholehearted sorrow for sin (Joel
2:12). Jesus said: 'Blessed are those who mourn' (over sin)
(Matt. 5:4). Christians are to encourage one another daily
so that none may be hardened by sin's deceitfulness (Heb.
3:13). On the other hand there is a distinction between a
godly sorrow which brings repentance and salvation and a
worldly sorrow that brings death (2 Cor. 7:10). God does
not want anyone to wallow in guilt in an unhealthy way. It is
good that there should be a deep sense of 'brokenness' in
spirit and emotions, but this should be for a limited time. It
is wrong for Christians to wallow in misery and failure,
which will encourage them to give up trying.

Repentance also involves seeing our sin as against God.

Although David had sinned against Bathsheba and Uriah he says to God, in Psalm 51:4, 'Against you, you only, have I sinned and done what is evil in your sight.' He is not denying his sin against the two people involved but recognises that its most serious aspect is that it is against God. Until we see that all our sin is ultimately against God (even if it seems primarily against men), we shall not know true repentance. We need to see the blackness of our sin silhouetted against the brightness of God's glory. It involves seeing that our sin crucified Jesus. The Greek word for confess means 'to agree'. Confession of sin means to agree with God about our sin; to see it as he does – very serious and deserving judgment. Jesus said men will be judged even for every careless word they have spoken (Matt. 12:36).

We commit sins with our minds and bodies because, like all men, we have sin as a principle and tendency in our hearts (innermost beings). Jesus said: 'Out of the heart come evil thoughts, murder, adultery, sexual immorality, theft, false testimony, slander' (Matt. 15:19). True repentance then is to discover our heart's attitude to God (pride and rebellion), to see how it offends his holiness, and to turn away from it to the right attitude.

Repentance is not just sorrow: it also involves obedience. Repentance is proved by good deeds (Acts 26:20; Matt. 3:8). Daniel says to Nebuchadnezzar: 'Renounce your sins by doing what is right, and your wickedness by being kind to the oppressed' (Dan. 4:27). It was after the people were 'cut to the heart' through Peter's preaching that he called them to repent (Acts 2:37–38). Remorse means being upset about sin and regretting it, but it is not repentance. Remorse, not repentance, was shown by Pharaoh (Exod. 9:27), the Scribes and Pharisees (John 8:9) and Judas (Matt. 27:3). Christians are called to the obedience of repentance or, as Paul has put it, 'called to be holy' (1 Cor. 1:2). They should hunger and thirst after righteousness (Matt. 5:6), purity of heart (Matt. 5:8) and perfection (Matt. 5:44). With such a challenging standard of repentance it is most encouraging to find that repentance is a gift given by God (Acts 5:31; 11:18; 2 Tim. 2:25). Christians must not strive to bring about the emotional aspects of repentance. They may be given by God. He will also give the grace to obey and to manifest the fruit of the Spirit.

## The undermining of obedience and holiness in the church

By way of illustrating the problems and weaknesses in the church let me introduce you to St Agatha's in the Marsh, a typical local church. The vicar is a pleasant friendly sort who is deeply conscious of his responsibilities to the whole parish, not just to the congregation. He wants the parishioners to feel welcome at church: to regard it as their church, even though most seldom, if ever, attend. And he certainly does not want to lose the faithful who attend regularly. So he does not present a challenge to discipleship. The congregation is treated to mild moral exhortations in his sermons. When mothers ring up to arrange a christening he readily agrees, even though none of the family attends church or shows any evidence of faith, except a vague belief in God. He tries to do a preparation session and finds the parents agree to anything and make the promises; but he never sees them in church after the christening. Young couples ring to arrange a wedding and in some cases the man and woman give the same address. The vicar is too discreet to ask the obvious question. The parishioners know the situation and think the church does not bother about such things nowadays. Sometimes the church members know the couple are living together but they maintain a discreet silence.

Of course there are the usual tensions: older folk prefer the old Prayer Book, the Authorized Version and the good old hymns; the young know the Alternative Service Book better, and the livelier modern hymns. Then the group of charismatics want spontaneous prayer and modern worship songs. The vicar too is attracted to the modern ways, even to some aspects of the Renewal Movement. In fact in his more discouraged moments he feels that without such developments the future and mission of the church might be in jeopardy. But to go that way might create a split in the church. Some of the traditional folk might leave. What is more the PCC would never agree to it. It would create unpleasantness and make him unpopular. So he resigns himself to wistful thinking about the new ways which could attract the younger generation of adults though he cannot help feeling a bit guilty about it.

St Agatha's is all too typical of the state of the modern church. I am not blaming church members, many of them well-meaning people who know of nothing better. The fault lies more with the clergy and the ecclesiastical system which has wandered away from the biblical norms. Many clergy give way to their fear of men and so soft-pedal obedience to God. They are deeply afraid of division in the church, of losing people, and of unpopularity. And they seek to avoid it at the price of disobeying God. They become men-pleasers. Yet they follow Christ who, as we have seen, said he came to bring division – between those who obey God and those who do not. Many of the clergy balk at challenging people to a biblical standard of discipleship. Yet Jesus said that one could not be his disciple without 'hating' our nearest and dearest and our own life. Little wonder he lost most of his congregation in John 6:60–66. However there is a subtle variation of this problem. Some clergy do expound scripture and proclaim a powerful challenge to obey it, and some church members enjoy this ministry and revel in the challenge it contains. But they do not act on it. The exposition is a sophisticated form of ecclesiastical entertainment. People do not really expect it to change their lives. In fact I have frequently found that clergy and 'mature' Christians, including some who are or have been in full-time Christian work, enjoy a good challenge. But they react negatively when they realise they are expected to 'do' the Word not just hear it. They run away from such practical obedience and even become negative to the person who has challenged them. Sadly they sometimes misrepresent him and criticise him unfairly as a method of self-defence. The blame is put on him for their own unwillingness to obey the Word.

The local church is not helped by the wider church in this matter. The pastoral Epistles (Timothy and Titus) lay down detailed lists of qualities a potential Christian leader should display before he is appointed to office. But the church does not take these standards seriously in the selection and training of clergy. Little wonder then if they do not keep to biblical standards of behaviour. One quality the New Testament demands is that a leader should be a faithful husband, effective manager of his family affairs and the father of believing children (see 1 Tim. 3:2–5; Tit. 1:6). However we see some fifty clerical marriages a year break down. I realise sometimes the clergyman will be largely innocent. But the fact remains that on many occasions he is the offending party. An editorial in *The Times*[3], seeking to be compassionate, says:

> The community at large makes the easy assumption that those who would preach morality must live morally and, therefore, in holy matrimony; and there is some spiteful pleasure to be had at the Church's expense when one of its public representatives falls from grace, whatever the reason for the end of wedlock. This must increase the pressure for the people concerned. It is even possible that it helps to destabilize some clergy marriages; a person with a public duty to be seen to be good may not make an easy partner to live with. The burden is an unfair one, surely. The church should be careful not to cultivate it unthinkingly.

How sad that the low standards in the church have encouraged such comment from the world. Similar thinking has infected the church and is directly contrary to biblical teaching. I prefer the modern worship of the ASB but am saddened at the comparatively superficial confessions in the new book. They are not just a modern version: they indicate a rather superficial view of sin, which goes hand in hand with a lack of stress on Christ bearing our sins and God's wrath upon our sins. In a recent radio programme in which I was involved an archdeacon said such a view of the cross was not Christian! In many churches there seems to be no realistic expectation of members growing in holiness.

## A practical way to encourage obedience and holiness in the church

Years ago I vowed never to teach elsewhere the principles and lessons that we are not fulfilling, albeit imperfectly in Hawkwell. So in this part I shall try to illustrate a practical way forward, based on our own experience.

We are very concerned to be a parish church, not just an eclectic congregation. We want newcomers and visitors to attend our services, especially when they live locally, and they do so. But we do not believe that anyone is won to Christ by soft-pedalling the challenge of biblical teaching. Jesus himself, as we have seen, regularly challenged the crowds to a radical discipleship. It is interesting that religious groups which challenge people tend to grow in numbers. As Jesus found, there are always those who will withdraw when challenged, but I believe we are bound to follow Jesus in proclaiming the challenge of God's Word. When someone requests a baptism we follow a policy agreed by most churches in the deanery. We offer the Thanksgiving Service as a first step, whether the couple are regular attenders or not. With non-attenders we seek to get to know them, inviting them to church, and to share the gospel with them. However we regard it as important for at least one parent to be attending church regularly and to have made a profession of faith before we proceed to the baptism. Similarly with a wedding couple. If we become

aware that they are living together, we explain that it is
necessary for them to repent before they proceed further
towards a church wedding. It is also important that they
believe in God and regard marriage as a lifelong exclusive
commitment.

More important than all this, though, is the conviction
that it is not our church or my church. It is not the church of
the traditionalists or the radicals; the old or the young; the
long-standing members or the newcomers. It is God's
church. This is not playing with words: it is a vital piece of
theological thinking. The criterion becomes: what does
God want for his church? What is he telling us to do? How
does he feel about our worship, fellowship, evangelism,
service, and so on? The primary source of discovering
God's will for the church is scripture. We shall look at other
ways of discerning God's will later.

Another challenge we have had to face is the danger of
division or losing members. Unity and peace in the body of
Christ are such high priorities that we must take great pains
to maintain them. Through prayer, careful teaching and
explanation, patient encouragement and sensitive timing,
we must seek to carry people with us. But if in the end
individuals dig their heels in and resist what God is clearly
saying to the church, then obedience becomes a priority
over unity. At this point Jesus' statement that he came to
bring division (even within the family) becomes relevant, as
does his experience of losing most of his congregation in
John 6:60–66 because they could not receive his hard
teaching. Sometimes acting in a genuinely Christ-like way
will result in division. And it may upset even longstanding
members. But that is no excuse for disobedience to Christ.
After all he was the one to make it clear that to love him
means to obey him. Jesus was the one who made himself of
no reputation. And he calls us to have our treasure in
heaven, not on earth. Reputation is one of the greatest of
man's treasures. A Christian leader will be of limited
effectiveness in the service of God until he lays down his
earthly reputation and looks for a reputation in heaven.

Sadly many ministers are short-sighted enough to give way to their fears of doing this.

In Hawkwell the biblical teaching from the pulpit or in housegroups is intended to be practical. We expect people to act on the Word of God, not just hear it. We encourage each other to obey the teaching of the Bible and, as we shall see later, we correct one another. At the same time we seek to be patient, understanding and forgiving. The congregation is united in a practical commitment to 'doing' the Word. This is not legalistic or Pharisaical: it is done in the power of the Holy Spirit. We all fail, but failure is something to be corrected, not tolerated. Repentance is important and on various occasions the whole congregation has come together to repent on some specific failing we have fallen into as a church. Always this has led on to the joy of forgiveness and a new effectiveness in God's service.

# 13

## Power and Praise

It is characteristic of the ministry of Jesus to baptise people in the Holy Spirit (Matt. 3:11; Mark 1:8; Luke 3:16; John 1:33). God said to John the Baptist: 'The man on whom you see the Spirit come down and remain is he who will baptise with the Holy Spirit' (John 1:33). Jesus does this on the basis of 'the Lamb of God, who takes away the sin of the world' (John 1:29).

Jesus told his disciples 'in a few days you will be baptised with the Holy Spirit' (Acts 1:4–5). Shortly afterwards the Spirit descended on the disciples on the day of Pentecost (Acts 2:1–4). On that day Peter preached that through repentance and baptism in the name of Christ his hearers would receive the gift of the Holy Spirit: 'The promise is for you and your children and for all who are far off' (Acts 2:38–39). In other words it is for every believer. When he began to preach to Cornelius and his friends 'the Holy Spirit fell on them just as on us at the beginning' (Acts 11:15). Since modern Christians and churches receive the same gift of the Holy Spirit we must look for the same effects of his presence and one of these effects is spiritual power.

### The local church should experience the power of the Holy Spirit

Before Pentecost the disciples lacked power. Therefore in fear they deserted Jesus after his arrest and Peter denied him (Mark 14:50, 66–72). They found it difficult to believe in the resurrection (Matt. 28:17; Mark 16:14; John 20:24–29). The main thing Jesus promised them when they received the baptism of the Spirit was *power*. He said before the ascension: 'I am going to send you what my Father has promised; but stay in the city until you have been clothed with power from on high' (Luke 24:49). 'You will receive power when the Holy Spirit comes on you, and you will be my witnesses' (Acts 1:8). Sure enough the power came when they were baptised in the Holy Spirit at Pentecost. They were so filled with power that critics accused them of being drunk (Acts 2:13,15). The Spirit given was not 'a spirit of timidity, but a spirit of power, of love and of self-discipline' (2 Tim. 1:7). The power at work for us and in us is 'incomparably great' (Eph. 1:19), 'able to do immeasurably more than all we ask or imagine' (Eph. 3:20). It is in fact the power of his resurrection (Phil. 3:10) and we are to be strong in his mighty power (Eph. 6:10).

The apostles exemplified all this. With great power, including the power of signs and miracles, they testified to Christ (Acts 4:33; Rom. 15:19; cf. 2 Cor. 6:7; 13:4). They became bold witnesses (Acts 2:14ff). Their preaching was 'with a demonstration of the Spirit's power' (1 Cor. 2:4–5; 1 Thess. 1:5) and was very effective (Acts 2:41). They offered great praise to God (Acts 2:11,47). They experienced the gifts of the Holy Spirit including speaking in tongues (Acts 2:4), prophecy, visions (Acts 2:17) and healing (Acts 3:1–10). The power of God also moulded them into a close loving community (Acts 2:44–46; 4:32).

The baptism in the Spirit is part of conversion. A person cannot receive eternal life and become a Christian without receiving the Holy Spirit: 'Anyone who does not have the Spirit of Christ does not belong to him' (Rom. 8:9; 1 Cor. 12:13); to become a Christian is to be 'born of the Spirit' (John 3:5–6). The first experience of the Holy Spirit is the baptism in the Holy Spirit and is pictured by baptism in water. But the baptism in the Holy Spirit is not just theological theory. It should be a dynamic experience, as

the testimony of the apostles shows, and it is an experience
for every believer. It is a fact of life however that often
Christians do not enter into this experience until after their
conversion, sometimes years afterwards. This is mainly
because of unbelief in the church as well as in the individual
– a lack of expectancy that we can and should experience
God's power.

## The local church should live adventurously by faith

The Christian way was never intended to be a safe, moder-
ate commonsense approach to life. Important though the
community of faith is, we are not to base our trust and
security on human beings. It is foolish to trust in one's own
abilities and understanding (Prov. 3:5; 28:26) or in other
people (Ps. 146:3; Jer. 17:5), let alone material possessions
(1 Tim. 6:17). Rather we are to find our security in God our
eternal refuge (Deut. 33:27) who 'surrounds' his people
with his protection (Ps. 125:1–2). Then we need not fear
(Heb. 13:6).

Jesus described as blessed those who are 'poor in spirit',
that is, who know their poverty without God. But he did
not expect them to limp through the Christian life, playing
it safe. Rather he expected them to step out in adventurous
faith. In fact he rebuked his disciples for being afraid in the
storm on the lake (Matt. 8:26), and Peter for giving way to
fear when he walked on the water (Matt. 14:31). He
rebuked the disciples again for being unable to deliver the
demonised epileptic boy (Matt. 17:17–20) and for not
immediately believing in the resurrection (Mark 16:14; cf.
Luke 24:11; 24:25). In John 14:12 Jesus says: 'I tell you the
truth, anyone who has faith in me will do what I have been
doing. He will do even greater things than these, because I
am going to the Father.' The context is concerning miracles
(v. 11). Jesus expects the church to be a miracle-working
organisation. Miracles were so normal in the early church
that Paul is described as doing 'extraordinary miracles' in

Acts 19:11. Jesus expected his disciples to have a faith which could move mountains (Matt. 21:21; Luke 17:6). He taught them to pray expecting an answer (Matt. 21:22; Mark 11:24).

## The local church should offer wholehearted praise and worship to God

Part of the fruit of the Holy Spirit is joy (Gal. 5:22; Acts 2:46–47) and it is therefore to be a characteristic of the church and a sign of the kingdom of God (Rom. 14:17). Jesus gives his joy to his disciples and wants their joy to be complete (John 15:11; 16:24; 17:13). Christian joy is 'an inexpressible and glorious joy' even in the context of suffering (1 Pet. 1:8; cf. Phil. 4:4; Jas. 1:2; 1 Pet. 1:6). Although this joy is ultimately 'inexpressible' the fulness of the Holy Spirit will issue in singing and making music in one's heart to the Lord (Eph. 5:18–20; Col. 3:16; 1 Cor. 14:26). Such worship will be wholehearted and self-forgetful (Ps. 9:1; 111:1). Some worship is adoration, part of loving God with all our heart. It includes ascribing to God glory and power, worth and honour, wisdom and strength, justice and truth (Rev. 1:6–7; 5:9–14; 7:10–12; 15:3–4). Adoration may also be expressed in silence – simply by being still and lifting our hearts to God (Ps. 46:10).

However worship may also be expressed in the form of exuberant praise. The Psalmist records that this can be expressed with lifting hands (Pss. 63:4; 134:2), clapping (47:1), joyful processions (118:27), dancing (149:3; 150:4) to the accompaniment of various instruments, for example harp, lyre, lutes, strings, tambourine, trumpet, pipe and cymbals (150), and so on. The Psalms give us a deep insight into the way God leads his people in worship. He calls for wholehearted self-forgetful worship, more concerned for God's desire that people worship him in spirit and truth (John 4:23–24) than for our feelings of shyness, dryness or depression, which sometimes are mistaken for legitimate personality or cultural factors.

## Undermining power and praise in the church

Back to St Agatha's! The congregation is very English and not given to displays of emotion or enthusiasm. Of course there are the few charismatics but they are considered rather unstable. To the rest of the congregation there seems to be something faintly improper about the intimacy with which they talk about God. The majority prefer the quiet formal liturgy which seems to keep God at a slight (and safe) distance. Then there is that talk about being 'born again'. It seems out of place to the congregation of St Agatha's and more appropriate to the Free churches or to the United States. After all to claim to be a born-again Christian is surely pretentious. The charismatics also claim to have experienced the baptism in the Spirit and some of them speak in tongues. This all sounds unbalanced and élitist to the rest of the congregation. All sorts of wild stories circulate and, although no one has checked if they are true, they provide good reasons for keeping away from such experiences.

It is all right for the vicar to pray for the sick in the intercessions, and privately with a sick person. But the church members have conditioned themselves not to expect too much. The prayer will probably give spiritual benefit and peace. However St Agatha's would not want healing services. They feel that claims of physical healing are probably inaccurate or unproven. Better to stick to the general intercessions and the National Health Service. In fact this is rather the attitude the congregation has to prayer in general. It seems a little presumptuous to expect too much from it. Not that it does no good: but it is difficult to define what good it does.

Christianity, for the people of St Agatha's, is essentially common sense. In the PCC there are three regularly quoted reasons for deciding against a new project. They have tried it before and it did not work. They have never done it before and it would not work. It would be too difficult and too expensive. One of these normally wins the day. So church life at St Agatha's is restrained and unexciting. Highlights tend to be from money-raising events like jumble sales. In the services the congregation appears to be an exclusive club. No page numbers are announced and that causes confusion to newcomers. They tend not to return because the services are frankly boring.

There are churches more spiritually alive than St Agatha's, but which nevertheless display some of the same weaknesses. True, people experience conversion/new birth as a result of biblical preaching but they seem singularly lacking in the dynamic power of the Spirit. There is not much evidence in individuals or in the church of the 'inexpressible and glorious joy' Peter talks about (1 Pet. 1:8). And there is little expectation of supernatural divine intervention – other than, perhaps, by way of conversion. Prayer is an obligation, but it is hard work, with few rewards expected. The church's attitude to prayer for healing is very low key and again with little expectation of obvious physical healing. The PCC is not that different from St Agatha's. In fact one could be forgiven for asking with St Paul, 'Are you so foolish? After beginning with the Spirit (conversion/new birth) are you now trying to attain your goal by human effort?' (Gal. 3:3).

## A practical way to encourage the experience of power and praise in the church

The fact is that individuals tend to experience the level of faith present within the congregation generally. If conversion/new birth is preached and generally experienced by the church members then newcomers are likely to experience it. But if that is not the case then a deliberate attempt to rectify it is called for. In Hawkwell we pray regularly for people to experience the conversion/new birth. We preach about it and encourage people to enter into it. In outline we urge them:

(i) To realise that, like the rest of us, they are sinners and fall short of God's standards.

(ii) To believe sincerely that Christ in his love died for them, experiencing hell in every sense of the word, and to ask his forgiveness.

(iii) To make a commitment to following Jesus as Lord, asking for the new birth and eternal life.

They may need further help to do all this. We provide this through private counsel or through the Faith Sharing Group – a home fellowship where the matter is discussed informally.

*The baptism in the Holy Spirit.* The baptism in the Spirit or 'fulness of the Spirit' is an experience of God's power, love and joy, resulting in a heightened spiritual awareness (particularly concerning scripture); a deep yearning to adore God; a profound sense of fellowship with others open to the Spirit and an expectancy of the supernatural intervention of God. The experience often results from specific prayer with the laying on of hands and can be instantaneous and overpowering. Many receive the gift of tongues and go on to experience other gifts. In order to encourage people to enter into the baptism of the spirit:

(i) We teach about it, using material such as the biblical study (above, pp. 158–160).

(ii) We ensure people find out more about it by reading books or mixing with people who have experienced it. In some churches this would be achieved by people attending Renewal meetings or conferences or by having a Renewal team visit the church.

(iii) We pray that this teaching and experience will encourage people:

- to expect more from God
- to yearn for an experience of God's power

- to repent of known sin (including the renunciation of anything occult)
- to ask God to release his power in them
- to seek specific prayer for the baptism in the Holy Spirit. Many people find it helpful to be prayed for by another person. This encourages an attitude of humility, faith and obedience
- to be open to receiving the gifts of the Spirit
- to praise God with enthusiasm and feeling.

Through such prayer many thousands of Christians have entered into a far greater depth of adoration and worship. Their faith is stimulated so that they expect God's supernatural intervention in gifts and miracles. A much greater sensitivity and intensity in prayer and a far deeper appreciation of God's Word also result. This depth of experience of God is sadly lacking in many Christians. Yet it is their birthright for they have received the Holy Spirit. It is not 'haves' and 'have-nots'. It is those who have entered into the depth of experience of their riches in Christ and those who have not. However we need to ask for the daily filling with the Spirit according to Ephesians 5:18, which can be translated 'go on being filled with the Spirit'.

*Adventurous faith.* Jesus clearly expects his disciples to 'live by faith'. That means to go beyond the safe, commonsense, humanistic way of thinking and acting. It means to take risks and to step out in a way which stretches our faith. Obviously it is vital that we are sure such action is biblical and God's will for us, otherwise we fall into presumption. Here is advice from our own experience over the years:

- Rely on prayer and direct giving rather than fund raising.
- Believe that money will be available for projects you are confident are in God's will.
- Begin to step out in more definite prayer with the laying on of hands for healing (perhaps in a communion service).

- Record answers to prayer and, where appropriate,
  publish them to stimulate faith (and thanksgiving).
- Be more adventurous in evangelism and wider mission,
  praying that you will be used to bring many to faith.

*Wholehearted praise and worship*. Basically this will be the
result of the work of the Holy Spirit in the lives of members.
It will no doubt begin in their private worship at home. But
various practical steps can be taken in church:

- teach about praise and adoration
- use more joyful hymns and songs
- use prayers and songs which express adoration to God
- allow brief 'spontaneous' thanksgivings or expressions
  of adoration from the congregation.

All of this can be done within the context of the liturgy. For
example, in Hawkwell we often use modern songs in place
of hymns, and either in place of, or in addition to, the
canticles. We regularly have a time of sung praise after
the absolution and versicles in morning prayer or after the
Gloria in the communion. Then we normally have some
quieter songs leading into the sermon at morning prayer or
into communion. During these times an opportunity is
given for members to lead in spontaneous thanksgiving
prayer or the spoken gifts of the Spirit.

# 14

# Prayer and Discernment

## Intercession

Jesus often withdrew to solitary places where he could pray (Luke 5:16; cf. Matt. 14:23; Luke 9:18,28). Sometimes he went out very early to pray (Mark 1:35). At other times he spent the night in prayer (Luke 6:12). Have modern Christians less need to pray than their Lord?

The early church members followed Christ's example and devoted themselves to prayer (Acts 2:42; Col. 4:2). Their prayer was earnest and sometimes accompanied by fasting (Acts 4:24; 12:5; 13:3; 14:23). The apostles delegated pastoral work in order to give attention to prayer (Acts 6:4). Paul assures the churches that he is constantly praying for them (Rom. 1:9–10; Eph. 1:16; Phil. 1:4; Col. 1:3,9–12; 2 Thess. 1:11; 2 Tim. 1:3; Philem. 4). He urges them to pray for him (Rom. 15:30–32; 2 Cor. 1:11; Col. 4:2; 1 Thess. 5:25; 2 Thess. 3:1; cf. Heb. 13:18), for all the saints (Eph. 6:18) and for those in authority (1 Tim. 2:2). He commends Epaphras who was always 'wrestling in prayer' for the Colossians (Col. 4:12). He urges the church to pray 'in the Spirit' (Eph. 6:18) who 'intercedes for us with groans that words cannot express' (Rom. 8:26).

Although he is against vain repetition (Matt. 6:7) Jesus encourages his disciples to persist in prayer (Matt. 7:7, where the tense is present continuous, 'keep on asking'; Luke 11:5–13; 18:1; cf. 1 Thess. 5:17). Of course their motives must be unselfish; his words must remain in them and they remain in him (John 15:7,16) and they must be in a

right relationship with others (Mark 11:25; cf. 1 Tim. 2:8;
Jas. 4:2–3; 1 John 3:22; 5:14–15). They must also believe
they have received what they ask for and it will be theirs
(Mark 11:24; Matt. 21:22; Jas. 1:6–7). In this context Jesus
promises: 'I will do whatever you ask in my name, so that
the Son may bring glory to the Father. You may ask me for
anything in my name, and I will do it' (John 14:13–14). He
also says: 'Again, I tell you that if two of you on earth agree
about anything you ask for, it will be done for you by my
Father in heaven' (Matt. 18:19). In the Lord's Prayer he
specifically urges them to pray for God's rule to be accepted
on earth; for God's provision for their needs, and forgiveness; for his protection in temptation and deliverance from
Satan's power (Matt. 6:9–13). He encourages them to pray
for evangelism (Matt. 9:38) and for deliverance for those
bound by Satan (Mark 9:29).

The Psalms provide a deep insight into disciplined, intensive intercession. The Psalmist often implores the Lord to
look at his problems; to see how his enemies persecute him
(Pss. 9:13; 25:19; 59:3–4,6–7; 83:1–5). He reverently expresses his complaint to God: 'Why, O Lord, do you stand
far off? Why do you hide yourself in times of trouble?'
(10:1); 'How long, O Lord? Will you forget me for ever?'
(13:1); 'Why have you rejected me?' (43:2); 'O Lord, how
long will the wicked be jubilant?' (94:3; cf. 22:1–2; 42:9–10;
44:23; 74:1; 80:4–6; 88; 142). He beseeches the Lord to
listen to him: 'Give ear to my words, O Lord, consider my
sighing' (5:1); 'Hear my cry for mercy as I call to you for
help' (28:2; cf. 17:1,6; 39:12; 54:2; 55:1–2; 64:1; 69:16,17).
The cry for mercy is an important emphasis (6; 51; 130:1–4;
143:2). The Psalmist often pleads with God to remember
his mercy, love, faithfulness and his covenant: 'Remember,
O Lord, your great mercy and love' (25:6); 'Remember the
people you purchased of old . . . remember how the enemy
has mocked you, O Lord . . . have regard for your
covenant' (74:2,18,20). Another way of putting this is to
plead God's 'Name' or his character and nature. He has a
name for holiness, goodness, love, power, justice, mercy,

faithfulness, and so on, and he cannot deny himself. We can reverently urge God to act in accordance with his revealed character and nature. The Psalmist writes: 'For the sake of your name, O Lord, forgive my iniquity, though it is great' (25:11); 'save me, O God, by your name' (54:1); 'Help us, O God our Saviour, for the glory of your name; deliver us and atone for our sins for your name's sake. Why should the nations say, "Where is their God?"' (79:9–10). The Psalms often contain affirmations of faith in God – an important part of intercession. God is a shield (3:3–4), he takes no pleasure in evil (5:3–6,12); he notices the afflicted (10:14,17). His love is unfailing (13:5); he is the eternal sovereign who will fulfil his purpose (90:1–6; 102:12–13, 25–28; 138:6–8).

Another aspect of prayer in the Psalms is the call for vindication – crying out for God to vindicate his holiness, sovereignty and power. Also we can ask God to vindicate his people. 'May my vindication come from you' (17:2; cf. 26:1; 31:17; 35:22–25;43:1). 'Rise up, O God, and defend your cause: remember how fools mock you all day long' (74:22). In New Testament terms any calling for judgment which the Psalms contain can be applied to the destruction of demonic forces behind the 'flesh and blood' enemies (Eph. 6:12) and to the frustration of evil words, deeds, and intentions.

In Daniel 9 the prophet takes up many of these themes in praying for the nation. He confesses the sin, rebellion and shame of the nation. As a consequence they have experienced the curses and judgments about which God's Word has warned them. But he reminds the Lord that he is merciful and forgiving (Dan. 9:9) and he is their redeemer (9:15). He asks God to remove his wrath for his name's sake and because the city and people bear his name (9:17–19).

Clearly the biblical tradition of prayer is one which includes disciplined intensive, persistent intercession. If we are to obey God today we are not at liberty to break with this tradition.

## Hearing God

When Peter confessed Christ, Jesus replied: 'Blessed are you, Simon son of Jonah, for this was not revealed to you by man, but by my Father in heaven. And I tell you that you are Peter ('Petros'), and on this rock ('petra') I will build my church, and the gates of Hades will not overcome it' (Matt. 16:17–18). The rock on which Jesus will build his church is the revealed truth about Christ as received and confessed by Peter. Peter had 'heard' God and this is foundational to the church. Also as Jesus is the architect of the church it follows that we need to consult him and 'hear' him for the instructions as to how he wishes his church to be built. Furthermore the church is in a situation of spiritual warfare, up against the 'gates of Hades' which makes hearing his instructions all the more urgent.

Paul warns church leaders to be careful how they build the church on the foundation of Christ for they will be judged on how they have built (1 Cor. 3:9–17). He says the church is built on the foundation of the apostles and prophets – ministries to which hearing God is fundamental (Eph. 2:19–20). In the church at Antioch there were prophets and teachers and as they were worshipping the Lord and fasting, the Holy Spirit spoke to them and instructed them to send Paul and Barnabas on a missionary journey (Acts 13:1–3). Similarly after the Council of Jerusalem the leaders were able to say 'it seemed good to the Holy Spirit and to us not to burden you'. The early church knew what it was to hear the Lord.

Jesus describes his sheep as knowing his voice (John 10:4–5). Through the Holy Spirit believers have an inner ability to recognise God's revelation. It is part of the Holy Spirit's work as a Spirit of truth who guides us into all truth (John 16:13). We have the mind of Christ (1 Cor. 2:16), a renewed mind which is able to test and approve what God's will is, his good, pleasing and perfect will (Rom. 12:2). The Holy Spirit also gives the gifts of wisdom, knowledge, faith, prophecy and discernment (see pp. 43, 274) which enable us to discern God's will. God will sometimes communicate with us through an inner conviction or dominant thought. On the road to Emmaus the two disciples said their hearts had been 'burning' within them when Jesus talked to them (Luke 24:32). Paul speaks about the Holy Spirit testifying with our spirits that we are children of God (Rom. 8:15–16). John states in 1 John 2:20,26–27:

> You have an anointing from the Holy One, and all of you know the truth . . . I am writing these things to you about those who are trying to lead you astray. As for you, the anointing you received from him remains in you, and you do not need anyone to teach you. But as his anointing teaches you about all things and as that anointing is real, not counterfeit – just as it has taught you, remain in him.

These passages clearly teach that God can and does communicate with us through an inner conviction. In addition God can communicate his 'now' word through the gift of prophecy to an individual, a church or even a nation. It is worth mentioning that some revelations may come in pictorial form: a mental picture, waking dream or vision. Such things characterise the last days as from Pentecost (Acts 2:17). These revelations must be checked by the church. However it is even more crucial that all revelations and gifts are checked by the teaching of scripture within the context of the community of faith. Scripture is the primary and normative way in which we hear God. Every claim to hear God in other ways must be judged by it. Individual Christians need the protection and teaching ministry of the body of Christ. A person who ignores or neglects this is very foolish.

## The local church should discern and enable every member's gifts

Paul writes that Christ gave to the church

> Apostles, prophets, evangelists, pastors and teachers to
> prepare God's people for works of service so that the
> body of Christ may be built up . . . [and] we will in all
> things grow up into him who is the Head, that is, Christ.
> From him the whole body, joined and held together by
> every supporting ligament, grows and builds itself up in
> love, as each part does its work. (Eph. 4:11–12, 15–16)

So the Lord's intention is that a team of variously gifted
leaders will use their gifts to discern and mobilise the gifts of
the church members, so that each part of the body of Christ
is functioning in ministry.

The New Testament is not very systematic about its lists
of gifts and ministries nor does it give us formal definitions
of them all. So we must not be dogmatic on details.
However the biblical material and modern experience
enable us to give some guidelines in this subject. The
leading ministries include:

*Apostles.* In addition to the Twelve and Paul, Barnabas is
called an apostle (Acts 14:14). It seems also that James, the
Lord's brother (1 Cor. 15:7; Gal. 1:19), Andronicus and
Junias (Rom. 16:7), Silas or Silvanus and Timothy (1
Thess. 1:1; cf. 2:6) were called apostles. Although the
apostleship of the Twelve and Paul was unique, other
pioneer missionaries were also styled apostles. This was
also the case for a time after the New Testament period. It
is clear from Ephesians 4:11 (cf. 1 Cor. 12:28) that the
apostolic ministry was intended to function throughout the
church's existence. (For a detailed defence of this assertion
and an extensive account of a modern apostolic ministry see
my Latimer study *The Challenge of the Housechurches*
1988.)[1] Apostles will be people with insight to be 'spiritual

architects' ensuring proper building, rebuilding or alter-
ation of the structures of the church, that is, an organised
local or wider grouping of the people of God. They will
have the authority, recognised by churches to which they
minister, to discern those with leadership potential; will
draw out this potential and care for the leaders concerned.
They will advise on overall policy and on problems of
discipline. They will encourage the local church to be
outward looking: to evangelise unbelievers and to share
unity with the wider church.

*Prophets.* Prophecy is a characteristic of the outpouring of
the Spirit (Acts 2:17–18). The prophets were a distinct
group from teachers (Acts 13:1; 1 Cor. 12:28–29; Eph.
4:11). They were found in Jerusalem, Antioch (Acts 11:27;
13:1), Caesarea (Acts 21:9), Rome (Rom. 12:6), Corinth,
Ephesus (Eph. 4:11) and Thessalonica (1 Thess. 5:19–20).
One main distinction from teachers is that prophets spoke
by immediate inspiration (1 Cor. 14:29–33). On occasions
they foretold the future (Acts 11:27–28; 21:10–11). It
seems a reasonable inference that they discerned and indicated candidates for office in the church (Acts 13:2; 20:28; 1
Tim. 1:18; 4:14). They also spoke words of encouragement
to the church (Acts 15:32; 1 Cor. 14:3–5,31) but the ministry may also have a powerful impact on unbelievers, revealing their sin, convicting them of it and of God's judgment
(1 Cor. 14:24–25).

However the words of prophets must be tested, particularly by other prophets (1 Cor. 14:29; 1 John 4:1). Their
words must be consistent with scripture (1 Cor. 14:37–38).
(For a fuller treatment of the ministry of the prophet see my
*Challenge of the Housechurches* mentioned above.) The
prophet has a regular ministry of conveying a specific vision
of God's will for the present and plans for the future, so that
God's people are challenged, rebuked, encouraged or
comforted.

*Evangelists.* This is a regular ministry of pointing people to a saving knowledge of Christ so that large numbers come to personal faith in him. Philip is called 'the evangelist' (Acts 21:8; cf. 8:5–7, 12–13, 34–35,40) and Timothy is called to do the work of an evangelist (2 Tim. 4:5). It may be a one-to-one or a public ministry (or both).

*Pastors.* This is a regular ministry of caring for, guiding and protecting God's people so that they are encouraged to maturity (John 21:15–17; Acts 20:28; 1 Pet. 5:1–3).

*Teachers.* This is a regular ministry of explaining biblical truth simply and accurately and ensuring the hearers understand and obey (Matt. 28:20; Tit. 1:9–11; 2 Tim. 2:2).

Leadership in the church is always corporate. Paul appointed elders in every church, and there is always more than one in each church (Acts 14:23; 20:17; Tit. 1:5). There may be a 'presiding elder' but he does not work in isolation from the others. An eldership may have one or more of the five leading ministries. They should see to it that all five are ministering into the church, which may mean calling on the ministry of someone outside the local church, particularly for the apostolic ministry.

The New Testament teaches that every church member has a gift or manifestation of the Spirit which is given for the common good (1 Cor. 12:7,11). An individual may have a different gift on different occasions. So when the church comes together there should be an opportunity for every member to speak (1 Cor. 14:26). We have already suggested definitions of some of these gifts (p. 43). There are further definitions in Appendix 3. Sometimes a member may exercise a gift on a regular basis and this becomes that member's ministry, although it may not necessarily be a leading ministry.

All these gifts need to be recognised, confirmed and mobilised by the church, especially through its leadership. This will require the leader(s) delegating, as Jesus delegated to the Twelve and the seventy-two (Luke 9:1; 10:1) and as the apostles delegated the care of widows so that they themselves could concentrate on the Word of God and prayer (Acts 6:1–6). It is instructive to note that when Jethro tells Moses similarly to delegate, he says that otherwise 'you and the people who come to you will only wear yourselves out' (Exod. 18:18; cf. Num. 11:13–17). Without delegation the church cannot mobilise its every member ministry. Also the leader(s) will be worn out and the church to that degree not properly cared for.

## The undermining of prayer and discernment in the church

The vicar of St Agatha's does not really pray much, apart from in church or when asked by a parishioner. The pressures and discouragements of ministerial life have undermined his commitment to prayer. Partly because of this the church does not really pray much either, except during the intercession in the services. It would be interesting to speculate as to whether, much of the time, the church really expects these intercessions to be answered. Many of the prayers are so general. When some urgent or tragic need arises the prayers have more feeling, but again it would be interesting to know what good they are expected to do. Of course the little group of charismatics pray together, but that is nothing to do with the church. Most of the congregation would not dream of being involved with them. Truth to tell, these folk are floundering in their prayers. When they meet they spend most of their time praying for each other: for personal needs and problems. So they hardly have time to pray for the church, let alone the world. When they do pray for issues outside their group their prayers flit from topic to topic. So there is no discipline, intensity or persistence in their prayers.

St Agatha's has never really thought much about gifts. True, Mrs Smith has a gift for embroidery and Mr Phillips

for playing the organ. But the vicar is the vicar. He is
expected to preach, lead services, visit, bring new people
into church, counsel the needy, do much of the administration, and so on. Did not the bishop say so at the institution?
What is more, he is paid to do it. Yes, the church members
can lend him a helping hand and it would be great if he had a
lay reader or even a curate, but there is not much hope of
that. The charismatics talk about gifts: speaking in tongues,
prophecy, healing. But this all sounds alien and even
dangerous to the people of St Agatha's. Far better to leave
the ministry to the professional man. He is trained for it. He
is not expected to specialise or to be an expert in one
particular side of the ministry. He is there to be a good
all-rounder: a sort of general practitioner.

Again – to be fair to St Agatha's – some churches which
would claim to be more biblical do not really major on
prayer. At best a few folk meet for a mid-week prayer
meeting; or a short time of prayer is included at the end of a
Bible study or housegroup. To be honest it is rather boring:
a religious duty so unattractive must be good for the soul!
The prayer is like a Cook's tour of the world: one minute
praying for the missionaries in Peru, the next for the parish,
the next for the government. It is a shopping list of requests
with no real sense of direction, no great depth of prayer or
perseverance in believing intercession. Little wonder most
people vote with their feet.

As for 'hearing' God, that sounds very mysterious to such
congregations. O yes, there are those irritating people who
are always saying 'The Lord told me to do this or that'.
Many of these churches understand God speaking through
the teaching of scripture or through conscience. But the
rest of the time they make decisions according to commonsense and democratic discussion. There is no waiting before
God in silence; no real expectation of his speaking. We
have said they understand God speaking through the
teaching of scripture. But it is surprising how certain areas
of biblical teaching are neglected. Instead the church uncritically follows hallowed tradition – even evangelical

tradition. For example there are still many 'biblical' churches dominated by the one-man ministry, which inhibits the discernment and encouragement of every member's ministry. The ministers of such churches often have a major blockage against delegation. They must do everything themselves. They could not possibly delegate: other people could not do it as well as they can – or so they think. One ministry the church is very reluctant to delegate is the celebration of communion. There is no biblical justification for limiting this ministry to some priestly order. It is encouraging that one diocesan bishop has said, 'I see no reason why any group of Christians should not invite one of their number to preside.' He also pointed out that the ministry of absolution and blessing should not be limited to a priestly order:

> God's forgiveness is always offered to sinners by his holy love. Why should not this truth be declared by any Christian to any sinner? The authority lies not in the person but in the truth. Again our forebears all took it for granted that any Christian could give a 'blessing'.[2]

Here again the wider church does not help the local church with an example of hearing God and disciplined intercession. The General Synod is a case in point. There are brief formal intercessions at the beginning of each day, followed by hours and hours of prayerless debate. Scripture is quoted very infrequently (even in much of the paperwork given to members). Emotional considerations often sway decisions: a powerful speech (even if not biblical) or an appeal to human sympathy can influence many people in their voting; emotive words like 'sectarian', 'fundamentalist' and 'witch-hunt' can effectively influence the Synod against making decisions which will bring the church more into harmony with biblical teaching. The Archbishop of Canterbury is held in affection, even something approaching awe, by Synod members. When he makes a speech they hang on his words and applaud enthusiastically. He has a powerful influence on the Synod even when, as is frequently the case, he is arguing for some liberalisation which is difficult, if not impossible, to substantiate from scripture. It is hard to go against the crowd and to act against the mood of the Synod. Human expertise and humanistic thinking are another major influence. Then there are political manoeuvres and procedural devices which can wreck an attempt to reach a sound decision. If only the Synod would learn to hear God and pray in depth we would save weeks of debate and reach helpful decisions. As it is, the procedures, and not infrequently the decisions, are remote from the teaching and example of the New Testament. Often we are not hearing God but we are certainly hearing man *ad nauseam*.

Another area in which the wider church does not help the local church is in discerning and using people's gifts. Again too humanistic an approach is taken to appointments in the church. Often the tempting carrot of a high salary is held out to get the 'right' person; for example a diocesan official may be paid more than the bishop himself. In 1987 the Church of England engaged an ICI personnel and management services director to be Appointments Secretary to the archbishops. His duties include being secretary of the Crown Appointments Commission, which recommends prospective bishops and advises on many other senior appointments. He had answered the advertisement in the journal of the Institute of Personnel Management. On his appointment he said: 'ICI is a very big system and so is the Church. The business of finding talent doesn't differ all that much between one big organisation and another.'[3] I disagree. Appointments and finding talent in the church should be on a different footing from industry. Not only are there aspects of the spirituality, theological persuasion and spiritual gifts of the candidates; there is also the need prayerfully to hear God over such crucial appointments. And this cannot be achieved by a quick prayer and a long discussion. Many of the church's councils, committees and synods function like the General Synod. No wonder they often get it wrong. The wonder is that they ever get it right. That can only be due to the mercy and overruling of God.

When a man is trained for leadership in the church, he is still trained to be a jack of all trades. Only weak attempts are so far being made to train him to draw out the gifts of the congregation and to delegate radically to those gifted to do what is needed. The parochial ministry is still in the pastor-teacher mould (with perhaps evangelistic connections). Yet not all clergy are pastors or teachers. Some have a prophetic ministry; others an apostolic ministry; others are evangelists. Little wonder the church is not making a real impact on the nation if its leaders are often square pegs in round holes, and are not trained or encouraged to change that situation. Charismatic Renewal is not just about deep spiritual experiences and new ways of worship. To think charismatically, that is, to structure the church with leaders and members majoring on using their particular gifts to the full, is vital if we are to win the nation back to Christ.

## A practical way to encourage discernment and prayer in the church

During my time in Hawkwell it was only after the first three years that we began to pray seriously. We started by designating Thursday as a parish day of prayer. Groups met at 6.30 a.m., 9 a.m., 1 p.m. and 7 p.m. In those days we knew no better than simply to pray through the prayer topics in our weekly prayer news sheet. Then eventually a few women became involved in the Lydia Prayer Fellowship and formed a Lydia Prayer Group. They began to learn to hear God and to intercede in a disciplined way. The time came when this group split up so that most of the members could lead new groups in the same sort of prayer. By 1988 there were twenty-four weekly prayer cells which involved about 140 adults. Each cell has five to seven members. Some meet early morning or early evening; others mid-morning. They have a limited scope, majoring

on a few subjects consistently week by week. The church
also calls evenings of prayer (often with fasting) when there
is a special need or challenge. Intercession is included in the
housegroup programme and in the evening services. It is
true to say that all we do is conceived, born and bred in
prayer. We would not have it otherwise.

We stress preparation for prayer. This includes worship
and praise (focusing our attention on the Lord); confession
of sin and asking the Holy Spirit to fill us. Then it is
important to submit our own feelings, thoughts and ideas to
God. After all they may not tally with the prayer topics he
wants us to pray about. For example, we called one special
evening of prayer because of an exciting possibility which
had suddenly occurred concerning a new church building.
It involved discussions with a secular business with a view to
sharing part of a new building complex. They seemed
interested in the project. They had told us that their
acquisition of the land was virtually completed. So we came
together to pray the night before their board meeting. As is
our custom, we submitted our ideas and feelings to God
then waited in silence before him. What happened was
totally unexpected. First one person then another said, 'It's
strange, but I just don't think God wants us to pray about
this project.' Yet that was the sole purpose of the evening.
Eventually it became clear that instead God wanted us to
pray for a breakthrough in the number of people coming to
faith in that area of the parish. We did this the whole
evening. Within a week we heard that the secular business
had unexpectedly pulled out of the building project. Had
we spent the evening praying about it we would have been
wasting our time. The Lord knew and managed to communicate it to us. The positive result was that we have since
seen a good number of people in that area of the parish
come to faith.

When we are sure what we should be praying about the
leader encourages the group to be disciplined. This involves keeping to the point and praying for that aspect until
it seems there has been enough persistent prayer and it is

right to move on. The answers have been remarkable, at times spectacular.

God communicates through:

(a) the teaching of scripture. He may bring a particular passage forcibly to mind
(b) a gift of prophecy, a word of wisdom or knowledge, and so on (see p. 43). This may take the form of a mental picture or parable, or it may be that words are given
(c) a dominant, recurring conviction (of something to be done or something to be avoided).

All of these must be checked by the fellowship and its leaders, especially to see that they are biblical.

The way that most of our important decisions are made in the parish is as follows:

 (i) Some individual or group takes the initiative to suggest what God may be saying to the church or simply to draw attention to a need or problem.
 (ii) The overall leaders of the parish prayerfully consider the matter and call together the leaders' fellowship (PCC members, housegroup leaders, and so on), having informed them of the matter in hand so that they can pray and think about it before the meeting.
 (iii) The leaders' fellowship (over fifty people) meets for further prayer and hearing God, and comes to a united mind about what God is saying.
 (iv) The PCC later comes together to formalise the decision and work out any details and implications.

How can a church begin to learn to pray together? Here are some suggestions:

(a) The minister prays for a spirit of intercession for the church.
(b) He gathers a few people who are concerned to pray.

(c)  Prayer should not be attached to another meeting, but should be a separate time.

(d)  Full preparation is important.

(e)  Disciplined, intensive, persistent intercession (for needs outside of those of the members of the prayer group) is the aim.

(f)  The members should learn to hear the Lord.

(g)  Answers to prayer and what is heard from the Lord should be conveyed to the whole church, where appropriate.

(h)  It is encouraging to involve people in larger intercession events (for example the Lydia Prayer Fellowship, Intercessors for Britain, Evangelical Alliance, and so on.)

(i)  Eventually the small group can be split up so that the members can lead other groups as interest grows in the church.

Discerning gifts and ministries: This cannot be isolated from the spirituality of church members. The deeper their experience of the Holy Spirit, the deeper will be their experience of the gifts of the Spirit. The procedure we have followed to discern gifts is simple but effective:

(a)  We provide teaching about the gifts.

(b)  We ask the individual to have a quiet half day, providing them with guidelines on a spiritual check up; on giving back to God any jobs they are already doing or any preconceived ideas they have; and on discerning their gifts.

(c)  At the same time we ask the individual's housegroup to pray (individually) about that member's gifts.

(d)  The group comes together and shares first what it sees the member's gifts are. Then the individual concerned shares what he or she has discerned.

(e)  The results are conveyed to the elders who try to ensure that the individual's gifts are encouraged and used.

## Commitment to One Another

On the night he was betrayed Jesus prayed for his disciples. The main burden of his petition was that they may be united. Four times he urges the Father: 'that they may be one as we are one' (John 17:11,21,22); 'that they may be brought to complete unity'. This unity is not to be some exclusive, cosy, inward-looking sect. Far from it. Jesus also says: 'My prayer is not that you take them out of the world but that you protect them from the evil one . . . As you sent me into the world, I have sent them into the world' (John 17:15,18). In fact Jesus' prayer for their unity in him is 'so that the world may believe that you have sent me' and 'to let the world know that you sent me' (John 17:21,23). However 'the world has hated them, for they are not of the world any more than I am of the world' (John 17:14; cf. v. 16).

So the main burden of Jesus' prayer in the traumatic and urgent situation on the night he was betrayed was that the disciples should be perfectly united, as united as the Father and Son are in the Trinity. Unity was not an optional extra or some superficial friendliness. To Jesus it was a vital priority; a necessity so that the world would believe. And his concept of unity was so deep that it could only be compared with the unity in the Trinity. Earlier he had commanded the disciples to love one another as he had loved them. This was to be a mark of their discipleship: a proof that they were disciples of Christ (John 13:34,35; 15:12,17). His love for them was such that he laid down his life for them (John 15:13). This then is to be the standard of love between Christians.

Paul teaches that in the body of Christ 'each member belongs to all the others' (Rom. 12:5). He prays that God will give the Romans a spirit of unity 'so that with one heart and mouth you may glorify the God and Father of our Lord Jesus Christ' (Rom. 15:5–6). He writes to the Corinthians: 'I appeal to you, brothers, in the name of our Lord Jesus Christ, that all of you agree with one another so that there may be no divisions among you and that you may be perfectly united in mind and thought' (1 Cor. 1:10). He urges the Philippians to 'stand firm in one spirit, contending as one man for the faith of the gospel' (Phil. 1:27) and to be 'one in spirit and purpose' (Phil. 2:2). Paul's standard for the church is therefore that the members belong to one another; they are one in their thoughts, convictions and words; they are united for spiritual warfare. The early church manifested such characteristics: they were 'one in heart and mind' (Acts 4:32). We should aim at this level of unity first in the local church, then we are more likely to achieve it in the wider church.

The New Testament teaches other characteristics of commitment in the local church.

## Submitting to one another

Submission is part of love, so if we love someone we submit to them. As Paul puts it: 'Submit to one another out of reverence for Christ' (Eph. 5:21); 'honour one another above yourselves' (Rom. 12:10); 'do nothing out of selfish ambition or vain conceit but in humility consider others better than yourselves. Each of you should look not only to your own interests but also to the interests of others' (Phil. 2:3–4). It is important to stress that Paul is not encouraging Christians to have an inferiority complex. He is not saying 'regard yourself as inferior'. Rather he is saying 'yes, you are all equal, but decide to put other people first. Renounce your rights and emphasise your responsibilities'. As he puts it in 1 Corinthians 10:24: 'Nobody should seek his own good but the good of others.'

Peter urges Christians to clothe themselves with humility towards one another (1 Pet. 5:5–6). Paul teaches that every member of the body of Christ is important and no one should be despised. Rather all the members 'should have equal concern for each other' (1 Cor. 12:21–25). They should give way to one another in exercising their gifts (1 Cor. 14:26–29). Paul stresses the need for patience, kindness, gentleness, compassion and forgiveness in Christian relationships (1 Cor. 13:4–7; Eph. 4:2–3,31–32; Col. 3:12–15). Submission is therefore to be a way of life for Christians: it is part of their duty to love. This raises the controversial issue of submission to those over us. Referring to the secular Roman authorities, Paul says that the authorities that exist have been established by God, so to rebel against them is to rebel against God (Rom. 13:1–2). However this is no blind submission. Paul defines the authorities as doing good and punishing the wrongdoer (Rom. 13:5). Peter says a similar thing (1 Pet. 3:13–14) and interestingly, unlike Romans 13, this passage was written in a context where Rome was persecuting the church. Titus 3:1 (again in the context of persecution) urges believers to be subject to rulers and 'to be ready to do whatever is good'. The clear implication of these verses is that we are to submit to rulers only in so far as they do good and punish evil. However if the authority demands that we do evil we must disobey. The apostles refused to obey the authorities who demanded that they stopped evangelising (Acts 4:19; 5:29).

What does the New Testament teach about our attitude to those over us in the church? It is interesting that the main relevant teaching is that leaders must be servants. The one who humbles himself is the greatest (Matt. 18:4; 23:5–11; Mark 9:35; Luke 9:48; 22:24–27). The Christian leader will not lord it over people but will be a slave (Matt. 20:25–28; Mark 10:42–45; 1 Pet. 5:2–3). He will not yearn for the limelight, walking round in flowing robes, being greeted in the marketplace and having the most important seat in the place of worship or at banquets (Mark 12:38–39). Rather he will take the lowest place (Luke 14:7–11) and 'wash the feet' of the saints (John 13:1–17).

This is not to say that the Christian leader has no authority and deserves no special respect. As we shall see later, he has a duty to correct people and to discipline the persistently impenitent. Paul writes to the Thessalonians: 'Now we ask you, brothers, to respect those who work hard among you, who are over you in the Lord and who admonish you. Hold them in the highest regard in love because of their work' (1 Thess. 5:12–13). Timothy is told: 'Don't let anyone look down on you because you are young' (1 Tim. 4:12). Similarly Titus is told: 'Encourage and rebuke with all authority. Do not let anyone despise you' (Tit. 2:15). The writer to the Hebrews urges his readers to 'Obey your leaders and submit to their authority. They keep watch over you as men who must give an account. Obey them so that their work will be a joy, not a burden, for that would be of no advantage to you' (Heb. 13:17). 'The elders who direct the affairs of the church well are worthy of double honour, especially those whose work is preaching and teaching' (1 Tim. 5:17).

## Guidelines to authority and submission

Because of the controversy over authority and submission it is important to draw out what the New Testament teaching means in practice. Here are some guidelines:

- We should honour church leaders as instituted by God, even though they are of course imperfect. It is not right to pick and choose which of the leaders in the local church we will honour. Our responsibility is to honour all of them. If we are not convinced that they have been instituted by God and cannot become convinced, then we must question whether we are in the right church.
- Leaders only have authority over matters of clear biblical teaching or issues which benefit or harm the church. They can only advise and urge in other areas.

They must not be domineering or authoritarian but act lovingly in the Spirit. It is important that leaders consult the church and weigh disagreements and criticisms carefully.

- In areas of life where Christian leaders have no formal authority it is wise and right to give due respect to their spirituality, integrity, experience, biblical and theological knowledge, and discernment. This does not mean their judgment is infallible or that we are bound to accept it. It is wise but not mandatory to seek prayer and advice over major personal decisions.

- It is quite possible to agree to disagree with leaders over secondary issues. But if the disagreement is very important, it may be necessary to consider moving to another church.

- The exercise of authority or reactions to authority must not be such as to keep Christians dependent upon their leaders. Rather they must be enabled to mature and to hear God for themselves without becoming isolated. There is however a right interdependence within the body of Christ.

- Submission does not mean we should not express disagreement and fair criticism. If, given full information, it is clear that leaders are involved in unbiblical teaching or behaviour then those they lead have a duty to take appropriate action. This should not be over secondary issues which Christians who genuinely accept the full authority of scripture interpret differently.

- Submission is an attitude of heart based on relationships of love and trust. It is wrong to be suspicious and judgmental or legalistic. It is sinful to engage in negative gossip or destructive criticism. It is wrong not to share questions and constructive criticism with leaders. Rebellion is not an attitude Christians should entertain. It is likened to divination in 1 Samuel 15:23. To avoid a proper submission to leaders by claiming that 'no one is infallible' or 'I am submitted only to God' is thinly veiled rebellion.

## Being loyal to and trusting each other

Gossip and slander are strongly condemned in scripture. The temptation to gossip is very powerful: 'The words of a gossip are like choice morsels' (Prov. 18:8; 26:22). But gossip and slander are signs of human depravity, listed alongside God-haters, murderers and practising homosexuals (Rom. 1:29–30; cf. 2 Cor. 12:20). John tells us of Diotrephes who loves to be first in the church and is gossiping maliciously about him (3 John 9–10). Gossips betray confidences, separate close friends and maintain quarrels (Prov. 11:13, cf. 20:19; 16:28, cf. 17:9; 26:20). Slander is not only a sign of human depravity but of foolishness (Prov. 10:18). In 1 Corinthians 6:9–10 slanderers are listed with idolaters, adulterers, male prostitutes, homosexual offenders, thieves, drunkards and swindlers as those who will not inherit the kingdom of God. In fact slander will be one characteristic of the 'terrible times in the last days' (2 Tim. 3:1–3). So God's people are to get rid of slander (Eph. 4:31; Tit. 2:3; 3:2; Jas. 4:11). They should not associate or eat with anyone who calls himself a brother but is a slanderer (1 Cor. 5:9–13). There again the slanderer is listed with the sexually immoral, greedy, idolater, drunkard and swindler.

A suspicious, judgmental attitude is often associated with gossip and slander. Jesus tells us not to judge or we too will be judged (Matt. 7:1–2). Paul adds that we are not to judge or look down on a brother because we shall all stand before God's judgment seat (Rom. 14:4,10,13; 1 Cor. 4:5). However the New Testament also teaches that we are to judge righteously concerning those for whom we are responsible. So Christians are clearly warned not to be suspicious or judgmental in their relationships and to avoid gossip and slander, which are signs of human depravity in those who will not inherit the kingdom of God. Put positively, this means Christians are to be loyal to each other and to trust each other.

## Encouraging and correcting one another

The New Testament emphasises encouragement. There is a gift of encouraging (Rom. 12:8) and leaders are called to encourage their congregation. But all church members have this responsibility. Paul urges the Thessalonians to encourage one another with the sure hope of eternity with Christ (1 Thess. 4:18; 5:11). They are also patiently to encourage the timid while warning the idle and helping the weak (1 Thess. 5:14). The writer to the Hebrews urges his readers to encourage one another daily so that no one will be hardened by sin's deceitfulness and turn away from God with a sinful, unbelieving heart (Heb. 3:12–13). He appeals to them to continue meeting together to encourage and spur one another on to love and good deeds (Heb. 10:24–25). Paul affirms the importance of mutual encouragement between leaders and members (Rom. 1:12). He says 'I long to see you . . . that you and I may be mutually encouraged by each other's faith'. The gift of prophecy, which is widespread in the church, is given 'for strengthening, encouragement and comfort' (1 Cor. 14:3). Paul says 'You can all prophesy in turn so that everyone may be instructed and encouraged' (1 Cor. 14:31).

This mutual encouragement by the whole church is matched by the ministry of its leaders. The church at Antioch was encouraged not only by the letter from the Council of Jerusalem, but by the ministry of the prophets Judas and Silas (Acts 15:30–32). Barnabas encouraged the church at Antioch to 'remain true to the Lord with all their hearts' (Acts 11:23). Paul and Silas met the Philippians 'and encouraged them' (Acts 16:40). Paul travelled throughout Macedonia 'speaking many words of encouragement to the people' (Acts 20:1–2). He longs for the Colossians and Laodiceans and all who have not met him personally to 'be encouraged in heart' (Col. 2:1–2). He encouraged the Thessalonians like a father (1 Thess. 2:12). Timothy is sent to them to encourage them (1 Thess. 3:2), and Tychicus is sent to the Ephesians for the same purpose (Eph. 6:22).

One qualification for an elder is the ability to encourage others by sound doctrine (Tit. 1:9).

So in a church functioning on biblical principles in the power of the Spirit there will be an extensive ministry of mutual encouragement – by the whole church, members and leaders. Part of this encouragement however will be the ministry of correction, otherwise the encouragement will be superficial. We have seen that suspicious, judgmental attitudes are sinful. So are quarrelsome, resentful attitudes (2 Tim. 2:24). We are nevertheless to correct one another. It does not mean that we make an issue out of every tiny imperfection. No, we are to 'bear with each other' (Col. 3:13); not being hard, critical and irritable but kind and merciful – ready to forgive. We should approach an offending brother privately and show him his fault just between the two of us (Matt. 18:15). Jesus says we have a duty to rebuke him (Luke 17:3) but we should seek to restore him gently (Gal. 6:1; cf. Jas. 5:19–20). Jesus made it plain that we are to forgive the penitent readily – up to seventy-seven times (Matt. 18:21–22; cf. Luke 17:3–4). If we do not forgive then we cannot receive forgiveness from God (Matt. 6:14–15; 18:23–35; Mark 11:25). We discuss later the next stage of correction if someone refuses to repent.

## Sharing needs and possessions

In the body of Christ 'if one part suffers, every part suffers with it' (1 Cor. 12:26). Paul appeals to the Galatians to 'carry each other's burdens' and to 'do good to all people especially to those who belong to the family of believers' (Gal. 6:2,7–10). In Matthew 25:35–40 Jesus describes judgment day as a time when assessment is made on the basis of provision for the hungry and thirsty, hospitality to the stranger, clothing the naked and visiting the prisoner. In the context of the rest of the New Testament we can see this as the outworking of saving faith – but very necessary for 'faith without works is dead' (Jas. 2:17,20). Jesus puts this duty to care for the needy on a high level by saying that what we do to the needy, we do to him (Matt. 25:40,45). Jesus challenges his disciples to invite the poor, crippled, lame and blind to a meal – those who cannot invite them back. James defines pure faultless religion as looking after orphans and widows in their distress and keeping oneself from being polluted by the world (Jas. 1:27). We are also to remember those in prison as if we were fellow-prisoners, and those who are ill-treated as if we ourselves were suffering (Heb. 13:3). Part of our responsibility for other Christians is always to pray for them (Eph. 6:18). We are also to show hospitality (Rom. 12:13) including to strangers (Heb. 13:2). An overseer in the church must practise hospitality (1 Tim. 3:2), as must a candidate for the order of widows (1 Tim. 5:10).

James strongly condemns rich people who oppress the poor: they stand in line for God's judgment for their injustice (Jas. 5:1–6). He also forbids the church to show favouritism to the rich. This is to insult the poor whom God has chosen to be rich in faith and to inherit the kingdom. It is after all the rich who were exploiting the church (Jas. 2:1–13). Similarly Paul rebukes the Corinthians for selfishness at the Lord's supper when one person remains hungry and another gets drunk. They 'despise the church of God and humiliate those who have nothing' (1 Cor. 11:17–22). A Christian is to share with others (Heb. 13:16). The early church had everything in common (Acts 2:44); 'No-one claimed that any of his possessions was his own, but they shared everything they had' (Acts 4:32). Jesus teaches that believers should sell their possessions and give to the poor (Luke 12:33–34; cf. Matt. 5:42), which the early church did (Acts 2:44–45). This early practice does not appear to have been perpetuated. Even while it continued it did not necessarily involve a person selling all his possessions. Those who owned lands or houses sold them; Joseph sold a field; Ananias sold a piece of property (Acts 4:34–5:1) but was judged for lying about the profit. However when famine hit Judea hard the disciples in Antioch gave according to their ability for famine relief and Paul took the gifts to Jerusalem (Acts 11:30; 24:17). He took gifts given by the Gentiles for the Jewish church too (Rom. 15:25–28).

The New Testament teaches that giving should be un-ostentatious (Matt. 6:1–4); very generous (Luke 6:38); cheerful (2 Cor. 9:7); regular, proportional to income (1 Cor. 16:1–4). The Macedonian Christians however gave beyond their means for famine relief; they urgently pleaded with Paul for the privilege of giving to the saints. This sort of giving was based on obedience to the teaching of Jesus and the apostles against the love of money. Jesus comman-ded his disciples not to love money or to store up treasure on earth because it is impossible to serve God and money (Matt. 6:19–24; cf. Luke 16:13). The love of money is a trap which causes people to wander from the faith and into all sorts of evils (1 Tim. 6:9–10). So the rich are not to trust in their wealth (1 Tim. 6:17; Heb. 13:5; cf. Luke 12:15–21) but to be generous and willing to share (1 Tim. 6:18–19). Greed and love of money is idolatry and is improper for God's holy people. It is listed alongside sexual immorality, impurity and lust, all of which, including greed, incur the wrath of God. No greedy person has any inheritance in the kingdom of God (Eph. 5:3–6; Col. 3:5–6). Instead of worry and greed concerning money and possessions, Christians should seek God's kingdom and trust him to provide for them (Matt. 6:25–34). They should be content with food and clothing (1 Tim. 6:6–8).

Paul defines equality as sharing so that everyone has enough. 'At the present time your plenty will supply what they need, so that in turn their plenty will supply what you need. Then there will be equality' (2 Cor. 8:13–15). He defines a rich Christian as one who has enough so that he is able to abound in generosity: not as someone who stores up riches – as we have seen (2 Cor. 9:6–11).

So the church is to share its possessions; to care for the needy; to pray for one another constantly and to practise hospitality. It is to stand against oppression of the poor by the rich and, far from showing favouritism to the rich, it is to give special attention to the poor. Christians are not to love money or be greedy; they must not store up treasures on earth. Rather they are called to give a proportion of their income regularly, generously (even sacrificially) and cheerfully. The ancient custom of tithing (Gen. 14:20; 28:22) was included in the later Old Testament law (Lev. 27:30; Deut. 12:6; 14:28; 26:12). There is no legalistic compulsion on believers under the new covenant. However if the people of the Old Testament, who had fewer spiritual privileges than we enjoy, gave at least a tenth, surely we cannot be content or right to give less.

## The undermining of commitment to one another in the church

The people of St Agatha's regard their faith as a personal matter. It is not something to be talked about even with other church members. They believe in being friendly but keep a polite distance from one another. It is best that way: they avoid the tensions that would arise if they tried to get too close to each other – tensions from different views of the church or the faith. Church is something they go to in order to meet God and to make their communion. However there are exceptions. The Christmas Fayre is one. There is not always an abundance of Christmas spirit at that: but at least it happens in November, well before the festive season. Every stallholder feels the Fayre brings the worst out in other people. It's all right for the vicar to describe it as a time of fellowship; he does not know all that goes on. There is bickering over who gets the best position for their stall; bad feeling over who helps on which stall; resentment over who gets the most contributions and therefore makes the most money. The gossip that goes on is something awful. Hardly anyone is immune. It seems that the character and reputation of everyone in the church is run down. The vicar and his wife are watched with an eagle eye to detect if they show a bias towards any stall. And of

course there are those who do not bother to do anything –
even to turn up on the day. Some of the holy Joes even
disapprove of the whole thing and say it should be replaced
with direct giving. But many adults already put £2 in the
collection on Sunday, some more (the average giving per
person attending the Church of England in 1984 – the last
year for which statistics are available – was £1.95 per week).

Another exception to the not-getting-involved-with-
one-another rule is the PCC. Meetings have been known to
be stormy at times, especially where money is concerned.
Everyone seems to have their own vested interest. The
representatives of the traditionalists want everything in the
church to stay the same. In fact they would like some
changes that have taken place to be reversed. They are
always present in force to torpedo any suggestion for
change which disturbs them. Having discussed the matter
fully with many of the influential people in the congregation
they are able to claim they represent many people who
would object to the proposed change.

There was the time when the vicar wanted to introduce
the peace into the communion. Everyone would be expected to shake hands during the service. The thought of
such intimate contact intruding into the reverent atmos-
phere of the communion service was horrifying to some.
Reactions among these ranged from a refusal to join in the
peace to threats to leave the church. By the time the PCC
met, the vicar could see the case was lost. Of course the
younger element on the PCC, including the one charismatic, were all for the peace. The argument raged for half
the evening and eventually the vote was lost.

After that vote some of the younger members spoke
to the vicar privately, expressing their frustration at the
fuddy-duddy attitudes of the older members. The vicar
expressed some sympathy with their frustration. But soon
afterwards the churchwardens, who felt duty bound to
support the traditionalists, reminded him that it was the
traditionalists who had supported the church over the
decades, giving to it, cleaning it, caring for it. So they had a

right to have their wishes respected. The arrogant young-
sters needed to recognise this and to stop rocking the boat.
The whole incident deepened the division that was normally seething underneath the surface at St Agatha's.
There was resentment, suspicion and gossip. On the rare
occasions when newcomers attended the church, unless
they followed the not-getting-involved-with-one-another
rule, they were quickly drawn into one or other of the
factions.

However the many churches who would regard themselves as far more biblical than our mythical St Agatha's
and would not have fund-raising events, suffer from similar
weaknesses – the factions, the vested interests, the resentment, suspicion and gossip. For all their claims these
churches are clearly not acting on the biblical passages we
have just looked at. We could go a stage further and say
that many churches who are into charismatic renewal also
face the same problems and weaknesses, even if they are
less traditional in worship, fellowship and outlook. Still
there can be factions, vested interests, resentment, suspicion and gossip. What is more (as mentioned earlier) we
can find other weaknesses not infrequently present in
charismatic churches: being hearers of the Word rather
than doers in some matters; clergy being men pleasers and
giving way to their fears of unpopularity or division;
worship becomes stale; prayerlessness or at least a rather
ineffectual, undisciplined and intermittent prayer life; the
gifts not being discerned and encouraged; the spoken gifts
not being used in the services or being rather chaotic; clergy
not delegating; some of the leading ministries of Ephesians
4 not ministering into the church; members acting independently and 'doing their own thing' in terms of gifts, ministries and discerning God's will, and so on. I have seen these
problems many times in 'renewed' churches up and down
the country.

Practical ways to encourage commitment to one another:

- A deep work of the Holy Spirit must be prayed for and

welcomed. For St Agatha's especially, and for churches not experiencing the fulness of the renewing work of the Holy Spirit, this is vital. But churches into renewal facing the problems I have outlined also need a new breath of the Spirit.

- A clear consistent teaching of the biblical material – such as at the beginning of this chapter – must be given. But there must be a determination to obey the Word, not just hear it. As many as possible in the church must be encouraged to commit themselves in practice to doing this; urging one another on and gently correcting one another when necessary. In Hawkwell we have a Commitment Course which we produced ourselves. The majority of it expounds the biblical teaching on the characteristics of the church. It was initially done with the whole congregation (in groups) and is now done with all newcomers and new converts. People are invited to make a sincere and practical commitment to working out this biblical teaching in the life of the congregation, particularly through the housegroups. Simple though the course is, it has been used by God to transform Hawkwell Church and many others which have ongoing links with us.

- A determination to obey God, whatever the cost, is required of church leaders. There will of course always be patient encouragement and counsel available to members who misunderstand or are fearful and hesitant. But in the end the leader must prayerfully and carefully risk unpopularity and even losing people to other churches. If people are digging in their heels against obedience to the Word of God the risk is justified, however painful to all concerned.

In Hawkwell we have seen God bring a deep unity and mutual commitment within the church. This was far from the case some years ago. There is now a high degree of submitting to one another, of respecting those in leadership, of acting as a member of the body, not in a spirit of independence. Members do trust one another and are loyal to each other. Gossip and judgmental attitudes are discouraged. There is an acceptance of responsibility for each other's growth in maturity and holiness. This leads people to encourage and, when necessary, gently correct one another. The congregation also shares financially and practically with those in need. Members are encouraged to tithe their income but only the treasurer knows who does this. The church is by no means perfect but we thank God for the remarkable work he has done among us.

## The ABWON Link Church Ministry

Many churches would find it helpful to have outside help and encouragement to go the way of obedience to scripture in the power of the Spirit. So in Action for Biblical Witness to our Nation (ABWON) we have developed what we call the ABWON Link Church Ministry. We are unashamedly aiming to make an impact on the church in this nation. We aim to encourage wholehearted obedience to scripture in the full power of the Holy Spirit. As churches throughout the nation move into such obedience this will have a major impact upon the 90 per cent of the population who never attend church. We are under no illusion about ourselves. We are an ordinary church but God has done a remarkable work among us by the power of his Spirit as we have sought to obey him. We never go to other churches to teach principles we are not putting into practice in Hawkwell.

Increasingly we are finding churches up and down the nation who are beginning to experience Renewal or have experienced it for some time. They want to go forward but various challenging questions face them: How can we reach a deep level of unity and commitment to one another in the church? How can we reach the point where the members are loyal to each other, keep confidences and are not judgmental or gossips? How can charismatic worship be blended with the liturgy? How can we encourage the

manifestation of spiritual gifts within the church and its
services? How can we encourage our people to pray
together in a disciplined intensive way? How can we learn
to hear God and practise spiritual warfare? How can we
reach the balance between authority and individual freedom? How can we encourage the development of every
member ministry? How can the clergy delegate in order to
be free to exercise their particular gifts? How can we gently
correct people in error? How can we deal with hypocrisy,
divisiveness and rebellion? How can we be truly effective in
evangelism as a church?

We have practical recommendations to make on these
and other questions, in our Link ministry. They are based
upon practical experience in our ordinary parish. And they
are being proved in a growing number of other churches of
various denominations linked with us. These include village, town and inner city churches and churches abroad.
We are learning a great deal and broadening our experience as we share with all these different churches. We are
not empire-building or seeking to take over anyone else's
church. The Link is a voluntary and temporary association
set up on the initiative and under the authority of the local
clergyman or minister. We firmly believe that any church
can find the practical answers to the above questions. So we
provide courses, literature, advice, counselling and other
resources for our Link churches.

Our present approach to this ministry enables us to
be more flexible and to minister to a larger number of
churches. In outline we cover the following items:[1]

1  An introductory audio or video tape about the Link
   Church Ministry.
2  Once a decision has been made to embark on a link, our
   Commitment Course on 'The Nature and Function of
   the Local Church' is made available for the Link church
   to use (this course is only available to our Link
   churches). It is intended to move the church into the
   practical answers to the above questions.

3 Where possible a visit to Hawkwell for the leaders of the church is arranged. It affords an opportunity to consider further the principles we teach and to see how we work them out in our own church. Counselling and training in counselling are also offered.

4 At some stage a team from Hawkwell may visit the Link church for a workshop weekend.

5 My wife and I or other full-time colleagues make one or more private visits to the leader(s) of the Link church for discussion, encouragement, advice and prayer (as geography permits).

6 Throughout the whole link a prayer cell devotes time every fortnight to specific intercession for the Link church.

7 Tapes (audio or video), guidance leaflets, other literature and advice are available throughout the period of the link, which lasts from one to two years. In all there are fourteen packs of such materials, related to the various stages of restoring a church to biblical principles.

(The materials themselves are adequate for churches where visits are not practicable.)

# Commitment to Mission

## Urgent evangelism

God loves the world, not just the church (John 3:16). He 'wants all men to be saved and to come to a knowledge of the truth' (1 Tim. 2:4). He is patient with mankind, 'not wanting anyone to perish, but everyone to come to repentance' (2 Pet. 3:9). Consequently Jesus did not come to condemn the world but to save it (John 12:47). He came as the Light of the world – not just the church (John 8:12). He is 'the Saviour of all men, and especially of those who believe' (1 Tim. 4:10). He is the atoning sacrifice not only for our sins but for the sins of the whole world (1 John 2:2; cf. John 1:29). God was reconciling the world to himself in Christ. It is important to note that although salvation is universally available, it is only received by those who repent and put their faith in God's one and only Son as the only Saviour (see pp. 10–11, 106–108).

It follows that the church is to share the Lord's love for the world and passion for its salvation. Jesus had compassion on the crowds who were harassed and helpless like sheep without a shepherd. He urged the disciples to pray for workers to go out into this ready harvest field (Matt. 9:37–38). At his ascension he sent out his disciples to make disciples of all nations (Matt. 28:19–20; cf. Mark 16:15). They were to preach repentance and the forgiveness of sins in his name to all nations (Luke 24:47–48). The purpose of Pentecost was to empower them to witness to the world (Acts 1:8). Jesus has called the church to be the salt and light of the world (Matt. 5:13–16). The proclamation of the gospel to the ends of the earth will herald the end times when Jesus returns (Matt. 24:14; Mark 13:10).

During his earthly life Jesus sent out the Twelve and the seventy-two to proclaim and demonstrate the kingdom of God (Luke 9:1–2; 10:1). After Pentecost the apostles felt so compelled to proclaim the gospel that they risked imprisonment and physical punishment rather than obey the authorities, who had forbidden them to preach (Acts 4:19; 5:29). Paul declared: 'Woe to me if I do not preach the Gospel' (1 Cor. 9:16). He could report that 'all over the world this gospel is producing fruit and growing' (Col. 1:6). Jesus had never intended the church to be inward-looking. Even its very unity was to win people to belief (John 17:21,23). The local and wider church was originally a dynamic missionary organism with a passion for winning the world.

The message of Jesus and the early church was the message of the kingdom of God: repent for the kingdom of heaven is near (Matt. 4:17,23). And he sent his disciples out to preach the same message (Matt. 10:7). It is the kingdom prepared since creation (Matt. 25:34), already within (or among) them (Luke 17:20–21) but finally to be revealed at the end of the age (Luke 21:31). Between his resurrection and ascension Jesus discussed much about the kingdom with his disciples and gave them 'many convincing proofs that he was alive' (Acts 1:3). His words were accompanied by signs.

## Signs and wonders

The mission of the church was not just to proclaim the kingdom in words. For the kingdom is not a matter of talk but of power (1 Cor. 4:20). It is demonstrated in righteousness, peace and joy (Rom. 14:17) and in signs and wonders. Jesus performed miraculous signs to accompany his preaching and many people who saw them believed in his name (John 2:23; 3:2; 6:2,14; cf. Luke 4:36). He was saddened that some people would not believe without seeing signs and wonders (John 4:48). Some would not believe even when they saw the signs (John 12:37). He urged people: 'Believe me when I say that I am in the Father and the Father is in me; or at least believe on the evidence of the miracles themselves' (John 14:11; cf. 10:38). Jesus clearly expected his disciples to do the things he had been doing and even greater things (John 14:12). He sent them out with authority to heal, cast out demons and raise the dead (Matt. 10:1,8; Mark 6:7; Luke 9:1; 10:9). These actions were all signs of the kingdom (Matt. 12:28; Luke 10:9; 11:20) and of the defeat of Satan (Luke 10:17–19). At his ascension with the promise of the power of the Holy Spirit to come at Pentecost, Jesus repeated that miraculous signs should and would accompany the preaching of the gospel including exorcism, healing, tongues and miraculous protection (Mark 16:17). So the Lord confirmed the message by enabling Paul and Barnabas to do miraculous signs and wonders (Acts 14:3). The writer to the Hebrews states that God testified to the message 'by signs, wonders and various miracles, and gifts of the Holy Spirit distributed according to his will' (Heb. 2:4; cf. Acts 2:43; 5:12–16; 8:5–7,12; Rom. 15:18–20; 2 Cor. 12:12).

Of course one of the basic signs of the kingdom is the new birth. No one can enter the kingdom simply by intellectual assent to the message of the gospel. As the gospel is proclaimed and received in the power of the Holy Spirit, people are born again (John 1:13; 3:3–8; Tit. 3:5; Jas. 1:18; 1 Pet. 1:23). This miracle of receiving eternal life enables a person to die to self, receiving the ability to overcome the temptations and pressures of the world by faith, and to obey God (1 John 3:9; 4:7; 5:1–5). It is after all a sign of the kingdom or rule of God that people gladly obey God. We are to teach people to obey all that Christ has commanded us (Matt. 28:20). It will not be the people who simply call Jesus 'Lord' who will enter the kingdom, even if they claim to have prophesied and performed exorcisms and miracles in his name. It is only those who do the will of God (Matt. 7:21). Obedience does not earn salvation. Obviously we all fail and need to repent and ask daily for forgiveness.

So the church is called to proclaim the gospel with the demonstration of signs and wonders. But it should also be aware that there are false signs and wonders, increasingly in the last days (Matt. 24:24; 2 Thess. 2:9–11; Rev. 16:14). However these counterfeits are another indication of the availability and importance of the genuine signs and wonders from the Holy Spirit. They also indicate the need for the church to be involved in spiritual warfare.

## Spiritual warfare

Satan is a real personal power of evil as the story of Jesus' temptations shows. And he has the world in his power (Matt. 4:8–9). He is the 'prince of this world' (John 12:31; 14:30; 16:11); the 'god of this age' (2 Cor. 4:4); the 'ruler of the kingdom of the air, the spirit who is now at work in those who are disobedient' (Eph. 2:2). As 'the god of this age' he has 'blinded the minds of unbelievers, so that they cannot see the light of the gospel of the glory of Christ' (2 Cor. 4:4; cf. John 8:42–47). He masquerades as an angel of light to deceive people and cause them to fall into his trap (2 Cor. 11:14). Paul was sent to turn the Gentiles 'from darkness to light, and from the power of Satan to God' (Acts 26:17–18; cf. Eph. 5:8; Col. 1:13; 1 Pet. 2:9).

In Daniel 10 the prophet has a vision of an awe-inspiring angelic messenger who brings a message of reassurance. He explains to Daniel that as soon as he began to pray, he (the archangel) was sent in response to the prayer. But he was resisted 'for twenty-one days' by the 'prince of the Persian kingdom' (Dan. 10:12–13). This 'prince' is obviously a supernatural being able to contend with an archangel and can therefore be described as a 'principality'. He is a high-ranking demonic power with control over a geographical area, namely Persia. Michael the archangel came to the rescue and took over the battle with the principality of Persia.

Later a 'prince' of Greece will come. It seems therefore that whenever there is a concentration of human power (for example a kingdom or empire) which is not under the lordship of Christ, there is a powerful demonic influence behind it. It seems reasonable to suppose that such powers govern certain aspects of evil, such as violence. However God has authority over Satan and his evil angels. All the heavenly powers whether they remain good or have re-belled were created by and for Christ (Col. 1:16). He came into the world to destroy the works of the devil (1 John 3:8) including his power of death which holds people enslaved to fear of death (Heb. 2:14–15). He defeated Satan by his perfect life (Heb. 4:15) and disarmed the powers and authorities making a public spectacle of them, triumphing over them by the cross (Col. 2:15; cf. John 12:31; 14:30; 16:11). Now the angels, authorities and powers are in submission to him (Eph. 1:19–22; Col. 2:10; 1 Pet. 3:22). So the one who dwells in believers is greater than the one who is in the world (1 John 4:4) and God will soon crush Satan under our feet (Rom. 16:20). Meanwhile nothing, not even 'heavenly rulers' or 'powers' can separate us from the love of Christ (Rom. 8:38).

This does not mean that the church can sit back and wait for the final victory. We are called to do battle in this interim period between Satan's defeat and his final removal from the scene. 'Our struggle is not against flesh and blood, but against the rulers, against the authorities, against the powers of this dark world and against the spiritual forces of evil in the heavenly realms' (Eph. 6:12). Like Timothy we are to be soldiers of Christ (2 Tim. 2:3) who do not fight with worldly weapons but weapons which have divine power to pull down strongholds (2 Cor. 10:4); the weapons of righteousness (2 Cor. 6:7). We must put on the whole armour of God to stand against the devil's schemes (Eph. 6:11–18; cf. Rom. 13:12). The belt of truth refers to sincerity and honesty (cf. Isa. 11:5). The belt bound the clothes under the armour to ensure the soldier's unimpeded movement (Exod. 12:11; 1 Kgs. 18:46). The breastplate of righteousness protects the heart (cf. Ps. 132:9; Isa. 59:17; 61:10; 1 Thess. 5:8; Rev. 19:8). The sandals of the gospel of peace speak of both the experience of peace and the proclamation of peace in Christ (cf. Isa. 52:7; Nah. 1:15; Rom. 10:15). The shield of faith quenches the flaming arrows of the evil one, that is, reliance on the promises of God overcomes Satan's insinuations. The helmet of salvation (or of the hope of salvation, 1 Thess. 5:8) protects the mind from doubts.

The offensive weapon is the sword of the Spirit which is the Word of God spoken out against the enemy. The Word of God is sharper than any double-edged sword and judges thoughts and attitudes (Heb. 4:12). Jesus is pictured in Revelation 1:16 as having a sharp double-edged sword coming out of his mouth. He fights against evildoers with the sword of his mouth (Rev. 2:16; 19:15,21), that is, with his powerful word. Similarly scripture speaks of God or Christ defeating the enemy by his 'breath' (2 Thess. 2:8; cf. Job 4:9; 15:30; Isa. 11:4; 30:28,33; 40:7,24; Ezek. 21:31). We are able to use this same powerful weapon against the enemy. So the Christian battle is the fight of faith – faith in God's Word (1 Tim. 1:19; 6:12; cf. 2 Tim. 4:7). Satan seeks to take away the seed of the Word (Luke 8:12) and to destroy faith (Luke 22:31–32).

Believers are urged to resist Satan, standing firm in the faith and he will flee from them (Jas. 4:7; 1 Pet. 5:6–9). Evil powers can be 'bound' by the authoritative Word of faith (Matt. 16:19; 18:18). It is important to note though, that Matthew 18:18 says literally: 'whatever you bind on earth, will have been bound in heaven'. This emphasises the need for the church, through prayer, to reach the conviction that the Holy Spirit has given the authority to bind the particular evil in question. Evil powers are also bound through exorcism or deliverance (Luke 10:17–20).

Satan seems to have a particular strategy to disgrace

leaders (1 Tim. 3:7; cf. Luke 22:31–32) and to trap people into wrongly opposing their leaders (2 Tim. 2:24–26). But one of his main methods is to deceive people into false teaching (1 Tim. 4:1). There are many false teachers and prophets in the world and, sadly, in the church (Matt. 7:15–16; Luke 6:26; 1 John 2:18–22;2 Pet. 2:1; 2 John 7) and there will be more in the end times (Matt. 24:24; 2 Thess. 2:9–12; Rev. 16:13). So the gift of discernment of spirit is vital (1 Cor. 12:10). It is important to test the spirit by which people prophesy to see it is from God.

It is essential that Christians do not give the devil a foothold by disobedience or lack of self-discipline. (See Eph. 4:26 where anger is mentioned; Jas. 3:14–16 where 'wisdom', which is accompanied by bitter envy and selfish ambition, is said to be of the devil, and 2 Cor. 2:10–11 where unforgiveness could give Satan an opportunity.) Paul urges believers not to eat food they have been told has been offered to idols (demons) for the sake of the conscience of the person who told them or of a Christian with a more sensitive conscience over such matters (1 Cor. 10:20–21; cf. 8:1–13). It may be worth saying that Christians should beware excusing themselves by claiming the devil made them do something. As James puts it: 'each one is tempted when, by his own evil desire, he is dragged away and enticed. Then, after desire has conceived, it gives birth to sin' (Jas. 1:14–15).

The battle which the church is called to fight is intended to show the manifold wisdom of God to the rulers and authorities in the heavenly realms. We are being watched by both good and bad spiritual authorities.

## Undermining the commitment to mission in the church

St Agatha's congregation seems to have more than enough to cope with simply to keep the church going. They have busy social and business lives. With services on Sunday, jobs around the church, PCC and committee meetings, and fund raising, there is no time for anything else. The vicar has a lot of contact with parishioners who do not attend church, of course. And that has occasionally brought new people into the church. The attitude of some members is: 'If they want to come to church, they know where it is. It's up to them!' However the church does advertise its festival services in the local press, and of course the fund-raising events too. There is Christian Aid Week when some of the members collect from house to house. Then there was the Tower Repair Appeal when a leaflet was delivered to every door. Christenings, weddings and funerals bring people to church – but not normally at the time when the regular congregation is there. Some of the younger members and the charismatics say that St Agatha's should be doing evangelism, but it is difficult to see what else could be done. Besides they are not fond of the Billy Graham approach.

Actually there is another strange thing about those charismatics. They often talk about the devil as if he is a real person, alive and active in St Agatha's and its parish. But this seems naive and rather medieval to the rest of the congregation. The charismatics have criticised various things in the church as 'of the devil' but they have had no impact on St Agatha's. The churchwardens are Freemasons, as are one or two other men, but hardly any of the members see anything wrong in that. Many of the members read their horoscopes. The majority would not see anything harmful in spiritualism – for those who like that sort of thing. The charismatics also criticised rock music and games the youth group play like Ouija and Dungeons and Dragons. Most members of St Agatha's thought this was extremism.

However, as before, we must be fair and see similar problems in some churches that regard themselves as more biblical than (and, if they are honest, superior to) St Agatha's. Oh, they believe in evangelism all right; they regard it as a good thing. In fact they have spent many hours discussing it, and heard many a sermon on it. All sorts of ideas have been suggested and everyone has agreed that the congregation should be witnesses. The vicar preaches evangelistically at festival services, and, all in all, there are occasional conversions. But if they are brutally frank the members would have to agree they have not really done any evangelism since they took a coach to Mission England. In fact they do not know how to do it and are scared of the prospect. The vicar is frustrated because he preaches on the subject with great feeling but all that seems to be achieved is that the congregation agrees with him in theory and goes home feeling somewhat condemned.

These churches do believe in the devil, of course, because the New Testament does. They know about temptation and the occult and have heard of demon possession. But somehow the influence of the devil seems rather remote from them in practice. They certainly would not want to become extremists and see demons behind every blade of grass.

One of the main problems with charismatic churches is that they become inward-looking, and really no further on in evangelism than the churches we have just described. The fellowship is so great and the worship so enjoyable. And of course they are into ministry to the individual. They have not seen the trap that church members can provide enough personal needs to keep one another busy in counselling until the second coming. Some of these needs are produced by inward-looking attitudes so it is a vicious circle. And it effectively crowds out evangelism. What some needy people require is not more counselling but a determination, by the grace of God, to look outside themselves to a world that largely does not know Christ. It is amazing how some personal problems dissolve when people do that. But, even from a self-interest point of view, charismatic churches which become inward-looking will find their experience of Renewal going stale and running into problems, perhaps serious ones. They are casualties of the subtle spiritual warfare Satan wages especially against churches which are experiencing the renewing life of the Spirit.

Thank God for some churches (whether charismatic or not) that are actually doing evangelism, and seeing results. However there may be weaknesses in them which render this evangelism less effective than it could be. Sometimes the prayer backing for the evangelism is weak. Perhaps the evangelism is being done by a minority in the church and the rest have not got the same concern and vision, so they do not pray with any great depth and intensity about it. Maybe also these churches are not sufficiently aware of the Satanic strategy against them. Because they are involved in evangelism they are prime targets for Satanic attack. And it is a no-holds-barred battle. Also they may have forgotten that Jesus sent out his disciples not only to proclaim the kingdom but to heal the sick. In other words the signs of the kingdom (which include healing) should be associated with the evangelism. God has renewed the gifts of the Spirit not just for the benefit of the church, but so that these gifts can be taken out to the non-Christians outside the church.

The wider church seems to suffer from the same weaknesses as we have noted above: talks, reports, debates, committees but all too little actual evangelism. Similarly the wider church is not much help in the area of spiritual warfare. In 1937 the archbishops appointed a committee to investigate spiritualism. But the bishops did not publish the Report. In recent years it has been put out in more than one publication, though not by the church officially. The majority of the committee (three signed a minority report) were fairly favourable towards spiritualism:

It is necessary to keep clearly in mind that none of the fundamental Christian obligations or values is in any way changed by our acceptance of the possibility of communication with discarnate spirits. Where these essential principles are borne in mind, those who have the assurance that they have been in touch with their departed

friends may rightly accept the sense of enlargement and
of unbroken fellowship which it brings[1] . . . The view has
been held with some degree of Church authority, that
psychic phenomena are real but that they proceed from
evil spirits. The possibility that spirits of a low order may
seek to influence us in this way cannot be excluded as
inherently illogical or absurd, but it would be extremely
unlikely if there were not also the possibility of contact
with good spirits.

If spiritualism, with all aberrations set aside and with
every care taken to present it humbly and accurately,
contains a truth, it is important to see that truth not as a
new religion, but only as filling up certain gaps in our
knowledge, so that where we already walked by faith, we
may now have some measure of sight as well.[2]

In his autobiography Dr Mervyn Stockwood, former
Bishop of Southwark, claimed he communicated with his
dead parents through a medium and speaks of another
experience with a medium as well as his own telepathic
powers. Commenting on this Michael Perry, Archdeacon
of Durham and editor of *Christian Parapsychologist*, was
quoted in the *Daily Telegraph* as saying,

There is no Church of England orthodoxy on this matter,
and no official pronouncement on mediums. But many
church leaders would look askance on it. The Churches
Fellowship for Psychological and Spiritual Studies is
trying to keep an open mind on these phenomena, and
many of us recognise going to a medium is allowable,
although it is very easy to be deceived, and self-deceived.
In effect we still say: 'Yes – but take care.'

This contrasts with the biblical statement 'let no-one be
found among you . . . who practises divination or sorcery,
interprets omens, engages in witchcraft or casts spells, or
who is a medium or spiritist or who consults the dead.

Anyone who does these things is detestable to the Lord'
(Deut. 18:10–12; cf. Lev. 19:31; 20:6).

However, occult influences are introduced into the
church in more subtle ways. Many church youth groups
have played Dungeons and Dragons. Psychiatrist Dr John
White said:

'Dungeons and Dragons is a game of fantasy role playing. Because the fantasy is acted out . . . it has more
potent psychological effects than fantasy that is read, or
watched on television. Role-playing differs even from
acting in a play, because there is a much greater blurring
of the difference between fantasy and reality in the mind
of the player in fantasy role-playing and because players
identify even more intensely with the role they have been
given. Role-playing in psychodrama is a fairly powerful
technique designed to enable someone to behave differently. It helps to break down any inhibitions a person
might have that would prevent the change from taking
place . . .

He continues that involvement in Dungeons and Dragons:

will involve fairly intensive education in the world of
witchcraft and sorcery, and repeating spells and incanta-
tions aloud. It can at advanced levels demand spells . . .
or even to be involved in fasting and imaginary sacrifices.
While these activities are make-believe activities, the
fact that they are part of role-playing, with its powerful
potential for modifying character, cannot be viewed
lightly.[3]

There are of course other profoundly unhealthy fantasy
role-play games today, some of them for computer users.
A game like Ouija is more obviously occult and very
dangerous.

Then there is rock music. Bob Larsen in his book *Rock*
says:

An incessantly driving pulsating beat pattern is not inherently evil but when applied for a protracted period of
time at high volume level, its spiritual effect can be
devastating. Like any repetitious assault on one's
neurosensory apparatus it may shut down the
neurosensory processes. This is the same technique used
in Eastern meditative techniques such as Transcendental
Meditation. The result is an inroad to the mind open for
evil invasion. Heavier rock groups . . . can rhythmically
manipulate an audience until they reach a zombie-like
state. In that condition their minds are non-objectively
open to the message of the music and their bodies are
possible prey to evil spirits that readily operate through
such entrancing music.[4]

The Beatles made the connection with eastern mysticism
in the 1960s: for example the song 'My sweet Lord' is
addressed to Lord Krishna. Various groups are into the
occult as well as into immorality. Often there are explicit
references to the occult. The Rolling Stones produced an
album *Their Satanic Majesties Request* which contains a
song 'Sympathy for the Devil'. Much rock music is brainwashing people with non-Christian, even anti-Christian
philosophy and morality. Yet it is a major influence upon
church people today.

We have already mentioned the spiritual dangers of
yoga, which many Christians have become involved in, and
of transcendental meditation, and some counselling techniques (see p. 133). Since the 1960s so many have become
dangerously involved in the occult that Hallowe'en, which
years ago was celebrated as a harmless games evening,
must now be taken seriously. For example the Association
of Christian Teachers has produced a warning leaflet about
Hallowe'en in schools.

I am grateful that in 1987 the General Synod received
and commended a Report on Freemasonry with particular
reference to its final paragraph, which states that most of
the working party 'are of the mind that the Report points to

a number of very fundamental reasons to question the compatibility of Freemasonry with Christianity'.[5] People become Freemasons for laudable motives. It seems to them a moral, charitable organisation. However I believe they are spiritually deceived by an organisation which is heavily affected by spiritual influences alien to Christianity. Like many others I have found serious spiritual blockages in Freemasons. Now the church has produced this report and other helpful material,[6] Freemasons in the church are without excuse. They should resign from Freemasonry.

Finally there is astrology. Reading the horoscopes, as many church people do, is hardly the most serious misdemeanour. But it can be the thin end of the wedge. Many are superstitious, or at least affected by superstition. Horoscopes and astrology are alien to Christianity because they are saying that our lives are controlled by impersonal forces, not a loving heavenly Father. In an age when we have seen there is a great openness to the occult, astrology can lead people down the road to more serious practices. It is good to leave all such practices well alone because we are in a spiritual battle against the kingdom of darkness.

## A practical way to encourage commitment to mission in the church

In Hawkwell we started doing serious visitation evangelism in 1976. We began to learn various important lessons. One was that we were not convinced the church services were worth coming to. Some of us (myself included) got bored in the morning services and the arrangements for the Young Church almost seemed to have been planned for maximum inconvenience, except for families with children aged between five and seven. And there was no crèche. So we made important changes in the worship to make the church more attractive, especially for families. At various times since, we have made other changes, so that newcomers will gain the maximum benefit from a friendly welcome and joyful, relevant and inspiring worship.

Then we learnt that evangelism is linked with spiritual warfare. Not only did we begin to experience tangible attacks on the evangelism programme,[7] but also evangelism brought out the spiritual problems in the congregation. A backlog of such problems that had been half ignored, half tolerated came to the surface. They had to be dealt with, sadly not always with a positive outcome.

Although we arranged some prayer for the evangelism programme, it was minimal. It took us two years to realise that much more prayer was required. So it was that in 1978 we designated Thursday a parish day of prayer. One of the things we eventually began to pray was for the whole congregation to gain a vision and concern for evangelism. This prayer has been answered. In Hawkwell we run the church through the housegroups. They do everything from cleaning church buildings to leading the occasional service. Each group has its own clearly defined mini-parish for which it is responsible. They are involved in pastoral care, including of parishioners who do not attend church – the lonely, sick, housebound, bereaved, and so on. Also they do evangelistic visiting and literature distribution. Each month they spend an evening preparing for or doing evangelism. From time to time they hold evangelistic events within a local home – a harvest supper, Christmas carol evening, video evening, and so on. So the whole church membership is regularly involved in evangelism. In addition to this we have a weekly Teach and Reach programme of evangelism which involves several visiting teams drawn from the whole congregation. Weekly coffee mornings have proved fruitful evangelistically. The church has also organised street evangelism, a float in the local carnival and a stand at the local show. The leadership constantly monitors the evangelistic activities of the church.

Over the years we have learnt the importance of linking the gifts of the Spirit with our evangelism. Normally at the end of an evangelistic guest service, we offer prayer for healing. This seems to make the evangelism more fruitful, especially when on many occasions we have seen the Lord bring definite healing to people. Sometimes we hold special healing services. In the visitation evangelism we ask if there is any need in the household which we can pray about. Healing is relevant here. Visitors have prayed for people in homes and sometimes on the doorstep – with the agreement of the person visited, of course.

In addition to direct evangelism we are involved in a good deal of social outreach. We run a Lifeline scheme whereby parishioners can easily contact us if some special need or emergency crops up. A weekly cancer support group, with trained church members, meets each week for the benefit of cancer sufferers and their relatives. Other members are involved in the local Christian hospice, hospital services, clubs for the disabled, old people's welfare and homes for the elderly. Housegroups provide practical help for parishioners: shopping, housework, making meals, caring for children as well as general visiting, including of the bereaved. The young church members (under supervision) have evenings when they visit the elderly and do odd jobs or gardening. Members also keep in touch with local organisations such as the British Legion, local councils and schools. We run a Christian Business Fellowship. Various members who have been made redundant and have decided to become self-employed meet together for mutual encouragement and help. This benefits not only them but the local society for whom they provide goods and services, maintaining Christian standards and witness.

Little by little we have learnt more about spiritual warfare. Sometimes individuals are in need of prayer for deliverance, possibly linked with the ministry of healing. Often the results have been remarkable. We now see the need to check systematically for any occult involvement in the lives of converts. Always there seems to have been some involvement and sometimes it has been extensive.

However we have found God giving discernment on a larger scale. Fairly often when we have taken a team to another church for a weekend the Lord has revealed the particular main strategy Satan has against that church. We did not anticipate this happening but, like many other lessons we have learnt, we were taken by surprise. We have discovered that Satan has different strategies. For one church the main attack may be the way of rebellion, for another bitter criticism or discrediting the leadership or a divisive spirit or immorality. Not infrequently darker happenings in the history of the church are a cause of present problems. The remarkable positive results of the prayer after this discernment confirms its accuracy.

Part V

# GOD'S SOVEREIGNTY
# IN JUDGMENT

# The Kindness and Sternness of God

One of the most serious errors in the church is an un-balanced view of the nature of God and, in particular, his love. Neglect (or ignorance) of much of the biblical teaching on the subject encourages even Christian leaders to define divine love in terms of human sentiment. Love tends therefore to be defined solely as being nice, kind and gentle. This means that subjects like judgment, wrath, hell and church discipline are very unpopular in Christian think-ing. Yet they are integral parts of the biblical teaching concerning God who is love.

We might expect to find such superficial thinking amongst those who openly pick and choose which parts of the Bible to believe. They will arrogantly and subjectively let their thoughts and feelings judge scripture. But it is worse when Christians who claim to uphold the full inspira-tion and authority of scripture do the same thing unawares. Experience convinces me that many evangelicals, char-ismatics and others who claim to take a conservative view of scripture, in effect reject part of its teaching. Some of the most conservative Christians would regard what Jesus taught about church discipline as correct in theory but not to be practised, except perhaps in extreme circumstances. Many do not truly believe in the reality of eternal separa-tion from God. If they did, it would be one motive for them to be more committed to evangelism, both by word and example.

Jesus strongly rebuked Peter for his misleading human reasoning and sentiment (Matt. 16:22–23). Peter was so concerned that Jesus should not experience the humiliation, cruelty and 'defeat' of being killed, that he rebuked him for saying he would. Jesus replied, 'Out of my sight, Satan! You are a stumbling block to me; you do not have in mind the things of God, but the things of men.' The same criticism can be levelled against many Christians today. What does the Bible say about this?

## The kindness of God's love

People uninformed about the Old Testament think it portrays God as some primitive tribal deity. Far from it. God has loved his people with an everlasting love and drawn them with loving kindness (Jer. 31:3). 'He tends his flock like a shepherd: he gathers the lambs in his arms and carries them close to his heart; he gently leads those that have young' (Isa. 40:11). Like a mother bird covers her babies the Lord protects his people (Ps. 91:4); like the mountains surrounding Jerusalem he surrounds his people for ever (Ps. 125:2). He is kind, forgiving and abounding in love for all who call upon him (Ps. 86:15). Micah prays:

Who is a God like you, who pardons sin and forgives the transgression of the remnant of his inheritance? You do not stay angry for ever but delight to show mercy. You will again have compassion on us; you will tread our sins underfoot and hurl all our iniquities into the depths of the sea. (Mic. 7:18–19).

According to the New Testament God so loved the world that he gave his one and only Son (John 3:16) to die for us while we were still sinful rebels against him (Rom. 5:8). Jesus came to show the love of the Father pre-eminently by laying down his life for his friends (John 15:9,13). Paul speaks of the meekness and gentleness of Christ (2 Cor. 10:1). Jesus wept at the death of his friend (John 11:35) and expressed deep grief over the impenitence of Jerusalem

(Matt. 23:37; Luke 13:34). He had compassion on the crowds who were 'harassed and helpless, like sheep without a shepherd' (Matt. 9:36). No circumstance or power can separate us from the love of Christ (Rom. 8:35–39). He commands us to love one another with the same kind of love as his (John 13:14, 34–35; 15:12,17).

Everyone needs to hear this message of the kindness of God's love. It is at the centre of the gospel. One of the most important things that Christians can learn is that God is their loving Father. Many are limping through their Christian lives because deep down they do not really believe it – perhaps because of the hurts they experienced from a human father. The church must show this love to those who feel rejected and hopeless. Sometimes the church has, quite wrongly, hated the sinner as well as the sin. So it must bear some of the responsibility for driving those with homosexual tendencies into the gay community, or those with other moral problems or addictions into similar communities. But the love of God can redeem such people. In my own ministry I have seen the Lord redeem people from homosexuality, adultery, prostitution, drug addiction, crime, and so on. However there is another side to the love of God.

## The sternness of God's love

### The example of Jesus

Jesus is the supreme revelation of the love of God, so it is vital for us to study carefully the nature of his love. It was not all gentle and kind.

*He rebuked hypocrisy.* He publicly called the religious leaders of the day a 'brood of vipers' who were 'evil' and therefore could not say anything good (Matt. 12:34). He publicly called them 'hypocrites' (Matt. 22:18), 'sons of hell', 'blind guides', 'blind fools', 'whitewashed tombs'

(Matt. 23:13–17,19,23–32). He said, 'You snakes! You
brood of vipers! How will you escape being condemned to
hell?' (Matt. 23:33). He was angry at their stubborn hearts
(Mark 3:1–6). On another occasion he said to them: 'You
belong to your father, the devil, and you want to carry out
your father's desire . . . He who belongs to God hears what
God says. The reason you do not hear is that you do not
belong to God . . . I know (God). If I said I did not, I would
be a liar like you' (John 8:44,47,55). Then there was the
famous occasion when he drove the money changers and
their animals out of the temple court, overturning their
money tables (John 2:14–16).

*He rebuked unbelief.* After Peter had taken the courageous
step of faith to walk on the water and then began to sink,
Jesus did not commend him for this remarkable, if limited,
achievement. He rebuked his unbelief: 'You of little faith,'
he said, 'why did you doubt?' (Matt. 14:31). When the
disciples were terrified that they were going to drown in the
terrible storm on the lake, Jesus did not respond with
human sympathy. Rather he rebuked them: 'Why are you
so afraid? Do you still have no faith?' (Mark 4:40). When
the disciples, early in their ministry, could not deliver a
demon-possessed boy, Jesus said, 'O unbelieving and per-
verse generation . . . how long shall I stay with you and put
up with you?' (Luke 9:41). The two disciples on the road to
Emmaus were grieving at the death of Jesus. He appeared
and said, 'How foolish you are, and how slow of heart to
believe all that the prophets have spoken!' (Luke 24:25).
He also appeared to the disciples and 'rebuked them for
their lack of faith and their stubborn refusal to believe those
who had seen him after he had risen' (Mark 16:14).

*He advised urgency.* If someone was not prepared to receive the message and ministry of the gospel, Jesus did not
advise wasting hours and hours on them out of misguided
human compassion. Rather he said, 'If anyone will not
welcome you or listen to your words, shake the dust off

your feet when you leave that home or town' (Matt. 10:13–15).

*He demanded commitment.* We have already seen that Jesus demanded a whole-hearted commitment (pp. 148ff.), 'hating' nearest and dearest and one's own life; risking division in the family; practising self-denial; renouncing the ownership of possessions; rejoicing in persecution, and so on. Little wonder he lost most of his disciples, in John 6:60–67: 'On hearing this many of his disciples said, "This is a hard teaching. Who can accept it?" . . . From this time many of his disciples turned back and no longer followed him.' Jesus also let the rich young man go away sad because his money was an idol preventing him becoming totally committed to God (Matt. 19:16–23).

*He urged discipline.* Very little is recorded of what Jesus said about the church. But what is recorded is the importance of church discipline:

> If your brother sins against you, go and show him his fault, just between the two of you. If he listens to you, you have won your brother over. But if he will not listen, take one or two others along, so that every matter may be established by the testimony of two or three witnesses. If he refuses to listen to them, tell it to the church; and if he refuses to listen even to the church, treat him as you would a pagan or a tax collector. (Matt. 18:15–17)

Clearly the last sentence does not mean ignoring or being spiteful to the offender. After all Christians are to love (and do good to) even their enemies. But it means treating him as out of fellowship until he repents, when he should be readily forgiven (Matt. 18:21–35). In the messages to the churches in Revelation 2–3 repentance and discipline are also stressed. They must repent of losing their first love or they will experience judgment in the form of their 'lampstand being removed' (2:4–5). They must not tolerate false

immoral teaching within the church or they will experience
judgment (2:14–16,20–23).

*He proclaimed judgment.* Jesus made it clear that it was not
his *purpose* to condemn the world (John 3:17) and he did
not condemn the woman caught in the act of adultery (John
8:11) though he did tell her to leave her life of sin. He came
rather to save from condemnation those who would believe
in him (John 3:18,36; 5:24). However the *result* of his
coming was condemnation for those who did not accept him
(John 9:39; 3:18; 12:47–48). Jesus pronounces judgment on
the hypocritical Pharisees who will continue the long tradition of persecuting and killing the prophets. He says that
the judgment for all this will fall on their generation (Matt.
23:35–36; Luke 11:50–51). He goes on to speak of the
coming destruction of the temple (Matt. 24:1–2). It is
interesting that in Matthew 27:25 the people shouted to
Pilate, 'Let his (Jesus') blood be on us and on our children!'
Ironically in Acts 5:28 the high priest, speaking on behalf of
the Sanhedrin, accuses the apostles of being determined to
make them guilty of the blood of Jesus. It is worth noting
that in one case Jesus drew a connection between personal
sin and some personal misfortune. He said to the invalid
healed at Bethesda, 'See, you are well again. Stop sinning
or something worse may happen to you' (John 5:14).

It is interesting that out of seventeen specific references
to hell as a place of punishment, fifteen are made by Jesus
himself (Matt. 5:22,29,30; 10:28; 18:8,9; 23:15; 23:33;
25:41,46; Mark 9:43,45,47; Luke 12:5; 16:23; 2 Pet. 2:4;
Jude 7). Allowing for parallels in the gospels Jesus is
responsible for eleven out of thirteen. But Jesus makes
other less specific references to this subject. He teaches that
many take the broad road to destruction (Matt. 7:13; Luke
13:22–30). Unbelievers will be cast into darkness (Matt.
8:10–12; 13:42,48–50; 22:13–14). Those with a mere legalistic righteousness will not enter the kingdom of heaven
(Matt. 5:20; 7:21–23). Blasphemy against the Spirit will not
be forgiven (Matt. 12:30–32); the unforgiving will not be

forgiven (Matt. 6:15; 18:35). The cities who have not repented in spite of his miracles will face judgment (Matt. 11:20–24). Jesus says anyone causing believing children to sin would be better to have a large millstone hung round his neck and to be drowned (Matt. 18:6–9).

Jesus tells two vivid parables about heaven and hell. In Matthew 25:31–46 (the parable of the sheep and the goats) he says to the unrighteous, 'Depart from me, you who are cursed, into the eternal fire prepared for the devil and his angels . . . Then they will go away to eternal punishment, but the righteous to eternal life' (25:41,46). In the parable of the rich man and Lazarus (Luke 16:19–31) Jesus portrays the sinful rich man in hell as in torment (vv. 23,28) and agony (v. 24). A great chasm prevents any transfer from hell to heaven. Clearly these parables contain a good deal of symbolism. But if Jesus knew that hell did not exist why did he tell them? After all, if it does not exist then to teach it is a terrible mistake. The inescapable conclusion is surely that he knew hell was a reality.

## The teaching of the New Testament writers

*They teach the need for church discipline.* It is important for Church discipline to be carried out in the right spirit.

(i) *Negative gossip and slander are sinful*
Paul lists 'gossips and slanderers' as those God has given over to depravity (Rom. 1:29–30). He condemns 'quarrelling, jealousy, outbursts of anger, factions, slander, gossip, arrogance and disorder' (2 Cor. 12:20). Similarly he urges the Ephesian Christians to 'get rid of all bitterness, rage and anger, brawling and slander, along with every form of malice' (Eph. 4:31).

(ii) *Judgmental attitudes are sinful*
Paul urges the Roman Christians not to judge one another because we shall all be judged by God. He says similar things to the Corinthians (1 Cor. 4:5).

(iii)   *Nursing resentment is sinful*

'The Lord's servant must not quarrel; instead, he must be kind to everyone, able to teach, not resentful' (2 Tim. 2:24; cf. Lev. 19:17–18).

(iv)   *Bear with your brother*

See Col. 3:13: 'Bear with each other.' We are not to be hard, critical and irritable but kind and merciful; ready to forgive.

(v)   *Restore him gently*

Jesus taught that we should approach him privately (Matt. 18:15). Paul adds that the correction should be gentle (Gal. 6:1; cf. Jas. 5:19–20). It is clear also from Jesus' teaching that the penitent should be readily forgiven (Matt. 18:21–22,35; Luke 17:3–4).

(vi)   *Discipline the persistently impenitent*

Those who call for the restoration of church discipline are often accused of being judgmental. I find this rather tiresome. The 'accusers' quote Matthew 7:1 'Do not judge, or you too will be judged.' But the interesting fact is that wherever the New Testament urges us not to judge it tells us to judge in the context. For example, in Matthew 7:15–16 we are urged to watch out for false prophets. In v. 6 we are told to be discerning about those with whom we share our treasures. In v. 5 when the plank is removed from our eye we can deal with the speck in the brother's eye. Similarly in Romans 14:10,13 Paul tells us not to judge, but in Romans 16:17–18 he says: 'I urge you, brothers, to watch out for those who cause divisions and put obstacles in your way that are contrary to the teaching you have learned. Keep away from them. For such people are not serving our Lord Christ, but their own appetites. By smooth talk and flattery they deceive the minds of naive people.'

In 1 Corinthians 4:5 Paul tells them to judge nothing before the appointed time (when the Lord comes). But in 5:11–13 he says: 'I am writing to you that you must not associate with anyone who calls himself a brother but is sexually immoral or greedy, an idolater or a slanderer, a drunkard or a swindler. With such a man do not even eat. What business is it of mine to judge those outside the church? *Are you not to judge those inside?* God will judge those outside. Expel the wicked man from among you.'

Paul says the Corinthians are to hand this man over to Satan so that his sinful nature may be destroyed and his spirit saved (5:5) and he says he has done this with Hymenaeus and Alexander so that they be taught not to blaspheme. It seems that this involves the people concerned losing at least some of the protection of the Lord, and that the resulting pressures will lead them to repentance.

The New Testament clearly teaches that being judgmental (suspicious and tending to jump to conclusions) is wrong. However we are to make right, spiritual judgments of people's teaching and behaviour. So we are to keep away from people who are idle and disobedient (2 Thess. 3:6,14–15) or divisive (Tit. 3:10). Paul is strong in his condemnation of false teachers in the church. Of those preaching another 'gospel' he says 'Let them be eternally condemned' (Gal. 1:8–9). Similarly 2 John 10–11 commands us not to welcome or give hospitality to a teacher who denies the incarnation: 'Anyone who welcomes him shares in his wicked work.' The aim of keeping away from people who persist in disobeying the Lord is to make them feel ashamed, not regarding them as enemies but warning them as brothers (1 Thess. 5:14–15). To fail to do this is as unloving as not to discipline.

(vii) *Restore a disciplined brother who becomes penitent*
Paul urges this on the Corinthians lest the disciplined brother becomes 'overwhelmed by excessive sorrow' (2 Cor. 2:5–11). The clear implication of the passage is that he had repented.

(viii)  *Applying New Testament discipline today*
Jesus makes it clear that the whole church needs to
be involved in the disciplinary process (Matt.
18:17). So it is of primary importance to teach the
congregation about godly discipline. It needs to be
established that every member is accountable. So if
someone manifests unbiblical behaviour he will be
gently corrected and biblical teaching is seen to be a
practical rule of life, not merely an agreed theory
(see p. 99). If the offender ignores all approaches
and is regarded as out of fellowship (Matt. 18:17)
then, in the Church of England, this may involve
excommunication (which involves the bishop) or
may involve loss of non-statutory privileges such as
membership of a housegroup or involvement in
some job or ministry in the church. There should of
course be ready forgiveness and restoration when
the offender does repent.

*They teach the coming judgment of God.* Paul teaches that
the wrath of God is already revealed against all godlessness
and wickedness (Rom. 1:18). The wrath of God is not an
uncontrolled rage or bad temper but a consistent holy
reaction against sin. Those who suppressed the truth about
God by their wickedness were given over to sinful desires,
lust, idolatry and a depraved mind. Although Paul emphasises homosexual practice he also lists many other sins
(Rom. 1:18–32). In fact all who break the law are under a
curse (Gal. 3:10,13). 'Neither the sexually immoral nor
idolaters nor adulterers nor male prostitutes nor homosexual offenders nor thieves nor the greedy nor drunkards
nor slanderers nor swindlers will inherit the kingdom of
God' (1 Cor. 6:9–10; cf. Eph. 5:5–6; Col. 3:5–6). However
Paul points out that some of the Corinthians have been
delivered from such things by the cross of Christ (1 Cor.
6:11), so forgiveness is available for the penitent.
     The final judgment of God is on a fixed day in the future
(Acts 17:30–31; 24:25). After death men have an appoint-

ment with God as judge (Heb. 9:27). This day of the Lord will come like a thief in the night, with cataclysmic results (2 Pet. 3:7,10). The Lord Jesus will be 'revealed from heaven in blazing fire with his powerful angels. He will punish those who do not know God and do not obey the gospel of our Lord Jesus. They will be punished with everlasting destruction and shut out from the presence of the Lord' (2 Thess. 1:7–9; cf. 2:8–12; Jude 14–15).

'Nothing in all creation is hidden from God's sight. Everything is uncovered and laid bare before the eyes of him to whom we must give account' (Heb. 4:13). So God judges impartially and justly (1 Pet. 1:17; 2:23). We Christians will all stand before the judgment seat of Christ, give an account of our lives and receive what is due to us (Rom. 14:10–13; 2 Cor. 5:10). We must remember that God is a 'consuming fire' (Heb. 12:29) and heed the warning of judgment (Heb. 12:25), 'for it is time for judgment to begin with the family of God' (1 Pet. 4:17). 'If we deliberately keep on sinning after we have received the knowledge of the truth, no sacrifice for sins is left, but only a fearful expectation of judgment and of raging fire that will consume the enemies of God' (Heb. 10:26–31). We must make allowances for the highly apocalyptic language of the book of Revelation. However it does clearly speak of divine judgment through famine, plague, cosmic disturbance and earthquakes, which are related to the wrath of God and Christ (Rev. 6, esp. vv. 16–17). Similar judgments are described in Chapters 8,9,15,16. These are seen as the righteous judgments of God (Rev. 16:5–7; 19:1–3).

However for Christians it is true that 'God did not appoint us to suffer wrath but to receive salvation through our Lord Jesus Christ' (1 Thess. 5:9). 'Since we have now been justified by his blood, how much more shall we be saved from God's wrath through him?' Rom. 5:9. Even so we shall all stand before the judgment seat of Christ to receive what is due to us for things done while in the body, good or bad (2 Cor. 5:10). Some believers will 'suffer loss' but will be saved, although 'only as one escaping through the flames' (1 Cor. 3:15). These facts will also be a great incentive to evangelism.

*They teach the present judgment of God.* We have already noted that Jesus saw the destruction of Jerusalem in AD 70 as the result of centuries of rebellion by the Jewish people, culminating in the rejection of their Messiah. He also warned the healed invalid to stop sinning so that nothing worse happened to him. There are other examples of personal misfortune being seen as judgment on personal sin. Ananias and Sapphira were struck dead because they 'lied to the Holy Spirit' by falsely claiming to have given to the church all the money they had made on a property deal (Acts 5:1–11). Herod was struck by a fatal disease because he had accepted the crowd's attempt to proclaim him a god (Acts 12:21–23). Elymas the sorcerer was struck with temporary blindness for opposing Paul's ministry (Acts 13:6–12).

Paul teaches that God 'hardens whom he wants to harden' (Rom. 9:18). He uses the example of Pharaoh and the judgments meted out to him because of his hard-heartedness. Similarly Israel has experienced 'hardening' (Rom. 11:7,25). 'Those of mankind who suppressed the truth about God by their wickedness were "given over" by God to sinful desires and lusts, and a depraved mind' (Rom. 1:24,26,28). It is instructive to note that the Gentiles are said to have given themselves over to sensuality (Eph. 4:17–19). Similarly in Exodus Pharaoh is said both to be hardened by God (7:3; 9:12; 10:20,27; 11:10; 14:4) and to have hardened himself (8:15,32; 9:34). It seems therefore that God often works out his sovereign purpose of judgment through the decisions which men make themselves. A parallel on the positive side is Philippians 2:12–13: 'continue to work out your salvation with fear and trembling, for it is God who works in you to will and to act according to his good purpose'. Here again the sovereignty of God and the decisions of man are inextricably linked.

Finally Paul warns the Corinthians that, because of the

division, selfishness and lovelessness amongst them, they were unworthy in their approach to communion. He points out that as a result some of them have become sick and others even died (1 Cor. 11:17–34). Here again the New Testament regards sickness (in some cases) as a judgment on personal sin.

# The Sentiment and Cynicism of Man

Through sentiment and cynicism some Christians undermine belief in God's sovereignty in judgment. Because of this unbalanced view of God, which neglects or rejects the sternness of his love, many Christians have inadequate views of human authority and discipline, and lower their biblical standards of behaviour. We shall now look at three areas in which this tendency is predominant.

## An unwillingness to practise church discipline

In 1986 Canon Roy Yin of Singapore Cathedral preached a sermon in which he suggested that non-Christians could qualify for heaven. Some days later he received a letter from the bishop complaining that he had departed from biblical teaching and disturbed many in the congregation. In May 1987 the canon complained to the Archbishop of Canterbury that he was no longer asked to preach at the cathedral. The Archbishop raised the matter with the bishop.[1]

What a contrast this makes with the Church of England where a man who denies aspects of the creed is made bishop, and a clergyman who denies the existence of an objective metaphysical God is still allowed to minister within the church. The only encouraging signs are the recent statements by a few bishops that they will practise discipline concerning practising homosexual clergy and ordinands. Writing in his diocesan letter of December

1986, the Bishop of Southwark says: 'Anyone who resists authority runs the risk of punishment or censure. But in our church there is a long and honourable history of not using the law to stifle dissent, but relying on persuasion and the appeal of the mind of the whole church.' If the bishop is referring to secondary issues such as aspects of ceremonial or details of liturgy, well and good. But sadly this liberal attitude is adopted by the church towards clergymen who deny basic beliefs or live immoral lives.

Bishop Michael Baughen of Chester writes:

> All across the church, and not confined to evangelicals, are those who have had that opening up of their eyes to the truth of God by the Holy Spirit and need to show patience towards those who may be in a position, even of authority, within local churches but are still to a large extent spiritually blind. We do not condemn someone for being blind; we try to help them . . . we can end up as judgmental as verses 3,4,10 and 13 of (Romans) 14 demonstrate. Rather (14:9) we should aim at upbuilding (15:2) to edify him. It is not an easy path to walk. There must be a form of judgment regarding the truth of the Gospel. We have, for instance, the passage in Galatians 2:11 where Paul opposed Peter to his face because he 'stood condemned'.[2]

It is true that patience is required. I know from experience that some clergy have been brought up in a church which either takes a very liberal view of scripture or hardly refers to it at all. They go off to theological college where sometimes they are given more liberal theology, but very little teaching of the content of the Bible. Then in their turn they go out to parishes to reproduce the same approach as the churches they grew up in. I know this is true from the testimony of clergy who have subsequently experienced the renewing power of the Holy Spirit. This has brought them into an experience of relationship with Christ and the dynamic power of the Word of God. When this happens it is, to say the least, well worth waiting for patiently.

However there is a serious problem: what about the congregations and parishes which are not hearing the gospel (or are perhaps hearing denials of it) while we wait? The New Testament would clearly take a strong line on this. And what about those clergy and bishops determined to continue denying the truth of various vital biblical truths? The New Testament would surely call for discipline, if all else failed. Of course the church is mainly at fault, rather than the individual. If selection procedures were more biblical and spiritually discerning, such men would not reach leadership until they were living and teaching biblical Christianity.

As we have seen, the Bishops' Report on *The Nature of Christian Belief* in effect makes belief in the virgin birth and the empty tomb optional. I know many bishops do believe in those two doctrines, but why, with all the other bishops on General Synod, sign the report? Why not sign a minority report while still commending the great deal of good material in the main Report? Again the reason is an unwillingness to grasp the nettle of church discipline or to appear to exclude anyone. The Church of England prides itself on its inclusive nature.

The Report points out that 'if the Church of England does not proceed against its ministers for heresy this comes not from indifference but from a conviction born of experience that such proceedings do more harm than good. It would be foolish to say that there can never be a situation in which it would be right (or, more likely, unavoidable as the last resort) to take such a step. But such cases as there have been in modern times are not encouraging.'[3] This statement is a cause of great concern. It is true that legal proceedings against a heretical or immoral clergyman tend to be complex, highly publicised and possibly unsuccessful. However the question is, are we going to obey the Word of God or not? To proceed against such a clergyman and to fail is excusable. Not to proceed (when all else has failed) is inexcusable.

In January 1987 Chichester Diocesan Synod passed a motion stating:

> The Church of England has always allowed growth in understanding, and also for difference of interpretation of Scripture on secondary matters. However, the Ordained Ministry is committed, through the Ordinal, to uphold, guard and teach the faith contained in the Creeds. We welcome the assurance of the Bishops in their recent statement *The Nature of Christian Belief* (p. 4) that bishops, priests and deacons are only ordained or appointed to office on the basis of a Declaration of Assent, 'made in good conscience and without private reservation', affirming their 'belief in the faith uniquely revealed in the Holy Scriptures and set forth in the Catholic Creeds'.

It rejected the rest of the proposal which reads:

> We ask that anyone in Holy Orders, who can no longer honestly and unequivocally assent to the basic doctrines of this biblical and credal faith which they were ordained to uphold and teach, be encouraged as a matter of conscience to resign their office and/or Orders without ignominy; and that the Church show compassionate understanding and make proper pastoral provision for them. We also request the Bishops to arrange for the periodic public renewal of ordination vows by all those in Holy Orders.

That is typical of the Church of England attitude to church discipline. Dr Edward Norman, Dean of Peterhouse, Cambridge refers to:

> that characteristically English preparedness to put up with almost anything rather than raise principles which

¨might rock the boat – a natural disposition which Englishmen themselves attribute to tolerant realism but which many overseas observers have identified as bone idleness applied to the ideological sphere. [He concludes:] The Church of England may not, at times, appear all that religious, but then the State, pre-occupied as it is with such material considerations as inflation or the level of welfare benefits, does not appear as an institution in pursuit of a higher destiny for its citizens. They are not ill-matched.[4]

How does the man in the street view all this? One indication might be an editorial in the *Sun*, commenting on the appointment of David Jenkins:

> The Church is fighting against falling membership and empty pews in an age of doubt. The Bible says: 'If the trumpet gave an uncertain sound, who shall prepare himself for the battle?' Men without faith themselves can hardly appeal to the faithful. The Anglican Church has no trumpet at all![5]

A clergyman who calls himself 'a catholic' writes about the lack of commitment and discipline in the church:

> It seems to me that the Church of England is committed to a concept of 'pastoral' ministry, both in its structures and its hierarchy, which so fears the idea of 'sects' that it discourages clear proclamation of the gospel and deepening of commitment to our Lord, in favour of folk-religion, which is undemanding, tinged with sentimentality, and at best only sub-Christian. Many of the clergy are themselves embodiments of such a religion. They make no demands and find no adherents; they preach to empty churches . . . How can I believe that baptism has in fact taken place for the child in my arms, when those making promises on his behalf and professing the Christian faith are knowingly making false promises

and committing perjury by claiming to be Christians? I have never heard of a catholic leaving the Church of England over baptism, but I am finding it increasingly difficult to remain.[6]

However the Church of England loses all credibility in not having disciplined Don Cupitt. As we have already noted (pp. 16, 124), he calls himself a Christian Buddhist. He does not believe in an objective deity, but says if such a God exists we should reject him. Obedience is sin and, in the long run, the Fall is a step upwards. He does not think of Jesus as the divine Christ. 'Conservative religion of the sort that sets God authoritatively over the believer . . . is now false religion, for it no longer saves . . .'[7] It seems doubtful whether there is any immense cosmic or supracosmic Creator-Mind. Even if there is, it is hard to see what it or he could have to do with religion.'[8] Concerning the resurrection he says 'a dubiously-evidenced freak event (or even a strongly-evidenced freak event) two thousand years ago is in itself of no religious interest whatsoever'[9] . . . 'Historical' claims about walking corpses and empty tombs are foolish and irrelevant.[10] Cupitt states that: 'Many people do hold that faith rests upon supranaturalist assertions. They hold it so firmly that they cordially approve of the official persecution of theologians who try – ever so gently – to wean them away from their dependency on such ideas.'[11] I certainly do not 'cordially approve of . . . official persecution' but sadly it is necessary to call for Cupitt to be disciplined as a practising clergyman.

## A refusal to recognise God's present judgment

There are two recent examples of this attitude within the church.

### The fire at York Minster

John Habgood, Archbishop of York, wrote to *The Times*,

I feel I must point out the disturbing implications of those letters which somehow seek to link the fire with some remarks made by a bishop-elect on a TV discussion programme. What kind of God do your correspondents believe in? I grant that if we still lived in biblical times, and if it was customary to treat thunderstorms as some kind of messengers from God, then the connection might seem inevitable. But have we learnt nothing in the intervening years about how God works in the world?

Disasters may indeed be messengers, in that they force us to think about our priorities. They drive us back to God. They remind us of mistakes and failures, and they call forth reserves of energy and commitment which might otherwise remain untapped. Disasters also remind us of the fragility of life, and of our human achievements. But to interpret the effect of a thunderstorm as a direct divine punishment pushes us straight back into the kind of world from which the Christian Gospel rescued us.

Is illness a divine punishment? Ought we to ask after a car crash whether the car was carrying some outstanding sinner?[12]

The Archbishop of Canterbury, Robert Runcie, was said by the *Church Times*[13] to have 'firmly rejected a suggestion that the fire might have been caused by divine anger at the consecration of Dr Jenkins'.

Canon Ian Dunlop wrote in the *Church Times*:[14]

Nothing could have brought those protesters into greater disrepute with me than their resorting to this kind of argument [that the fire demonstrated the wrath of God]. If Professor Jenkins or the Archbishop of York had been struck dumb or blind or dead at the consecration, I admit that the coincidence would have been remarkable. But to strike the building two nights later?

The question that forces itself upon me is what sort of God would behave in this way? Presumably this would be no unique instance, not the only occasion on which God expressed his disapproval by lashing out. We must formulate the general principle that God always – or at least normally – expresses his disapproval by lashing out. To posit any general connection between human disobedience and divinely ordained disaster is quite beyond me . . .

There is a sense in which I believe that God's *wrath* expresses itself in human life. Just as virtue is its own reward, so selfishness is its own punishment. But both rewards and punishments are inherent in the process, not arbitrarily imposed from outside. The burning of the Minster would come in the latter category. I do not believe that it was of God.

A letter to the *Church Times*[15] said:

Recently in our town two children were killed by lightning during a thunderstorm, and nine people were injured. Is God passing judgment on them as well as York Minster? Or do we say that one is from God and the other not, because that happens to suit our feelings at the moment. Reading your letters page on this and other issues of conflict, I sometimes wonder what kind of God is worshipped and whether the Church is Christian at all.

Tim Lenton, writing in the *Church of England Newspaper*,[16] pointed out that the parish church of St Mael and St Sulien in Corwen, North Wales had also been struck by lightning and suffered some fire damage. He went on to poke fun at the idea of this expressing divine wrath.

In *The Times*[17] Clifford Longley wrote:

There are no schoolboy photographs of angels with flaming brands on the roof of the Minster last Sunday night; but on the other hand it was not Lincoln Cathedral's roof which caught fire, nor was it three weeks ago

or a month hence. It was York, and it was then. Enough
to unsettle; not enough to prove anything.

Conor Cruise O'Brien wrote about the fire in the *Observer*
under the heading 'Shivers down an agnostic spine'. A man
local to Hawkwell was brought from atheism to believe in
God through the fire. It seems the world is more ready to
believe in the intervention of God in judgment than the
church.

What are we to make of this? The argument is really
about the nature of God, as three of the critics of the 'wrath
of God' view recognise. We have seen that Jesus and the
New Testament writers taught extensively that God is
judge and that hell (eternal separation from God) is a
reality. They also saw judgment in the present: the fall of
Jerusalem related to the centuries of rebellion of Israel
culminating in the rejection of their Messiah; sudden death
through 'lying to the Holy Spirit'; a fatal disease because of
blasphemy; blindness for opposing the ministry of the
gospel; sickness and death because of selfishness, division
and lovelessness in the church. Then there is Revelation
prophesying judgment through famine, plague, cosmic
disturbance and earthquake. Against all these judgments
attributed to God by Jesus and the New Testament, at-
tributing the York fire to God's judgment seems fairly
minor. The New Testament most definitely portrays God as
one who could show his displeasure in such a way. This may
be embarrassing for the critics of the 'wrath of God' view,
but it is fact. So the answer to the question 'What sort of
God do we believe in?' is the God of the New Testament.

How can we tell which events are divine judgment? In a
real sense mankind is under God's judgment because of
human sin. The result is a disordered world where suffering
and disaster can affect the innocent as well as the guilty.
None of us is immune. We believe in the providence of God
but that is no insurance policy against suffering and trouble.
On the contrary, Jesus promises: 'In the world you will
have trouble.' However he goes on, 'But take heart! I have

overcome the world' (John 16:33). With apologies to those theologians who think 'conservatives' have everything tidily worked out and 'all the answers', we all have to live with questions. One of the most profound prayers I know is that of Mother Basilea of the Evangelical Sisterhood of Mary in Darmstadt. It says simply, 'My Father, I do not understand you but I trust you.'

Not all sickness is the result of the personal sin of the sufferer (as Jesus makes clear in John 9:1–3). Not every lightning strike is divine judgment on individuals adversely affected by it. We must look at the circumstances of these happenings and we must also seek prayerfully to hear God about them (see pp. 170ff., 176–178). Some people's theological and philosophical presuppositions shout so loudly about emotive subjects like judgment that they do not take time to hear what God is saying.

The relevant circumstances are in two areas. First there is an examination of the behaviour of the people adversely affected by some traumatic experience. In the case of the York fire, the context is disturbing. A man who publicly denied fundamental aspects of the creed, causing much hurt and scandal throughout the nation and the world was consecrated bishop in the Minster just over 48 hours previously. This was done by the Archbishop of York with dismissal of widespread protest from the church and without even any special requirements being made of the bishop-elect. Instead the service continued and included his affirming the very things he previously (and subsequently) denied. There have been other doubting bishops but David Jenkins was the first to express his doubts so publicly prior to his consecration without any special statement being required of him to correct the situation. Then the Minster caught fire in strange circumstances. This was the first time the Minster was empty (except for the night watchman) after the Archbishop had compounded his error by defending his action before the whole General Synod at the Sunday morning Eucharist. God's mercy is shown in that he allowed the consecration to take place: the

Minster was empty when the fire broke out and only limited damage was done: and that to a building, not people.

Secondly we should examine the circumstances concerning the occurrence itself. In this case they increase the likelihood that the event was a divine intervention. Witnesses described what happened. 'I've never seen anything like it before. There was no rain or thunder. The flashes got brighter and brighter. And they seemed to last for longer than normal lightning would,' said a teacher. 'It was like nothing I've ever seen before. It was forked and there were also big flashes in the sky. And it was coming down from all over the place. It was really quite frightening,' said another man. A third said 'Every so often we would have one very big flash which would travel from the sky down and sometimes, even, you would see some sort of kick-back. The lightning itself was very thin in comparison, but it was shielded with some sort of corona, glowing gas. And as these lightning streaks came towards us – close – this gas, this ionized gas would stay in the air longer with some orangey hue. (The lightning) almost seemed to come from the sky to the ground and then back up into the sky again.'[18]

C. G. Collier, an official at the Meteorological Office Radar Research Laboratory, Malvern wrote to *Weather* magazine in October 1984 about the fire:

Eyewitness reports suggested that the fire began around 0230 BST as a result of one or a number of lightning strikes on part of the church roof. However, there was some doubt as to whether or not a thunderstorm was located close enough to the city of York at the appropriate time . . . However, an isolated (rainfall) cell, which was first observed by the radar at 0156 BST, was also seen in the area of York . . . the cell moved northwards to York, appearing to decrease in intensity slightly and deviate a little to the east *after* passing over the city area . . . this cell was small, and, due to its rapid movement, would not have led to large rainfall accumulations. Since the cloud associated with the cell was not very deep, and the instantaneous rainfall not very heavy, compared with most mature thunderstorms, the cell was really a heavy shower rather than a thunderstorm. It is surprising that it apparently produced such devastating lightning.[19]

In the Spring 1985 edition of the *Chartered Insurance Institute Journal* there was an article on the fire by Peter Jacob, a group executive partner of a leading firm of chartered loss adjusters:

> As well as the insurance community, the government showed considerable interest in the cause of the fire and very detailed investigations have been carried out. Although all of the more common causes of fire – the dropped light, arson, an electrical fault, maintenance work and the like – have been looked at, each has been discarded for want of evidence. The possibility of a lightning strike has attracted much attention, but *there was in fact no evidence that the building had been struck. Currently, the forensic scientists appointed by the insurers are interested in a somewhat rarer climatic phenomenon involving the repeated release of a bound electrical charge from a cloud hovering over the South transept roof.*[20]

Charles Brown, Surveyor of the Fabric at York Minster, wrote in October 1985:

> The evidence of the cause of the fire was non-existent and after the most careful analysis, the official report had to record an open verdict. Lightning was the most likely cause but could not be proved. In fact the report talked not of lightning, but of electrical atmospheric disturbance. *The night had been full of strange flashing light but there was no rain and no thunder which must accompany the high electrical discharge which is usually the cause of fire.*[21]

He refers later[22] to 'The mysterious fire of July 9th 1984'.

So this beautiful historic building was damaged in spite of being as fully protected against lightning and fire as modern technology provides. I do not rejoice at that. However it seems to me that in one event God spoke into various sins of the Church of England:

- Toleration of heresy: it rebuked unbiblical compromise by the Church
- Academic arrogance: it made such academics seem very small.
- Idolatry of buildings: it damaged one of our treasured buildings (such 'idolatry' has often hindered the mission of the church and wasted its resources).

It was clearly redemptive in its intention, not destructive. It was a warning to the church: but one which has largely gone unheeded, even cynically dismissed. What next?

## Acquired Immune Deficiency Syndrome (AIDS)

The AIDS Faith Alliance is composed of three religious groups which favour homosexual practice. It produced a leaflet entitled *Is AIDS God's Wrath?* and more specifically *Is AIDS God's Wrath on homosexuals?* The leaflet states: 'God does not punish through disease . . . Jesus Christ had much to say about the correlation between sin and disease. In the Gospel of John, in just three verses, Christ changed the common assumption that suffering is the direct result of sin.' It quotes John 9:1–3: 'As he went along, he saw a man blind from birth. His disciples asked him, "Rabbi, who sinned, this man or his parents, that he was born blind?" "Neither this man nor his parents sinned," said Jesus.' The leaflet continues: 'We might ask a similar question in our own time: "Do homosexuals get AIDS because of their 'sin'?" Applying Christ's teachings in the Gospel of John, our response would be, "No".'

Archbishop Habgood writes:

However foolish, or immoral, or simply unlucky, AIDS victims may have been, surely no Christian would want to add to their suffering by describing it as some kind of punishment for sin. And if any are tempted to do just this, then it is well to remember where Christ is most likely to be found – among those who think themselves righteous or among those who know themselves to be sinners.[23]

Richard Holloway, Bishop of Edinburgh, thinks the view of AIDS as God's punishment is morally repugnant and illogical, 'it creates a picture of God as an enraged terrorist who fashions and throws bombs at his enemies, no matter who gets injured'. He asks why it is very unlikely to affect lesbians. 'If it is argued that God does reward wickedness so specifically, why is he taking so long to lob something at rapists or child abusers, groups that are infinitely more malign in their effects than gay men?' He asks, 'Can you imagine what it must be like to lie dying, knowing that there are people not far away who think you are getting what you deserve as your body becomes a viral battlefield? This is the central issue for many Christians.'[24]

The report *AIDS, Some Guidelines for Pastoral Care* published by the Board for Social Responsibility states:

Whatever the pastor's view of the morality of differing life styles the prime responsibility is not to obtain agreement of the boundaries of acceptable behaviours, but to reveal God's love for and valuing of each individual. Whatever the attitude of the pastor to homosexuality or drug abuse, the declaration of the love of God in word and action and touch does not require prior penitence on the part of the person with AIDS.[25]

At a conference at Southwark Cathedral on March 2nd 1987 the Bishop of Southwark spoke on 'Is AIDS the judgment of God?':

The idea of God as Judge has been out of fashion recently. That doesn't mean that there is no truth in it, but it at least suggests that we no longer wish to talk about it in the way that earlier generations did . . . (Jesus) does not encourage us to think that God's judgment is an overflow of anger directed at particular individuals by means of a particular illness or a particular accident.

He too quotes John 9:1–2. The bishop then refers to Romans 1 where 'there appears to be a direct link between God's wrath and homosexual practices'. He agrees with C. H. Dodd that God's wrath is a description of the consequences of sin, part of the inevitable cause and effect of a moral universe. He continues:

It is important not to speak of judgment in too impersonal a way, like some moral weighing machine. But it is also important not to make it sound as if each one of us is at the receiving end of a very precise judgment which will account for all the things that go wrong in our life or the suffering we undergo.

The speech concludes:

(1) AIDS is not a personal 'curse' or punishment, visited on individuals one by one . . . (2) AIDS *can* be described as part of God's general judgment on society, as long as we are clear that there are many other things which might be described in the same way: the evil results of drug addiction, alcoholism, the spread of venereal diseases, the rise in violence, the sufferings of the hungry . . . I hope I have said enough to make it clear that there is actually no Biblical or theological foundation whatever for regarding AIDS as the or a particular judgment of God against active homosexuals.

The Diocese of Worcester Board of Social Responsibility produced a leaflet entitled *A Christian Response to AIDS* (April 1987). It states bluntly, 'To believe that AIDS is the wrath of God on AIDS sufferers, is to accuse God of being the source of evil. God does not punish through disease and suffering, whatever the affliction – AIDS, cancer, arthritis or traffic accident.'

Writing in the Roman Catholic newspaper, the *Tablet*, Robert Nugent says that 'the leader of a large Baptist denomination in the United States' says:

that God has created AIDS to 'indicate his displeasure' over the acceptance by Americans of the homosexual life style. Nor are Catholic representatives of this position lacking. The Cardinal Archbishop of Philadelphia twice publicly declared that AIDS is an 'act of vengeance' of God for an immoral life style. The theological and pastoral implications of such positions are horrendous, to say nothing of the image of God which they project.

He goes on to quote Archbishop Raymond Hunthausen of Seattle as saying: 'given that our God is a God of love, we as Christians can in no way claim that AIDS is a punishment from God. This kind of explanation would be quite unworthy of our God.'[26]

Archbishop Habgood criticised James Anderton (Manchester police chief) who claimed the AIDS crisis was a result of gays, drug addicts and prostitutes 'swirling around in a human cesspit of their own making'. The archbishop said: 'Such comments had only succeeded in driving sufferers underground and away from seeking vital medical treatment . . . If one goes too far in stressing fear and guilt, one is simply adding to the burden which sufferers already have to bear and one is making notification of AIDS much less possible'.[27] Similarly the *Methodist Recorder* referred to the views of the Memorials Committee of the Methodist Conference: 'The opinions of the Chief Constable of Manchester, about the wrath of God, are not regarded by the committee as an adequate expression of Christian concern about AIDS. The harshness of such comments will not encourage those suffering from AIDS to come forward for testing.'[28]

Chris Medcalf, Director of Turnabout, the evangelical counselling service for homosexuals, who sees homosexual practice as wrong, does not see AIDS as judgment. If it were, he says:

> we would have to say that it was wildly inaccurate, and that God was 'missing' the target group. Many people who have never sinned homosexually are suffering or have died, and many more who have sinned homosexually and have been exposed to the virus have escaped the disease . . . Certainly God MAY act in judgment through particular affliction for particular sins (Acts 5:1–11), but we must not presume to know God's mind when we do not know it. The most that we can say is that the risk of catching the disease for the homosexual is a consequence of wrong behaviour, in the same way that other wrong behaviour may lead to the risk of affliction, e.g. lung cancer from smoking, venereal disease from sexual promiscuity, or heart disease from gluttony.[29]

We must now respond to these criticisms of the view that AIDS is divine judgment on a promiscuous generation. It is – in this country – predominantly a homosexual disease because homosexuals tend to be much more promiscuous than heterosexuals. As I shall explain later, I do not regard AIDS as a judgment inflicted personally on each promiscuous individual. However I do regard it as redemptive judgment on an immoral society. In passing though, I want to deal with the false idea that sickness is *never* a personal judgment:

The AIDS Faith Alliance leaflet simply ignores the biblical passages which teach sickness can be a personal judgment (see pp. 230f).

Archbishop Habgood twice regards talk of AIDS being

judgment as adding to the burdens of AIDS sufferers. I understand what he means but this must be weighed against the truly loving obligation, especially when a person is dying, to bring them to repentance and peace with God. He refers to AIDS sufferers as those who know they are sinners. But do they? It is vital that they are reconciled to God, therefore they need to know they are sinners (I refer here particularly to AIDS sufferers who contract the disease through wrong behaviour but, of course, all human beings are sinful). The Methodist comments on James Anderton are open to the same criticism. The General Synod Board for Social Responsibility report is correct in what it states but is seriously unloving not to stress also that guilty AIDS sufferers need to come to repentance and peace with God.

Bishop Richard Holloway caricatures the views of those who hold that AIDS is God's judgment. He asks why God does not also judge rapists and child abusers. Chris Medcalf asks why some innocent people suffer and some guilty of homosexual practice escape. It is a fact of life that some guilty people are punished here and now, others later; still others, not until they stand before God on the day of judgment. (Repentance is, of course, possible at any stage during this life.) We do not know why this is so. God alone knows why. The Psalmist faced this problem in Psalm 73. Why did the guilty sometimes prosper and why did the innocent sometimes suffer? In a fallen world we often suffer as a result of other people's sins. This is tragically so for some who contract AIDS. The Psalmist said, 'When I tried to understand all this, it was oppressive to me, till I entered the sanctuary of God; then I understood their final destiny' (that is, of the wicked; Ps. 73:16–17). In terms of New Testament references to judgment, innocent Jews and Christian believers were all adversely affected by the fall of Jerusalem. Yet they did not deserve such judgment.

The Bishop of Southwark is right in what he says about judgment being inherent in the way things are in a moral universe. But he is wrong to deny that sickness can be a personal punishment. The Bible includes the latter.

The Worcester Board of Social Responsibility ignores biblical teaching on judgment, as does the Archbishop of Seattle.

Regarding AIDS as God's judgment on a promiscuous generation does not and should not involve any lack of compassion. Anyone who has seen a documentary about people dying from AIDS cannot fail to be profoundly affected. Young adults with emaciated bodies and staring eyes face the inevitability of death. Fears of the disease isolate the patients as modern-day lepers. Some cases are made all the more poignant by their desperate involvement with some of the more bizarre forms of alternative medicine. Whatever one's view of the morality of homosexual practice, sexual promiscuity or drug abuse through which many contract AIDS, one's reaction to the individual sufferer can only be practical compassion. They need to experience the love and healing ministry of Christ.

But various important questions arise. Are those who justify homosexual practice the only ones to show compassion? True there are Christians who suffer from homophobia – a tendency to reject the homosexual person as well as homosexual practice. That is un-Christlike. So is 'heterophobia' – the irrational antagonism shown by many homosexuals to heterosexuals, especially those who believe the Bible teaches homosexual acts are sinful. But many who are convinced that scripture condemns homosexual practice seek to show a Christlike love to the homosexual and especially to the AIDS sufferer.

Another important question is what is Christlike compassion anyway? Is it true that the AIDS Faith Alliance, for example, is fostering, as it claims, 'a truly loving religious response to the problem of AIDS'? I do not doubt that they give a great deal of practical care and emotional support to AIDS sufferers. Perhaps sometimes they pray for healing (both physical and emotional) in the name of Christ. Like Christ they reach out to touch the 'leper'. But Christ's redeeming love and compassion includes another crucial element which it appears the AFA omits. In contrast to the hypocrites who only wanted to condemn her, Jesus showed acceptance and forgiveness to the woman caught in the act of adultery, *but* he told her to go and leave her life of sin (John 8:11; cf. John 5:14). Confronted with the paralytic Jesus gave him absolution before healing him physically (Mark 2:1–12). Christ can also bring healing to the emotional deprivations and traumas which some claim are contributory causes of homosexuality and can give spiritual strength for self-discipline in sexuality, which is of course required by heterosexuals too.

It is not loving to the practising homosexual and especially to the AIDS sufferer who contracted the disease through homosexual activity, sexual promiscuity or drug abuse to omit dealing sensitively and lovingly but definitely with the sin involved. The need to encourage penitence and then declare God's forgiveness is just as necessary in a loving ministry to the AIDS sufferer as is healing, acceptance and practical support. Peace with God through repentance and absolution is vital, especially in one facing death. To deny this by neglect, by false compassion, by justifying or even denying the sin is unloving. Although no one can earn healing, experience teaches that unconfessed sin can be a barrier against receiving Christ's gift of healing. It is certainly a barrier to peace with God.

The AFA claims to convey the message of 'the redeeming love of Christ to the gay community'. But unless they encourage the latter (as everyone else) to turn away from the sins for which Christ died including the sin of homosexual practice (Rom. 1:26–27; 1 Cor. 6:9–10; 1 Tim. 1:9–10) their message is fundamentally flawed. It is true that homosexual practice is only one of many sins, as these passages show, and it is forgivable – but that does not justify it.

I do not see AIDS as a judgment personally and indi-

vidually inflicted upon each promiscuous person. Rather I
see that God in his wisdom has chosen at this time to allow
this disease to develop within our promiscuous generation.
It is primarily spread by the misuse of the human body.
God's judgment is 'written into' the way things are. Misuse
of God's creation renders a person vulnerable to inherent
divine judgment. (This applies to other than sexual sins and
other results than AIDS.) The fact that AIDS is a new
disease indicates God has chosen to remove his protection
from our generation in this respect. AIDS is rapidly becoming pandemic but could be eliminated within a few years if
the vast majority adopted biblical standards of sexual
behaviour. It can therefore be seen as primarily an act of
redemptive judgment – to call our generation back to God
and his standards. The church must proclaim this prophetic
message, otherwise whole nations could be decimated.

Above all the Church should proclaim and demonstrate
the redeeming love and healing ministry of Christ to those
suffering the results of their sins. He bore our condemnation (Gal. 3:13; 1 Pet. 2:24). So there is no condemnation
for those who repent and are united with Christ by faith
(Rom. 8:1).

## A refusal to believe in eternal separation from God

John Hick, Professor of Theology at Birmingham University, writes:

> The contrast between the bad news of a God who
> deliberately makes creatures for whom he must also
> make a hell, and the good news of the God of love heard
> in the parables and sayings of Jesus, is so great that I
> cannot regard them both as true; and every instinct of
> faith, hope and charity responds to Jesus' Vision of the
> heavenly Father rather than to that of the omnipotent
> Scientist who deals so cold-bloodedly with his finite
> creatures[30] . . . the doctrine of hell has as its implied

premise either that God does not desire to save all his human creatures, in which case he is only limitedly good, or that his purpose has finally failed in the case of some – and indeed, according to the theological tradition, most – of them, in which case he is only limitedly sovereign.[31]

He believes this compels us to repudiate the idea of eternal punishment.

The rejection of the idea of a divine sentence of eternal suffering is not in itself equivalent to universalism (the ultimate salvation of all human souls), for there remains a third possibility of either the divine annihilation or the dwindling out of existence of the finally lost. In this case there would not be eternally useless and unredeemed suffering such as is entailed by the notion of hell as unending torment.[32]

However, Hick prefers another alternative,

namely that God will eventually succeed in his purpose of winning all men to himself in faith and love . . . The least that we must say, surely, is that God will never cease to desire and actively to work for the salvation of each created person. He will never abandon any as irredeemably evil. However long an individual may reject his maker, salvation will remain an open possibility to which God is ever trying to draw him . . . It seems morally (although still not logically) impossible that the infinite resourcefulness of infinite love working in unlimited time should be eternally frustrated, and the creature rejects its own good, presented to it in an endless range of ways.[33]

Don Cupitt says, 'It is spiritually important that one should not believe in life after death.'[34] He continues, 'if I make the mistake of supposing that heaven and hell exist and allow fear and hope to determine my conduct, I am ceasing to be moral.'[35]

Anyone who claims to believe in hell and can speak of it without a sense of deep sorrow and horror at its reality, either does not really believe in it or seriously lacks love. But the question remains – are we going to determine what we believe by human reasoning and feeling or are we going to submit to the sovereignty of God in revelation? Jesus and the New Testament writers clearly believed in hell. To say that Jesus was a man of his age and therefore knew no better than to believe in hell is surely blasphemous arrogance. To say that he simply used the current language about hell for effect, without meaning it, is surely to accuse him of being deeply unloving, because clearly his hearers would take him to believe in eternal separation from God in hell. To say that these comments were actually alien to Jesus' teaching but were put into his mouth by the gospel writers does not say much for their integrity. And this opinion is based upon a subjective theological presupposition (see Part I).

Although we may wrestle emotionally and theologically with the concept of hell and its implications, the fact is that Jesus and the New Testament writers believed in it. We are therefore not at liberty to reject it. God respects man's free will, including when he chooses to reject his creator. As Professor S. H. Hooke puts it, 'The torment of hell consists in the consciousness of a self-imposed separation from God.'[36] One might add that this consciousness is without repentance.

## Submitting to God's Sovereignty in Judgment

We have examined how the New Testament teaches that God is judge. It speaks of the 'wrath' of God – a consistent holy reaction against sin. It describes the present and coming judgment and sternness of God. In this chapter we give some practical guidance as to how to gain a balanced view of the two sides of God's nature.

### Reject the humanistic view of God

Reject the modern sentimental idea that God's love is solely gentle and kind. Jesus is the ultimate revelation of God and he shows us sternness as well as kindness. We have noted (pp. 221–225) his devastating criticism of religious hypocrites; his firm rebuke of his disciples; his call for church discipline and his clear teaching on divine judgment and hell.

### Submit to a fully biblical description of God

This means seeing him as:

*Father.* It is vital for Christians to have a heartfelt belief in the kindness of God's love, such as we briefly alluded to (pp. 220ff.). Meditate on those and other similar passages, asking the Holy Spirit to impress them upon your mind and heart. If there are emotional blockages to your truly accepting this (for example hurts inflicted by your human father), ask God for healing. It may be necessary to seek some experienced person to pray for inner healing. Even some of those who vehemently reject the sternness of God's love may not, deep down, really believe he loves them personally in the way the Bible teaches he does. A belief in the kindness of God's love is vital for a properly balanced view of God. Otherwise believing in God's sternness can become a harsh, vindictive concept.

*Judge.* It is equally vital to have a heartfelt belief in the sternness of God's love. Meditate on the other biblical material we have examined, asking God to impress it upon your heart and mind. Ask him to help you deal with any fears or resistance to this teaching you may experience. If necessary seek the help of someone you know to believe in this side of God's character.

## Ask God to purify your human love with his divine compassion

This will involve two aspects:

(a) Renouncing human sentiment in situations calling for firmness or rebuke. Jesus says, 'If your brother sins, rebuke him' (Luke 17:3).
(b) Renouncing gossip, slander, judgmental attitudes and resentment, which can undermine human love (see pp. 225ff.). Such attitudes may be in place of a willingness to be firm or may make an attempt to be firm become harsh and unloving.

## Accept the responsibility of mutual correction within the body of Christ

Instead of gossip or resentment begin to accept some responsibility for the growth of holiness in your friends in the church. Have the courage to correct them gently when necessary. Have the humility to seek and receive their gentle correction. We are to restore an erring brother gently (Gal. 6:1) and to bring him back to the truth (Jas. 5:19).

## Support the practice of godly discipline

Self-discipline is of course primary. Then there is discipline of children, inside and outside the home. There is also church discipline. Meditate on what Jesus and the New Testament writers teach on this (see pp. 223, 226–8) and be prepared to support the church in carrying out discipline when necessary. If you are in responsibility in the church, ask God to deal with your fears of unpopularity and of negative reactions. Decide to go the way of faith and obedience to the Word of God, leaving the consequences to God. Moral support, prayer and advice from a Christian leader experienced in this area is a great help.

## Teach about God as judge

You will not want to continually roast people over hell with fire and brimstone sermons. But it is neither obedient to God nor loving to people (Christians or non-Christians) to omit teaching on God as judge, final judgment, heaven and hell. The Alternative Service Book funeral service retains a prayer that we should be spared 'the bitter pains of eternal death'. How terrible to think of people standing one day before the judgment seat of God when we had not warned them in a loving way.

## Stress the need of repentance

Sin is serious. It presumes upon the kindness of God and is an affront to his holiness. We should practise and teach the depth of repentance David expressed in Psalm 51. He saw his sin as ultimately against God and justifying God's judgment (v. 4). He comes before God with 'a broken spirit, a broken and contrite heart' (v. 17).

## *Ask for a sense of urgency in evangelism*

There are various motives for evangelism. The reality of
God's judgment and hell is one of them, and it should add
urgency to our efforts. To say we believe in these truths and
not to be urgent in evangelism is to be either self-deceived
or disobedient.

# Conclusion: Our God Reigns Over the Future

We have looked in some detail at five major areas of Christian belief. In conclusion it is important to regain a sense of perspective. For some years in Hawkwell we have summarised our message in terms of 5 Rs.

## Repentance

Although God is much more willing to forgive than we are to repent, yet repentance is not just some quick, superficial apology. It is seeing our sin silhouetted against the brightness of God's glory: he who dwells in unapproachable light. It is remembering that (as we saw in Part II) he is the almighty, sovereign Creator who spoke the universe into existence and sustains all things by his powerful word. On the one hand we should remember our creatureliness as we bow in awe before him. On the other we recall the dignity for which he specially created us in his image: a dignity we so often fail to achieve or maintain. We are also bound to remember our accountability as the high point of his creation. For (as in Part V) he is the judge before whom we must stand and give account. Repentance is therefore a deep and solemn subject. Yet remembering God's infinite kindness (as we did briefly in Part V) the confidence of being forgiven makes repentance bear the promise of joy.

## Renewal

In the last twenty-five years the church has experienced a move of God's Spirit unparalleled since Pentecost. It has been truly worldwide and has affected every denomination of the Christian church. Charismatic Renewal is still spreading, and some estimate that 85 per cent of Christians will have had a charismatic experience by the end of the century. The work of the Spirit is the real answer to liberalism, radicalism and general unbelief. The effects of Renewal are various:

It renews (or creates) an appreciation of biblical authority – though not a dead neurotic orthodoxy. I know of those from a thoroughly liberal background who have suddenly come to a conservative appreciation of scripture through Renewal. We can expect this for the Holy Spirit is the Spirit of truth who inspired scripture (see Part I).

It renews (or creates) an expectancy and experience of miracles. The old unbelief and rationalistic cynicism fades away, being replaced by an anticipation of divine intervention. We can expect this because the Holy Spirit is the Spirit of power.

It renews a devotion and allegiance to the Christ of the Bible: a new intimacy of relationship with him, a new certainty that the fulness of salvation is in him and only in him (as in Part III). This is to be expected as the Spirit is the Spirit of Christ who glorifies Christ.

## Restoration

Sadly this word has recently been narrowed in its meaning to the approach of certain strands in the housechurch movement. However it is a good word for the rest of the church to use. I use it to refer to the restoring of the church to biblical principles, by the power of the Spirit. We saw some of them in Part IV: obedience and holiness, power and praise, prayer and discernment, commitment to one another and to mission. I want to affirm, loud and clear, that such restoration can be achieved, albeit imperfectly, within existing denominations such as the Church of England. It has been our experience of what God has done in Hawkwell. And because he has done it, he gets the credit.

But what are repentance, renewal and restoration all about? Ultimately of course they enable us to glorify God more effectively. That will always be the first priority. But is the only other purpose to have a more joyful, pure, powerful, exciting and biblical fellowship? Looking at some churches, one might be forgiven for answering yes. But that is a travesty of the truth. Similarly the ultimate purpose of this book is not to encourage the church to be more biblically orthodox and spiritually powerful. No, second to glorifying God the purpose in both cases is to further his mission to the world. It is estimated that over half the population of the world have never heard of Jesus: some calculate about 2.7 billion people. It is for this reason that we must stop playing church, whether it be a stale theoretical, evangelical orthodoxy; an arid, irrelevant liberalism; a barren, ritualistic catholicism or a burnt out, introspective pentecostalism.

The God we believe in 'wants all men to be saved and to come to a knowledge of the truth' (1 Tim. 2:4). Is he going to wait for the Christian church to win the unevangelised billions? He certainly requires the church to go all out to achieve this, but God is both a realist and a merciful Father. It is the conviction of many Christians that, because of the desperate spiritual needs of the world, God is planning a new and greater move of the Spirit. That is why he is renewing the Church and restoring it to biblical principles, so that when the new move of the Spirit occurs at least a large number of churches will be ready to disciple the new believers. We call this new move of the Spirit a revival.

## Revival

This has happened at various times in history. The history
of revivals is instructive but we must not assume that what
God does in the future will be identical with what happened
in the past. However, revival is such a powerful move of the
Holy Spirit that many thousands are brought into the
kingdom of God by it – often without any human mediation
such as evangelism. It has been defined as 'an outpouring of
the Holy Spirit upon a prepared people of God, and the
subsequent flow of spiritual power through them to the
inhabitants of the surrounding district, so that sometimes a
whole locality or even the whole nation is transformed'.[1]
This took place for example in England in the time of
Wesley.

But we cannot sit back and wait for it to happen.
Although revival is a sovereign act of God we should not
just assume it will happen without our obeying the prompt-
ing of the Holy Spirit to prepare for it. Essential preparation is by persistent sacrificial prayer, as well as repentance,
renewal and restoration.

Some Christians on the other hand believe we face
judgment, not revival. The result could be, as often in
church history, Christians arguing with one another about
the two possibilities. Yet I believe both are true. Because I
believe we live in the end times it is exceptionally urgent
that the unevangelised billions in the world should be
reached. I believe therefore that God has a plan for revival.
However, just to speak of this country, we live in a society
which has slaughtered two and a half million unborn babies
(the vast majority without any justification) since 1967.
Their blood cries out to God for judgment. The flood of
homosexual practice and propaganda as well as heterosexual promiscuity and perversion is engulfing our nation.
Then there is the violence, the godless materialism, the
selfishness vis-à-vis the poor at home and especially in the
third world while we spend billions on weapons. The nation
is already under judgment with much more to come, and, as

usual, it will begin at the house of God. Unless the church repents I believe we shall see this judgment working out within the next few years.

So I believe that revival and judgment will go hand in hand. Jesus foretold that in the end times, 'because of the increase of wickedness, the love of most will grow cold' (Matt. 24:12). We can therefore expect great apostasy and falling away from God. But those individuals and churches who 'endure to the end' will be used by God in his purpose of reaching those who have never heard. The division between these and the formal traditional church will become so acute that the latter may persecute the former.

All of this needs to be viewed against the background of the return.

## Return

That is, the return of Christ as so extensively foretold in the New Testament (see p. 109). When Christ first came only two old people (Simeon and Anna) had the spiritual discernment to recognise the fact. (The shepherds had an angelic choir and the wise men the star!) History is likely to repeat itself regarding the signs leading to the second coming, given the cynicism of many in the church: 'Where is this "coming" he promised? Ever since our fathers died, everything goes on as it has since the beginning of creation' (2 Pet. 3:4). Such scoffing will be a characteristic of the last days (2 Pet. 3:3). People point out that Christians throughout history have often thought they were living in the last days. For example they have thought that various evil figures like Hitler were the antichrist, only to be proved wrong – or were they? John points out that many antichrists had come in his day (1 John 2:18). Prophecy throughout scripture can have a multiple reference. Hence the antichrist concept can rightly refer in a secondary way to numerous historical figures. However, it also has an ultimate fulfilment (see 2 Thess. 2:1–12).

What signs are there that we live in the last days? (Bearing in mind that the last days began at Pentecost [Acts 2:17] we should clarify that by 'last days', strictly, we mean 'the end of the last days', that is, the period shortly before Christ returns). We could, of course, ourselves make these the Last Days. We have the nuclear power to achieve that at any time. It is calculated that we have 6,000 times all the fire power used in the Second World War including the atom bombs. We are living on a time bomb and must thank God for his restraining hand. I cannot but see this as significant as a new factor on the human scene. One can speculate as to whether we could fulfil 2 Pet. 3:12 without supernatural intervention. Jesus himself, in answer to the question, 'What will be the sign of your coming and of the end of the age?' (Matt. 24:3), referred to war as one sign. There have been wars throughout history so what did Jesus mean? Looked at in the context of other 'signs' it cannot be without significance that we live in a century which has seen two horrific world wars and the threat of a third (nuclear) war. Also since 1945 there have been some 200 wars and major armed conflicts throughout the world. Even non-Christians speak of Armageddon as a possibility. (It is perhaps necessary to say that such a prospect is not to be 'welcomed' as an interesting prophetic sign but to be prayed and worked against.)

Jesus also gave another sign of the end of the age. 'Watch out that no-one deceives you. For many will come in my name, claiming, "I am the Christ" and will deceive many . . . Many false prophets will appear and deceive many people. At that time if anyone says to you, "Look, here is the Christ!" or "There he is!" do not believe it. For false Christs and false prophets will appear and perform great signs and miracles to deceive even the elect – if that were possible' (Matt. 24:4–5,11,23–26). There are thousands of cults in the world – including about 100 in this country. Many of them have arisen since the middle of this century. We have seen (Part III) the growth of the occult New Age Movement and its infiltration into the church and otherwise laudable groups such as the conservation movement. We have noted the spiritual dangers of yoga, transcendental meditation, astrology, some rock music, Freemasonry and games such as Dungeons and Dragons – all of which are not only widespread in the world but also in the church. In the New Age Movement we see the widespread expectation of a messiah: but certainly not the Messiah of the Bible. If we link the huge growth in the occult and in cultic prophets and messiahs with the moves towards world government (aided by the peace and interfaith movements) it does not seem unreasonable to say that the stage is being set for the figure Paul refers to in 2 Thessalonians 2. He predicts the rise of the 'lawless one' who will be revealed with 'all kinds of counterfeit miracles, signs and wonders' and who 'opposes and exalts himself over everything that is called God or is worshipped, and even sets himself up in God's temple, proclaiming himself to be God' (2:4,9).

Another prediction Jesus made was concerning the Jewish people. He said, 'They will fall by the sword and will be taken as prisoners to all the nations' (Luke 21:24). This was fulfilled literally in AD 70 with the destruction of Jerusalem by the Romans and the exile of the Jews to all parts of the world. Then Jesus added, 'Jerusalem will be trampled on by the Gentiles until the times of the Gentiles are fulfilled.' It is a fact of life that the survival of the Jewish people is unique. No other people has survived exile from its country for so long. That this people has now set up a nation in its original land after 2,000 years is amazing. In 1967 they regained possession of Jerusalem. Unlike some Christians, I do not ignore the fact that Israel is no more religious than Britain and that she manifests all the sins of a secular state. Nevertheless I cannot but recognise the 1967 regaining of Jerusalem as a fulfilment of Jesus' words.

To rest all this on one verse is precarious. Behind that verse is the prophetic teaching of the Old Testament. For example Isaiah in a context referring to the end times says, 'In that day the Lord will reach out his hand a second time to reclaim the remnant that is left of his people . . . He will raise a banner for the nations and gather the exiles of Israel; he will assemble the scattered people of Judah from the four quarters of the earth' (11:11–16; cf. 43:5–6; 60:4,9,10,21,22). I find any attempt to make such passages refer to any other event in history or to 'spiritualise' them to refer to the church thoroughly unconvincing. Rather such attempts imply God does not keep his promises and they ignore the remarkable 'coincidences' of the survival of the Jewish people and their return in large numbers to the renewed state of Israel.

Paul states: 'I do not want you to be ignorant of this mystery, brothers, so that you may not be conceited: Israel has experienced a hardening in part until the full number of the Gentiles has come in. And so all Israel will be saved' (Rom. 11:25–26; cf. vv. 12,15; Israel in this context clearly bears its literal meaning). God has a purpose in preserving the Jewish people and that is to bring about a widespread turning to Christ. There are, I believe, many evidences that the scene is being set for this. The passages we have looked at refer to 'the times of the Gentiles' being 'fulfilled' and the 'full number of Gentiles' coming in. Such statements, although not yet completely fulfilled, have a thoroughly eschatological sound, pointing to a late stage in the divine plan. They are signs of the end times.

However, our brief glance at some of the signs of the end times would be seriously incomplete without reference to another prediction by Jesus. He said 'this gospel of the kingdom will be preached in the whole world as a testimony to all nations, and then the end will come' (Matt. 24:14). In fact considering the long delay in the fulfilment of prophecies concerning the return of Christ, we are to remember that 'the Lord is not slow in keeping his promises, as some understand slowness. He is patient with you, not wanting anyone to perish, but everyone to come to repentance' (2 Pet. 3:9).

Today we have the technology to reach the whole world with the gospel. Satellite TV, radio, literature, and modern transport make the world a global village. We also have a renewal of the Holy Spirit's power unparalleled since Pentecost (itself a sign of the end times, I believe). Instead of undermining the message through an arrogant rejection of divine revelation or unwarranted scepticism about scripture, we must proclaim the gospel with conviction and certainty. Instead of capitulating to the denial of God's creative activity, or even his existence, we must point to the God who sustains the universe by his Word. Instead of denying the uniqueness of Christ crucified as the only saviour, we must uncompromisingly proclaim reconciliation through the cross of Christ appropriated by faith as the only way of salvation. Instead of perpetuating a church which is impure, powerless, prayerless, boring, divided and inward-looking, we must forge it into an instrument for spiritual warfare and mission. Instead of deceiving people with a sentimental image of God we must lovingly warn them of the sure prospect of judgment.

Jesus said, 'Yes, I am coming soon' (Rev. 22:20). Our radical obedience to his Word in the power of the Spirit can hasten his return, with its ultimate proof that 'our God reigns'.

# Appendix 1

## Books explaining and defending a high view of scripture

Craig Blomberg, *The Historical Reliability of the Gospels*. IVP, 1987.

F. F. Bruce, *The New Testament Documents: are they reliable?* Eerdmans, 1983.

Leon Morris, *I Believe in Revelation*. Hodder, 1976.

John W. Wenham, *Christ and the Bible*. IVP, 1984.

## Pro-Life organisations

CARE Trust, 21a Down Street, London W1Y 7DN.
  Opposes abortion, provides literature and keeps a register of private families willing to shelter unmarried mothers during pregnancy.

Life, 118–20 Warwick Street, Leamington Spa, Warwicks CV32 4QY.
  Provides literature and a confidential telephone service. Area groups advise on financial, housing, social security and medical problems. Offers private accommodation during pregnancy for unmarried mothers.

Society for the Protection of the Unborn Child (SPUC), 7 Tufton Street, London SW1P 3QN.
  Opposes abortion, provides literature and speakers, keeps a register of private families willing to shelter girls under pressure to have abortions.

## Counselling services for homosexuals

The following Christian counselling agencies are available
to give help and support to homosexuals.

Pilot, c/o Shankill Road Mission, 116 Shankill Road,
Belfast BT13 2BD. 0232-230743.
Provides telephone and personal counselling.

True Freedom Trust, PO Box 3, Upton, Wirral,
Merseyside L49 6NY. 051-653-0773.
Provides a confidential counselling service and a teaching
ministry on homosexuality, for churches and individuals.
The director is Martin Hallett, author of *I am Learning to
Love* (Marshall Pickering, 1987), which describes his
spiritual pilgrimage out of a homosexual lifestyle.

Turnabout, PO Box 592, London SE4 1EF. 01-460-2425.
Provides a similar ministry to TFT but in London and the
Home Counties.

# Appendix 2

## Our vision of the nature and mission of the local church

We aim:

1   To be wholeheartedly committed to Christ as Saviour and Lord (John 20:31; Rom. 10:9).

2   To be baptised in water and regular at Communion (Acts 19:5–6; 1 Cor. 11:23–26).

3   To read the Bible regularly, accepting its authority and acting on it by the power of the Holy Spirit so that the church may be made more true to the Bible under the Lordship of Christ (2 Tim. 3:16–17).

4   To seek personally and to encourage others to seek the release of the Baptism of the Holy Spirit as a definite experience, and daily filling with the Spirit, so that our eyes may be open fully to our riches in Christ and the vision God is revealing (Acts 2:17,38–39).

5   To seek personally and to encourage others to seek security in God (which is faith), not in our own understanding, efforts, other people, material things, circumstances or traditional patterns (Prov. 28:26; Jer. 17:5–8; 1 Tim. 6:17).

6   To seek personally and to encourage others to seek that spiritual 'brokenness' before God, so that our wills are submitted to his and his will is all that matters (Matt. 7:21–23). To aim at holiness of life based on the fruit of the Spirit, and to seek for inner healing as necessary, so that there are no barriers to spiritual progress (for example fear of commitment, other

people, circumstances or the future) (Ps. 118:6–9; Matt. 6:25–34).

7 To join regularly in worship and to encourage the building of a worshipping community which will know regularly what it is to adore God, being 'lost in wonder, love and praise' and to express this worship fully (Ps. 100).

8 To learn to intercede for others and to listen often in prayer for God's specific guidance and developing vision for the future (Rom. 8:26–27; Eph. 6:18; Isa. 30:15,18,21).

9 To seek the church's guidance to find our gifts and use them. To encourage the discovery of every member's spiritual gifts and ministries so that all the gifts of the Spirit will operate in the church; that people will only be doing the things which the leaders in the church have helped them to recognise or confirmed that God has called them to and gifted them for (Eph. 4:11–16; 1 Cor. 12).

10 To be deeply committed personally and to encourage others to be deeply committed to the church as a community, not each 'doing his or her own thing' in the rebellious spirit of the age; but aiming to achieve a unity of heart and mind in which the church moves enthusiastically as one in obedience to God so that the world may believe (Eph. 6:21; John 17:21–23).

- To accept the authority of the elders and other leaders, respecting them, obeying them in teaching and advice that the Bible clearly supports and in matters which affect the church (1 Thess. 5:12–13; Heb. 13:17).
- To be completely loyal to one another – keeping confidences, defending one another against negative criticism, not being judgmental or jumping to conclusions about each other (Gal. 5:13–15; Col. 3:12–15).
- To be open and honest with one another, including

giving and receiving prayerful encouragement and correction and putting right any gossip or negative criticism in each other (Matt. 18:15–17; Gal. 6:1–2; Eph. 4:15; Tit. 3:1–2, 10–11; Jas. 5:19–20).

- To encourage the sharing of important personal issues with others, particularly with leaders, confidentially, for prayer and guidance before making a decision (Prov. 12:15; 1 Pet. 5:5).

- To share material things with one another, to give at least a tenth of income to God and to ensure a fellow member is not left in serious financial need (Lev. 27:30; Mal. 3:8–10; Matt. 5:42; 2 Cor. 8:13–15; 9:6–8; 1 John 3:17).

- To encourage the church to become more caring by accepting pastoral responsibility being given to the many rather than the few, so that the church may become a truly loving community and a place where God's healing power will be operating in obvious ways (Matt. 4:18; Eph. 4:16).

- To base family life and to encourage others to base their family life on the biblical principles of love, fellowship, submission and discipline, and to see that single and widowed members are included in families (Eph. 5:22–6:4).

- To be involved regularly in one of the fellowship groups organised by the church (Acts 2:42,46,47; Heb. 10:24–25).


11   To support the church as it invades 'the gate of hell', enabling Christians to recognise and resist the enemy; bringing deliverance to people from bondage to sin, weakness, habit and Satan; by evangelism with 'signs following'; by giving prophetic messages from the Lord to the world (Matt. 16:18–19; 28:18–20; Mark 16:17–18; Amos 3:7–8; Ezek. 3:16–18; Rev. 1:3).

12   To support the church as it stresses the urgency of its mission to the world in the light of the return of Christ,

working with fellowships who share this vision and encouraging other fellowships into the vision (Acts 10:42; 1 Tim. 4:1–2; Heb. 10:24–25).

# Appendix 3

## The gifts of the Holy Spirit

### *General gifts (1 Cor. 12:8–10)*

Any Christian can expect any of these gifts to operate through him at any time. For the messages of wisdom, knowledge, prophecy, tongues and interpretation see p. 43.

(i) *Faith:* a supernatural ability to go beyond general and saving faith, and to believe the 'impossible' will happen (Acts 3:6–7).

(ii) *Gifts of healing:* a supernatural ability to bring Christ's healing and deliverance to those who lack mental, emotional or physical wholeness or are in spiritual bondage. A person may be used more in one aspect than in another (many NT examples).

(iii) *Miracles:* a supernatural ability to bring God's power to bear on an 'impossible' situation so that 'natural laws' are suspended (1 Cor. 12:28 and many other NT examples).

(iv) *Distinguishing spirits:* a supernatural ability to discern whether a particular manifestation comes from the Holy Spirit, the human spirit or a demonic spirit (various NT examples).

### *Gifts some Christians display*

(i) *Helping:* a supernatural ability to bear others' burdens, to strengthen the weak and to support them in prayer (1 Cor. 12:28).

(ii) *Administration:* a supernatural ministry of efficiently organising people and things for the achievement of a common aim. This can be a leadership gift (1 Cor. 12:28).

The following are found in Romans 12:6–8:

(iii) *Serving:* a supernatural ability to serve God and others beyond natural talent and strength.
(iv) *Teaching:* many Christians will be involved in teaching one or more people. But their ministry will not be so extensive and authoritative as the ministry of the Teacher.
(v) *Encouraging:* a supernatural ability to inspire others to give of their best and more than their best through Christ.
(vi) *Contributing:* a supernatural ability to give sacrificially and to manage money.
(vii) *Leadership:* a supernatural ability to lead, making decisions and helping others to fulfil those decisions.
(viii) *Showing mercy:* the supernatural ministry of showing compassion and identifying with those in distress; giving advice, emotional comfort and help.

# Notes

## Chapter 2    The God Who Intervenes

1   *The Nature of Christian Belief*. Church House, London 1986.
2   ibid. para. 65.
3   ibid. para. 50.
4   Interview on *The World at One*, BBC Radio 4, April 4th, 1985.
5   Sermon at St Paul's Cathedral, May 22nd, 1985.
6   General Synod, *Report of Proceedings*, vol. 17, no. 2, p. 467.
7   *Sunday Times*, May 12th, 1985.
8   Don Cupitt, *Taking Leave of God* (SCM, London 1980), p. 8.
9   ibid. p. 14.
10   ibid. p. 103.
11   ibid. p. xii.
12   General Synod, *Report*, op. cit. pp. 476–7.
13   *Sunday Times*, May 12th, 1985.
14   *Credo*, LWT programme, February 23rd, 1985.
15   John Wenham, *Christ and the Bible* (IVP, Leicester 1984), pp. 172–3.
16   General Synod, *Report*, op. cit. pp. 488–9.
17   ibid. p. 457.
18   ibid. pp. 466–8.
19   *Credo*, op. cit.
20   *Sunday Telegraph*, June 8th, 1986.
21   J. B. Phillips, *The New Testament in Modern English* (Collins, London 1975), p. 421.

## Chapter 3    The God Who Speaks

1   Wenham, *Christ and the Bible* (op. cit.), pp. 181–2.
2   F. F. Bruce, *The New Testament Documents: are they*

*reliable?* rev. edn (Eerdmans, Grand Rapids, Michigan 1960), p. 13.

3   ibid. p. 14.
4   ibid. pp. 46–61.
5   ibid. pp. 55–7.
6   ibid. pp. 57f.
7   ibid. p. 58.
8   ibid. p. 60 ff.
9   ibid. p. 20; qu. J. A. T. Robinson, *Redating the New Testament* (SCM, London 1976).
10  K. A. Kitchen, *The Bible and its World* (The Paternoster Press Ltd, Exeter 1977), p. 131.
11  Donald Guthrie, *New Testament Introduction* (Tyndale, London 1962), p. 43.
12  ibid. p. 88.
13  ibid. p. 120.
14  ibid. p. 173.
15  ibid. pp. 205–21.
16  ibid. p. 233.
17  ibid. p. 269.
18  General Synod, *Report*, op. cit. p. 469.
19  ibid.
20  ibid. p. 470.
21  ibid. p. 454.
22  *Church of England Newspaper*, February 22nd, 1985.

## Chapter 5   The God Who Created

1   For a fuller treatment of sexuality in scripture and the Fathers see Tony Higton, ed., *Sexuality and the Church*. ABWON, 1987. Available from Emmanuel Church, Main Road, Hawkwell, Hockley, Essex SS5 4NR.

## Chapter 6   Evolution Undermined

1   art. in *Daily Telegraph*, January 13th, 1987.
2   *The Creation*, Everyman, BBC 1, January 11th, 1987.
3   Reprinted by permission from *Nature*, vol. 290 p. 82. Copyright © 1981 Macmillan Magazines Ltd.
4   *New Scientist*, August 2nd, 1979.

5   For information in this para., and on the Natural History
    Museum, I am indebted to Alan Hayward (research physi-
    cist), *Creation and Evolution*. Triangle, 1985.
6   E. G. Conklin, *Man, Real and Ideal*. (Scribners, New York,
    1943).
7   Hayward, op. cit. p. 16; qu. C. R. Darwin, *Origin of Species*
    (1859), Foreword to Dent edn (London, 1971)
8   Hayward, op. cit. p. 20; qu. BBC Radio 4, October 1981.
9   Hayward, op. cit. p. 28; qu. *Implications of Evolution*.
    Pergamon (Oxford, 1960).
10  *Daily Telegraph*, January 13th, 1987.
11  *The Turn of the Tide*, BBC Radio 4, March 15th, 1986.
12  Everyman, op. cit.
13  *Daily Telegraph*, January 13th, 1987.
14  ibid.
15  *The Blind Watchmaker*, Horizon, BBC 2, January 19th,
    1987.
16  ibid.
17  qu. in *The Times*, September 2nd, 1987.

## Chapter 7    Evolution in the Dock

1   attributed to George Bernard Shaw. Exact source unknown.
2   *Daily Telegraph*, June 6th, 1985.
3   ibid.
4   ibid. December 6th, 1986.
5   *The Times*, June 3rd, 1985.
6   ibid. February 2nd, 1987.
7   See Prof. A. W. Liley in *The Tiniest Humans*, ed. R. L.
    Sassone (1977); H. B. Valman and J. F. Pearson, 'What the
    foetus feels', *British Medical Journal*, January 26th, 1980; G.
    L. Flanagan, *The First Nine Months of Life* (Heinemann,
    1970); G. Bergel and C. Everett Koop, *When You Were
    Formed in Secret* (Intercessors for America 1980; Koop is
    Surgeon General of the USA); all quoted in *Tynewald: avert
    this tragedy*. SPUC, 1985, London.
8   Letter in *Lancet*, June 1986.
9   *Open to Question*, BBC 2, January 15th, 1985.
10  Report in *Daily Telegraph*, January 15th, 1986.
11  *The Times*, November 30th, 1985.
12  *Daily Mail*, November 18th, 1985.

13 ibid. December 11th, 1985.
14 *The Times*, December 10th, 1985.
15 *Daily Telegraph*, December 9th, 1986.
16 *Viewer and Listener*, Autumn 1985.
17 qu. in *Moral Choice*, National Council for Christian Standards in Society, London May 1986.
18 qu. *Sex Education in Schools*. The Responsible Society. (Milton Keynes).
19 qu. in Valerie Riches, *Family Portraits*. Social Affairs Unit.
20 Seminar at North Manchester General Hospital, October 31st, 1986.
21 Graham Heath, *The Illusory Freedom* (Heinemann, 1978), qu. in *The Case for Responsibility*.
22 *Family Policy Studies Centre Report*, January 13th, 1986.
23 *Population Trends*. HMSO, London, September 16th, 1986.
24 FPSC Report.
25 Letter in *Church Times*, September 12th, 1986.
26 *Open to Question*, op. cit.
27 Letter repr. in *Evangelical Times*, January 1987.
28 Department of Education and Science Circular no. 11/87 states: 'There is no place in any school in any circumstances for teaching which advocates homosexual behaviour, which presents it as the "norm", or which encourages homosexual experimentation by pupils. Indeed encouraging or procuring homosexual acts by pupils who are under the age of consent is a criminal offence' (para. 22). It remains to be seen how effective this is, and for how long.
29 *Homosexual Relationships: a contribution to discussion* (CIO, London 1979), paras 106–7.
30 ibid. para. 111.
31 ibid. para. 115.
32 ibid. para. 168.
33 Graham Turner, 'There's a Moral in it Somewhere'.
34 York Diocesan leaflet, December 1987.
35 For further information see Tony Higton, ed., *Sexuality and the Church*, op. cit.

## Chapter 9   The God Who Saves

1 Bruce *The NT Documents – are they reliable?*, op. cit. p. 119.

2   *Annals* 15:44.
3   *Antiquities* 18:33.
4   *Epistles* 10:96.


## Chapter 10    Salvation Undermined

1   *Together in Prayer for Peace* (BCC, London 1987), p. 2.
2   *Towards a Theology for Interfaith Dialogue* (CIO, London 1984), p. 8.
3   ibid. p. 9.
4   ibid.
5   *Guidelines on Dialogue: with people of living faiths and ideologies* (WCC, Geneva 1984), p. 8.
6   *Can We Pray Together?* (BCC, London 1983), p. 10.
7   K. Cracknell, *Considering Dialogue* (BCC, London 1981), p. 13.
8   ibid.
9   *Towards a Theology for Interfaith Dialogue*, op. cit. p. 13.
10   K. Cracknell, *Why Dialogue?* (BCC, London 1980), p. 16.
11   ibid. p. 17.
12   *Towards a Theology for Interfaith Dialogue*, op. cit. p. 15.
13   in *The Myth of God Incarnate*, ed. J. Hick. SCM, London 1977.
14   ibid. p. 172.
15   ibid. p. 181.
16   *Towards a Theology for Interfaith Dialogue*, op. cit. p. 23.
17   *Can We Pray Together?* op. cit. p. 9.
18   *Towards a Theology for Interfaith Dialogue*, op. cit. p. 24.
19   ibid. p. 33.
20   Cupitt, *Taking leave of God*, p. 81.
21   ibid. p. 141.
22   Not all occultists and astrologers agree over the date of the start of the Age of Aquarius, but they are agreed we have entered it.
23   *The Golden Book of the Theosophical Society* (1925), pp. 28–9, qu. in C. Cumbey, *The Hidden Dangers of the Rainbow*. Huntington House, Shreveport, Louisiana, 1983.
24   Cumbey, ibid. pp. 166, 168.
25   Cupitt. *Taking Leave of God*, p. 83.
26   Cupitt. *The Myth of God Incarnate*, p. 142.
27   ibid. p. 144.

28  Steve Turner, 'Echoes of the age of Aquarius', *Times*, May 30th 1988.
29  Cupitt, *Taking Leave of God*, p. 14.
30  ibid. p. 85.
31  ibid. p. 3.
32  ibid. p. xii.
33  ibid. p. 4.
34  ibid. p. 9.
35  ibid. p. 66.
36  ibid. p. 91.
37  ibid. p. 64.
38  ibid. p. 156.
39  ibid. p. 160.
40  Vishal Mangalwadi, *The World of the Gurus* (Croom Helm Ltd, London), p. 107.
41  *Turning Points*, January 20th, 1986.
42  ibid. April 28th, 1986.
43  ibid. February 24th, 1986.
44  *The Whole Programme – September at St James* (1987).
45  Cracknell, *Considering Dialogue*, op. cit. p. 17.
46  *Towards a Theology for Interfaith Dialogue*, op. cit. p. 35.

## Chapter 12    Obedience and Holiness

1  qu. in Roy Pointer, *How Do British Churches Grow?* (Marshall, Basingstoke 1984), p. 67.
2  ibid. p. 10.
3  *The Times*, August 17th, 1985.

## Chapter 14    Prayer and Discernment

1  Tony Higton and Gilbert Kirby, *The Challenge of the House-churches*, Latimer House, 131 Banbury Road, Oxford, 1988.
2  John Baker, Bishop of Salisbury and Chairman of the Doctrine Commission, in his Selwyn Lecture at Lichfield Cathedral, October 2nd, 1986.
3  *Daily Telegraph*, January 9th, 1987.

## Chapter 15    Commitment to One Another

1   Procedures, correct at the time of going to press, are subject to development. Further details from Tony Higton at Emmanuel Church, Main Road, Hawkwell, Hockley, Essex SS5 4NR.

## Chapter 16    Commitment to Mission

1   Archbishop's Committee on Spiritualism, *Report* (1939) in *Christian Parapsychologist*, vol. 3 (1979), p. 64.
2   ibid. p. 65.
3   *Evangelical Times*, October 1985.
4   B. Larson, *Rock*, Tyndale House, Wheaton, Illinois (1980).
5   *Freemasonry and Christianity: are they compatible?* (Church House, London 1987), p. 40.
6   e.g. John Lawrence, *Freemasonry: a religion?* (Kingsway, Eastbourne 1987).
7   See Tony Higton, *That the World May Believe* (Marshall, Basingstoke 1985).

## Chapter 17    The Kindness and Sternness of God

1   There is no justification for the dreadful treatment of the Jews by the Christian Church throughout the ages, let alone other anti-semitism. True, the generation of Jewish people contemporary with Jesus had a special responsibility for his death, and the result of this, in terms of exile, has affected many subsequent generations. But Gentiles are also spiritually responsible for the death of Christ.

## Chapter 18    The Sentiment and Cynicism of Man

1   *Daily Telegraph*, May 18th, 1987.
2   *Church of England Newspaper*, February 7th, 1986.
3   *The Nature of Christian Belief*, op. cit. pp. 37–8.
4   *Daily Telegraph*, February 1st, 1982.
5   *Sun*, Summer 1986.
6   Private Letter to the author, qu. by permission.

7   Cupitt, *Taking Leave of God*, p. 5.
8   ibid. p. 8.
9   ibid. p. 41.
10  ibid. p. 45.
11  ibid. p. 140.
12  *The Times*, July 12th, 1984.
13  *Church Times*, July 13th, 1984.
14  ibid. July 27th, 1984.
15  *Church Times*, August 10th, 1984.
16  *Church of England Newspaper*, September 7th, 1984.
17  *The Times*, July 16th, 1984.
18  qu. from witnesses' statements on *The World at One*, BBC Radio 4, July 6th, 1984.
19  *Weather* (October 1984), pp. 326–7.
20  *Chartered Insurance Institute Journal* (Spring 1985), p. 135 (italics mine).
21  *Maintenance and Equipment News* (October 1985), p. 14 (italics mine).
22  ibid. p. 15.
23  York Diocesan leaflet, January 1987.
24  Reported in *Church Times*, December 12th, 1986.
25  *AIDS, Some Guidelines for Pastoral Care* (Board for Social Responsibility of General Synod, London 1987), p. 8.
26  *Tablet*, July 19th, 1986.
27  Reported in *Daily Telegraph*, January 7th, 1987.
28  *Methodist Recorder*, July 18th, 1987.
29  *Turnabout* newsletter, March 1985.
30  J. Hick, *Evil and the God of Love* (Macmillan, London 1966), p. 120.
31  ibid. p. 378.
32  ibid.
33  ibid. pp. 379–80.
34  Cupitt, *Taking Leave of God*, p. 10.
35  ibid. p. 68.
36  S. H. Hooke, *Alpha and Omega* (Nisbet, 1961), p. 184.

## Chapter 20    Our God Reigns Over the Future

1   Charles Clarke, *World Wide Revival* (priv. pub.), p. 4.

# Bibliography

Archbishop's Committee on Spiritualism, *Report* (1939) in *Christian Parapsychologist*.

Baker, J., Selwyn Lecture at Lichfield Cathedral, October 2nd, 1986.

BBC Radio 4, October 1981.

Bergel, G. and C. Everett Koop, *When You Were Formed in Secret* (Intercessors for America, Reston, Virginia, 1980); qu. in *Tynewald: avert this tragedy*.

*The Blind Watchmaker*, Horizon, BBC 2, January 19th, 1987.

Blomberg, C., *The Historical Reliability of the Gospels*. IVP, 1987.

Bruce, F. F., *The New Testament Documents: are they reliable?* Eerdmans, 1960.

*Can We Pray Together?* BCC, 1983.

*The Case for Responsibility* The Responsible Society (No date)

*Chartered Insurance Institute Journal*, Spring 1985.

*Christian Parapsychologist*, vol. 3, 1979.

*Church of England Newspaper*, September 7th, 1984; February 22nd, 1985; February 7th, 1986.

*Church Times*, July 13th, 27th, August 10th, 1984; September 12th, December 12th, 1986.

Clarke, C., *World Wide Revival*. Privately published. (No date)

Conklin, E. G., *Man, Real and Ideal*. Scribners, New York 1943.

Cracknell, K., *Considering Dialogue*. BCC, 1981.

Cracknell, K., *Why Dialogue?* BCC, 1980.

*The Creation*, Everyman TV programme, January 11th, 1987.

*Credo*, TV programme, February 23rd, 1985.

Cumbey, C., *The Hidden Dangers of the Rainbow*. Huntington House, 1983.

Cupitt, D., *Taking Leave of God*. SCM, 1980.

*Daily Mail*, November 18th, December 11th, 1985.

*Daily Telegraph*, February 1st, 1982; June 6th, December 6th, 1985; December 9th, 1986; January 7th, 9th, 13th, May 18th, 1987.

Darwin, C. R., *Origin of Species* (1859), foreword to Dent edn London, 1971, qu. in A. Hayward.

Department of Education and Science, Circular no. 11/87.

*Evangelical Times*, October 1985; January 1987.

*Family Policy Studies Centre Report*, January 13th, 1986.

Flanagan, G. L., *The First Nine Months of Life* (Heinemann, 1970); qu. in *Tynewald: avert this tragedy*.

*Freemasonry and Christianity: are they compatible?* Church House, 1987.

General Synod, *Report of Proceedings*, vol. 17, no. 2. London 1986.

*The Golden Book of the Theosophical Society* (1925), qu. in C. Cumbey.

*Guidelines on Dialogue: with people of living faiths and ideologies.* WCC, 1984.

Guthrie, D., *New Testament Introduction*. Tyndale, 1962.

Hayward, A., *Creation and Evolution*. Triangle, 1985.

Heath, G., *The Illusory Freedom*. Heinemann, 1978; qu. in *The Case for Responsibility*.

Hick, J., *Evil and the God of Love*. Macmillan, 1966.

Hick, J., ed., *The Myth of God Incarnate*. SCM, 1977.

Higton, T., *That the World May Believe*. Marshall, 1985.

Higton, T., ed., *Sexuality and the Church*. ABWON, 1987.

Higton, T. and Kirby, G., *The Challenge of the Housechurches*, Latimer House, 1988.

*Homosexual Relationships: a contribution to discussion*. CIO, 1979.

Hooke, S. H., *Alpha and Omega*. Nisbet, 1961.

Josephus, *Antiquities*

Kerkut, G. A. *Implications of Evolution*. Pergamon, Oxford 1960.

Kitchen, K. A., *The Bible and its World*. Paternoster, 1977.

*Lancet*, June 1986.

Lawrence, J., *Freemasonry: a religion?* Kingsway, 1987.

Liley, A. W. in *The Tiniest Humans*, ed. R. L. Sassone; qu. in *Tynewald: avert this tragedy*.

*Maintenance and Equipment News*, October 1985.

Mangalwadi, V., *The World of the Gurus*. Croom Helm, London.

*Methodist Recorder*, July 18th, 1987.

*Moral Choice*. National Council for Christian Standards in Society, May 1986.

Morris, L., *I Believe in Revelation*. Hodder, 1976.

*The Nature of Christian Belief*. Church House, 1986.

*New Scientist*, August 2nd, 1979.

O'Donnell, K. in *Church Times*, September 12th, 1986.

*Open to Question*, BBC 2, January 15th, 1985.

Phillips, J. B., *The New Testament in Modern English*. Collins, 1975.

Pliny, *Epistles*

Pointer, R., *How Do British Churches Grow?* Marshall, 1984.

*Population Trends*. HMSO, September 16th, 1986.

Riches, V., *Family Portraits*. Social Affairs Unit, 1986. Responsible Society.

Robinson, J. A. T., *Redating the New Testament* (SCM, 1976), qu. in F. F. Bruce.

Sassone, R. L., ed., *The Tiniest Humans*, (Santa Anna, California) 1977.

Seminar at North Manchester General Hospital, October 31st, 1986.

Sermon at St Paul's Cathedral, May 22nd, 1985.

*Sex Education in Schools*. The Responsible Society (No date).

*Sun*, Summer 1986.

*Sunday Telegraph*, June 8th, 1986.

*Sunday Times*, May 12th, 1985.

*Tablet*, July 19th, 1986.

Tacitus, *Annals*.

*The Times*, July 12th, 16th, 1984; June 3rd, August 17th, November 30th, December 10th, 1985; February 2nd, September 2nd, 1987.

*Together in Prayer for Peace*. BCC, 1987.

*Towards a Theology for Interfaith Dialogue*. CIO, 1984.

*Turnabout* newsletter, March 1985.

*Turning Points*, January 20th, 1986.

*The Turn of the Tide*, BBC Radio 4, March 15th, 1986.

*Tynewald: avert this tragedy*. SPUC, 1985.

Valman, H. B. and J. F. Pearson, 'What the foetus feels', *British Medical Journal*, January 26th, 1980; qu. in *Tynewald: avert this tragedy*.

*Viewer and Listener*, Autumn 1985.

*Weather*, October 1984.

Wenham, J., *Christ and the Bible*. IVP, 1984.

*The World at One*, BBC Radio 4, July 6th, 1984; April 4th, 1985.

York Diocesan leaflet, January, December, 1987.

# Index